Acting Power

An Introduction to Acting

Robert Cohen

Mayfield Publishing Company

Pages 1, 37, 38, 55, 82, 87, 99, 139, 199, 232: Quotations from *Showcase* by Roy Newquist. Page 2: Leonard Probst's *Off Camera* published by Stein and Day. Reprinted by permission of Mike Nichols. Page 3: From *Close Up* by John Gruen, published by The Viking Press, 1968. Pages 7, 70: From *Building a Character*, edited and translated by Elizabeth Reynolds Hapgood. Page 13: From *Actors Talk About Acting* by Lewis Funke and John E. Booth. Page 17: In John Cottrell's *Laurence Oliver*. Pages 23, 219: From *The Job of Acting* by Clive Swift. Page 39: From *Theatre in the Twentieth Century* edited by Robert W. Corrigan.

Pages 41, 51, 63, 64, 80, 90, 124, 202, 216, 217, 234: Quotations from *The Player*. Copyright © 1961 by Lillian Ross, © 1962 by Lillian Ross and Helen Ross. Reprinted by permission of Simon & Schuster, a Division of Gulf & Western Corporation.

Pages 43, 223: From Michael Billington, *The Modern Actor*. Page 44: From Leonard Probst's *Off Camera* published by Stein and Day. Reprinted with permission of Al Pacino. Pages 60, 223: From *Directing the Film*, by Eric Sherman. Page 62: From David Shipman, *Brando*. Pages 66, 91, 181: From *Letters From An Actor*. Page 66: From *Reflections on The Theatre*. Pages 69, 83, 130, 213: From Leonard Probst's *Off Camera* published by Stein and Day.

Pages 97, 44: From Liv Ullmann's *Changing*. Copyright © 1977 by Liv Ullmann. Reprinted by permission of Alfred A. Knopf, Inc. Pages 121, 122, 193: From *The Actor's Freedom* by Michael Goldman. Copyright © 1975 by Michael Goldman. Reprinted by permission of The Viking Press, Inc. Pages 130, 185: From *If you Don't Dance They Beat You*. Page 131: From *Directors on Directing*. Page 145: From *Theatre: A Rediscovery of Style*. Pages 154, 204: From "Method and Attitude," in *The Music Theatre of Walter Felsenstein*, translated and edited by Peter Paul Fuchs. Page 163: From *Distinguished Company*. Page 164: From *Tyrone Guthrie on Acting*. Page 183: From *The Empty Space*. Page 214: From *Great Acting* edited by Hal Burton. Page 219: From *Acting in the 60s* edited by Hal Burton. Page 227: From *The Presence of the Actor*. Page 233: From *Directing a Play*, by Willis. Page 235: From *Murder of the Director* by Willis.

Library of Congress Catalog Card Number: 77-089918
International Standard Book Number: 0-87484-408-8

Manufactured in the United States of America
Mayfield Publishing Company
285 Hamilton Avenue, Palo Alto, California 94301

This book was set in Trump and Helvetica Light by Chapman's Phototypesetting and was printed and bound by Kingsport Press. Sponsoring editor was C. Lansing Hays, Carole Norton supervised editing, and Gene Tanke was manuscript editor. The book was designed by Nancy Sears, with artwork by Mari Stein, and Michelle Hogan supervised production.

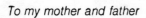

To my mother and father

CONTENTS

LIST OF EXERCISES

TO THE ACTOR:
THE AUTHOR'S PREFACE

I think we can all agree that there is bad acting, there is good acting, and there is great acting. And that we can all tell the difference when we see it, even if we can't exactly define the difference.

Most actors try very hard to become good actors. This is laudable, of course, but it is not enough. One must try to become a great actor.

Why? For two reasons.

The first is a professional one. Only great actors can develop, over the course of many years, a suitable and successful professional career. If you are good, *very* good, you can get cast from time to time, perhaps even regularly if you make yourself continually available. But nobody will be *dying* to cast you, and in a business as competitive as the theatre (or films or television) it is having people dying to cast you that is, over the long run, pretty much what it takes to ensure a permanent career. It takes directors, producers, and casting directors who will think of you when you're not around; who will take the trouble to hunt you out and negotiate with others for your services. That means that you are more than a good actor; it means you are an *exciting* actor; one who has the capacity to quicken their pulse and enliven their imagination— and, if theirs, an audience's as well. The only alternative to being a great actor is to be selling yourself day by day in what is clearly going to remain what it is today: a buyer's market. And this is a difficult way to have to spend your life.

The second reason is even more important. It is, for want of a better term, the artistic reason. Most professional actors—most *interesting* actors anyway—are not in the business solely for money, or fame, or exhibitionistic exploitation. They are actors because they have a tremendous need to *act*; a powerful urge to express themselves creatively and skillfully in a medium of high artistry, a medium with a twenty-five-hundred-year history and with a brilliantly exciting present. Merely good, competent, "B plus" acting will not satisfy this goal—either for actors or for their audiences. After all, there does not *have* to be a theatre. Theatre is not like government service, primary education, or agriculture. People can live perfectly good lives without theatre, and in most parts of the world they *do* live without it. Theatre only exists, and only continues to exist, because of great plays, great performances, and great actors. "Greatness" is what creates audience demand; "greatness" is in the theatre's very lifeblood. Without greatness, and the striving toward it, theatre would simply cease to exist.

What separates the "great" from the merely "good"? It is not easy to say, perhaps not even possible to define in absolute terms. But I think it can be approached.

Philosopher William James suggests that "the difference between the first- and second-best things in art absolutely seems to escape verbal definition—it is a matter of a hair, a shade, an inward quiver of some kind—yet [it] is miles away in point of preciousness."

What is greatness in acting? It is not necessarily becoming a "star" or playing lots of leading roles. There are great actors in every medium who specialize in small parts, locally seen, and who offstage are self-effacing to the point of anonymity. But they excite the emotions, the intellect, and the very physiologies of the audiences who see them, the actors who act with them, and the directors who direct them. They make audiences want to see them again, and directors want to cast them again—or steal them away from other directors. They have the capabilities to entertain, to move, to dazzle, to fulfill, and to inspire. They are men and women of wide-ranging powers; they are, if you ask someone, "Great!"

This book, above all else, is an attempt to explore the qualities of greatness; to take aim at that "inward quiver" which James mentions, and to suggest, to you the actor, an approach toward not merely good acting but great acting.

I am aware of a certain presumptuousness in this attempt; a presumptuousness in my writing of it, and in your thinking about it. We live in an age of professed egalitarianism, where "coolness" and "looseness" are publicly preferred to the apparent arrogance of transcendence. But art is not egalitarian. Art demands, or requires, the very best of every aspirant; it accepts only the maximum effort. An actor who wants to be part of the lifeblood of the theatre—the theatre of today and the theatre of the future—must set his sights at the highest, at greatness itself. Nothing less will really do.

I would like these words to serve as my preface to you—my personal remarks prior to your reading my book. But they could also serve as my remarks to you prior to your reading any book at all. Reading this book will not make you a great actor, nor will reading any book nor any group of books. But the foundation of your becoming an actor, I believe, will be your courage in reaching toward great heights. This is a courage which you need never express publicly (if you do it will earn you respect in some quarters, enemies in others), but which you must carry in your mind. It will be your inner passion, your energy source, and finally, perhaps, your greatest happiness regardless of ultimate success. Good luck.

R. C.

NOTES ON THE TEXT

I have given up any attempt to be fair to both sexes in the use of pronouns; in a study of this sort, which uses personal pronouns extensively, it would add at least three dozen pages of "his or her" redundancies. The male gender, therefore, always represents either sex in this book except where specified.

I have limited myself to discussing only those forms of acting in which the actor plays a human character, or an anthropomorphic character. For those rare occasions where an actor is asked to play a bookend or an ashtray, I imagine some of the discussions herein will appear irrelevant.

It has been convenient for me to draw many of my examples from two plays, *The Glass Menagerie* by Tennessee Williams and *Hamlet* by William Shakespeare. I have done so because these plays are well known, and I can expect the reader's general familiarity with them. In discussing the plays, I wish to make clear that I am not trying to interpret them, but simply showing how certain interpretations may best be played by the actor.

I have "illustrated" this book with what I believe to be pertinent quotations by (and occasionally about) actors themselves, mostly actors distinguished in both stage and film presentations. Some of these quotations have been slightly edited from their original sources.

Notes to the text—source citations, references, and comments—are collected at the back of the book (pp. 247–48), where they are listed by text page and line number (so that "45/12," for example, introduces a note to the material on page 45, line 12).

ACTING POWER

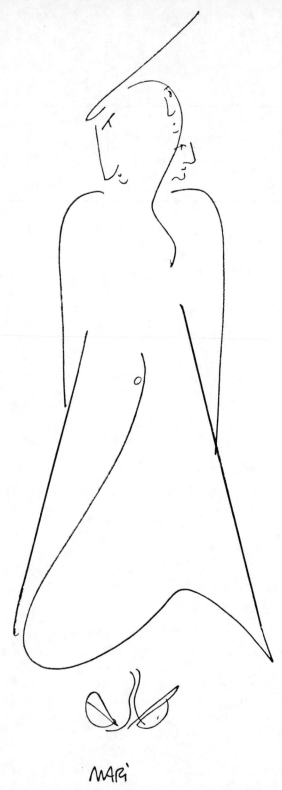

INTRODUCTION:
THE ACTOR'S VIEWPOINT

"People have said to me, from time to time, that they admire my 'technique,' or I can read in print that I have 'unusual technical abilities.' These comments aren't always complimentary because so often what people mean by 'technique' is some sort of artificial or mechanical approach to a role. The best definition of technique I know is this: that means by which the actor can get the best out of himself. It's as simple and as broad as that—and as personal and private."

—*Hume Cronyn*

For a great many years, acting has been discussed as some sort of delicate balance between two contradictory forces: the actor's "internal belief in his role," and his "external performance technique." Schools have arisen to claim that acting is predominantly one or the other; different schools have tried to combine the two in some sort of package, often a fairly awkward one. "You must live the life of your character, but of course you must also be heard in the back row," is the familiar packaging, with numerous variations. Clearly, belief and technique are both involved in successful acting, but if they are approached as complementary forces rather than contradictory ones, the package need not be so awkward, and a whole, integrated art of acting may develop.

The fact is that "internal belief" and "external technique" are fundamental aspects not merely of stage acting, but of the basic processes of living and communicating. They can, of course, be separated for reasons of analysis, and it is clearly to the advantage of the behavioral scientist or the dramatic theoretician to do so, given their goals of dissection, designation, and theoretical analysis. But the actor's goals are quite different from these: the actor's ultimate task is neither to dissect, designate, nor analyze, but rather to put together, to enliven, and to create a sense of life in a whole and fulfilling theatrical experience. To the actor, it is not the separation of "belief" and "technique" that is at issue, but their marriage.

In this book we will not, therefore, be concerned with dividing the actor's separate tasks into their various components, but with integrating the components into their most perfect possible alignment. In doing this, we will take, therefore, not the critical or theoretical perspective of the objective observer, but the perspective of the actor himself. We will take, that is, a subjective approach. We will approach acting from the inside, not the outside, and by so doing we will try to suggest ways in which the actor can direct his consciousness into a highly useful, productive, creative, and artistic instrument. A *real* instrument, that can be used in a real world.

"There is a kind of quiet terror that comes over everyone—actors, director, crew—when someone says 'Roll!' A little bit of life goes out of everyone and a lot of self-consciousness comes into everyone. I've always been concerned, as much as possible, with feeding the life and finding things for the actors to concentrate on so that the self-consciousness can be overcome or forgotten."

—*Mike Nichols*

ACTING IS REAL

Acting takes place in "plays," and is called "playing." These words connote deception and nonseriousness, and usually lead beginners to think that acting is wholly different from "real" behavior. There are, of course, many differences between acting on stage and behaving in life, but the differences are not exactly those between "reality" and "unreality" or between "honesty" and "dishonesty."

In the first place, reality is not a very simple concept to define. Certainly we can agree that reality includes trees, birds, rocks, the human skeleton, and the sky; but what place in reality do dreams, feelings, numbers, love, or despair occupy? They are real if only because we feel they are real; their realness, though subjective, is as influential in our "real" decisions as hard and fast tangible reality.

One of the basic questions about acting, however, has to do with whether or not an actor's feelings are or should be "real" or "honest." When looked at from the subjective aspect of reality, this question only gives rise to thousands more. "Real to whom?" "Honest to whom?" "To the actor?" "To the audience?" And even these questions are undermined when we start to question the "reality" or "honesty" of some of our own feelings. While, to be sure, we are often overcome by wholly spontaneous waves of emotion, there are also many times when we are vague and unsure about our feelings. We go to a funeral and wonder if we are weeping because we are sad, or because it's expected of us. We laugh at a comedy, and wonder if we are laughing at the joke, or to encourage the actors, or to convince others in the audience that we understand the point of the humor. We smile at someone

"Be yourself! You cannot be anyone unless you become yourself first."

—*Stella Adler*

and wonder if we "really" mean that we're happy, or simply wishing to make a show of fondness, or are even getting out of a sticky situation gracefully. To say that an actor should be "real" or "honest" is all well and good, but it's not clear that by saying that, we are in fact saying anything of substance.

Very interesting studies in the area known as "cognitive dissonance" have changed our understanding of psychological reality sufficiently to make these studies of great importance in an approach to acting. The principle of cognitive dissonance is that *we come to believe in what we find ourselves doing, regardless of the reasons we first started doing it!* In the most critical first experiments, people were paid to tell an innocuous lie: that they had enjoyed taking an examination which in fact they hadn't enjoyed. Later they were asked by other investigators if they had enjoyed taking the exam: they answered Yes. That is, having once said they enjoyed the exam, they came to believe they *had* enjoyed it. They had, in the common phrase that denotes cognitive dissonance, come to live their lie.* In the same way it can be shown that debaters who are paid to take a position tend to come to believe in the position as their own. So do lawyers, speechwriters, lobbyists, and commercial advocates. A person who joins a political group in order to meet people tends to come to believe in its cause, consciously and willingly. And, of course, actors tend to come to believe in their parts.

We are all familiar with the popular literature about actors assuming the characteristics of the parts they play. Romance onstage frequently leads to entanglements off; the celebrated affair of Richard Burton (Antony) and Elizabeth Taylor (Cleopatra) is only the best known example of a common situation on many film locations or the theatrical "road." Likewise, history records some fairly brutish offstage behavior by onstage heavies, including the real assassination of a beloved leader by the leading Richard III of his time, John Wilkes Booth. But there is concrete scientific evidence for this phenomenon as well, provided by Professor Philip Zimbardo at Stanford University. Professor Zimbardo invited a group of healthy, normal male college students to participate in a mock prison exercise, for which purposes he had constructed a full-scale model penitentiary in the basement of a Stanford laboratory building. Some of the students were designated— on an arbitrary basis—as "guards" in this exercise, and others were

---

*This experiment is discussed more fully in the Appendix.

designated "prisoners." Costumes were given out, "rules" posted, and the scientist experimenters withdrew behind their one-way windowed mirrors. Barely two days into the projected week-long experiment, Zimbardo had to call a halt. The "guards" were berating, assaulting, and even torturing the "prisoners." The "prisoners" were in states of deep depression and nervous exhaustion, exploiting scapegoats in their midst, developing psychosomatic twitches, and fraught with anxieties. One had a complete breakdown, others had already forfeited their stipends and begged out. Zimbardo's conclusion: "illusion had merged inextricably with reality." The "play" had become indistinguishable from the "real."

The Zimbardo experiment was originally undertaken to study the effects of prison life by "acting out" a prison situation: the most valuable result of the experiment, however, was the information it yielded on the "acting out" process itself. For here Zimbardo had created his own improvisational theatre: with situation, scenery, costumes, actors, and an audience. Zimbardo's theatre was a context for acting. The context was, of course, arbitrary—a scientific experiment—but the improvisation that went on within it, an interaction of psychological and physiological reality, was genuinely intense. And thus it is with all "play" which takes place within an effective context.

One may ask why the "prisoners" in the Zimbardo experiment failed to simply lie on their cots, reminding themselves that "this is only an experiment." Standing outside the context, it is hard if not impossible to understand its hypnotic effect on the participants' emotions. Within the context, one sees differently and thinks differently; one asks different questions and fails to question very obvious "outside" peculiarities. Within the context, a real, but different, universe exists. It is the universe of "play."

Consider, as a more common example of the universe of "play," the ordinary "playing field": a sports arena. A sporting game is also a context for improvisation: the sport with its rules and regulations, its dimensioned playing field, and its chosen teams of opponents. Everything in the context is arbitrary; there is nothing intrinsic about three strikes that makes them constitute an "out"; it is only that the rule book so designates them. And there is nothing particularly intrinsic about the team that should make it be seen—as it is—as representing a certain interest, because teams recruit outstanding players regardless of their regional or philosophical allegiances. And yet within this odd, arbitrary sporting world, interactions that are real, vital, and brutally

intense are daily engaged and passionately followed, both professionally and by amateurs, throughout the civilized world.

To the sports player and to his "fans," as to the Zimbardo "pris-
oner" and his "guard," the context is an absolute. During the hours of
competition, the reality within that context is total; it is the whole universe. If a ballplayer strikes out, you can offer him no comfort by saying
"It's only a game," for his look in response will be only astonishment—
"What world are you in?" Nor can you comfort him by suggesting,
"three strikes are an unreasonably unfair limitation: five at least should
be allowed." To the ballplayer within the game, such remarks are nonsense: within the context the rules are absolutes, and outsiders are suf-
fered rudely, if at all. And since the rules are absolutes, the energy
within the context is wholly deployed in winning the game; it is not
wasted on trying to change the rules.

What we can see from this is that the presence of a context surrounding an action, instead of fragmenting the passions, feelings, and
intensity of the action, heightens them. This is the way of the theatre.
A highly structured context—and a play is one of the most highly
structured there is, whether an "improvised" play or a fully staged and
scripted drama—acts as a crucible which intensifies everything within
it, and which makes the reality of every moment, from the viewpoints
of both the participant and the engaged observer, vivid and even overwhelming. It is a fact that "play experiences," whether in "child's
play," in sporting play, or in the plays of the theatre and film, are frequently the most remembered and most treasured moments of our
entire lives. Often they establish for us the models for what life's "peak
experiences" *should* be, and become the hallmarks against which we
measure the actual feelings and behaviors we experience in life's actual
events.

To suggest, therefore, that the actions within a "play" are somehow "unreal" in the sense that they are wholly separate from reality
is to miss, quite entirely, the most striking aspect of the theatre, which
is that insofar as it is different from everyday reality, it is different in
the direction of "more real" rather than "less real;" usually, hour for
hour, more rather than less intense, revealing, enlightening, evocative,
and even whimsical. The theatrical context, whether it is composed of
stage and scenery, street and trestles, celluloid and camera, is an arena
for goals intensely pursued, battles vibrantly engaged, loves eagerly
sought, and lives brilliantly lived. To separate acting from reality, therefore, is to diminish both.

"Our demands are simple, normal, and therefore they
are difficult to satisfy. All we ask is that an actor on
the stage live in accordance with natural laws."

—*Constantin Stanislavski*

ACTING IS COMMUNICATION

"Acting" is a word we use to refer both to stage acting and to offstage
behavior (as in "acting strangely," or "a heroic act"). As we have seen,
there is no solid line of demarcation between stage acting and offstage
acting.

Almost all of our actions are *communications,* or at least have a
communicative function. From rising in the morning to falling asleep
at night, our wakeful life is filled with millions of subtle and not-so-
subtle attempts to reach the world outside us; to make contact with
our fellow beings. We smile at people, walk and dress in certain ways,
exchange words, frowns, and raised eyebrows, snort, chuckle, nod, and
feign indifference hundreds of times a day in order to convey some
message to someone—or to rehearse conveying some message to
someone. What links all communications together is this: they are
all, consciously or unconsciously, *purposeful.* Most of our actions are
consciously or unconsciously intended to influence, in some way we
consider favorable (though it might not be), the attitudes and behaviors
of others.

To say this is not to say that all people are, at all times, exploitive,
manipulative, or particularly aggressive. It is only to say that we, as a
species, behave at least in large measure in ways that we think will be
helpful to ourselves; we have underlying purposes and intentions
which are directed toward increasing our own well-being. These purposes are usually unconscious, habitual, and entirely benign—the
"stuff" of ordinary human relations. We smile to engage others to
smile back at us, we "stroke" (as psychologist Eric Berne put it) in

order to be stroked in return. In the way that we walk down the street or into a room, or speak, or smile, or glare, or sit in a chair, we attempt to convey information about ourselves that will attract the kinds of attention we wish, and which will dissuade the kinds of attention we don't wish. In fact, as an axiom of communication theory has it, we cannot *not* communicate; we cannot *not* have purposes beneath our daily behavior.

It was an emphasis on the purposes and intentions of human behavior that distinguished the first great theory of stage acting, that of the Russian master Constantin Stanislavski. Stanislavski's approach to acting, both as a performer and the director of the Moscow Art Theatre, and as the author of seminal books on the acting process, was that stage acting rests on the actor's discovery of the intentions and purposes of his character, and his successful "playing" of those intentions. There is hardly an acting theory or an acting teacher today who does not, at least in part, accept this view. The book you are now reading accepts it. It is fundamental.

But the subject of character intentions is treated, by Stanislavski and others, as separate from the subject of actors and audience. This has led to the basic Stanislavskian package of "you must live the life of your character and also be heard in the back row," a combination which implies the need for a great deal of Scotch tape. Would it not be better if acting could be integrated in such a way that the character's intentions and the actor's technical demands could be part of the same whole—indistinguishable as the actor performs? Developing such an integration should be the primary goal of every actor.

THE FUNCTION OF AN AUDIENCE

What has created the apparent difficulties for the actor in trying to "live the life of his character" is, of course, the apparently artificial presence of an audience. The audience, which is the theatre's truest necessity, is also the source of its most perplexing set of paradoxes. Whether it is a true audience, as for a stage play, or a hypothesized future one, as for a film, actions that seem at first glance "sincere interactions" between two characters seem at second glance to be interactions contrived for the benefit of others. Obviously, it is necessary in this case to take a third glance, and see if we cannot find a way around this dilemma, or else everything on stage will have to be conceded as false, deceptive, affected, and hypocritical. Many people, of course, already find it so: the Greeks, we must remember, named the first actors *hypokrites.*

The route is this: audiences do not exist solely in the theatre, they exist in life. Communication is rarely a simple affair. Let us take a very simple example: a junior executive walks into a large office and, passing a secretary's desk, says "Good morning." This is a simple interaction—a "stroke," in Eric Berne's sense. But suppose the junior executive knows that his senior executive will overhear the remark. In that case, it is possible that his underlying purpose is to show the senior executive that he—the junior executive—is building company morale. The "good morning" is no longer a simple interaction—it is an interaction (with the secretary) played to an audience (the senior executive). Notice that sincerity and honesty are utterly irrelevant in this example: the communication situation is equally complex whether the junior executive is or is not genuinely fond of the secretary, whether or not he genuinely wishes to build morale, and whether or not it is genuinely a good morning. It does not even matter whether the senior executive is actually within earshot—it is only important that the junior executive thinks he is. The purposes of the junior executive's communication, therefore, lie at two separate levels: the level of interaction with the secretary, and the level of interaction-for-an-audience with the senior executive. This interaction-for-an-audience we can simply call a *performance.*

INTERACTION AND PERFORMANCE

Interaction and performance, then, are basic levels of communication in life as well as on the stage; "performance" is an activity in which we daily, routinely, and all but inevitably engage. Words do not even have to be exchanged in order for a person to interact and perform. For example, a young woman is seated at a lunch counter, and a man sits down next to her. She sits immobile and silent; some would say that she is not communicating at all, but that is not, of course, accurate: one cannot *not* communicate. What she is communicating, of course, is the very clear message, "I do not wish to converse with you."

Now at this level, her communication is simply an interaction with the man next to her. But suppose that she thinks her boyfriend might come in behind her at any moment, and might, in fact, be just approaching the door. In that case her immobility is not merely an interaction with the man next to her; it is an interaction-for-an-audience—a performance—for the boyfriend who might (or might not) be present. Whether her disinterest in the man next to her is sincere, feigned, or ambivalent does not alter the fact that her immobility and silence conveys a multiple communication: a simultaneous interaction and performance.

The point of these examples is this: interactions in life that are performed for an audience are not necessarily insincere, dishonest, or artificial. Entirely sincere actions can also be entirely sincere "performances." A student may ask a bright question in class both to get the answer from the professor (an interaction) and to show the rest of the class how bright he is (a performance). A director may speak sharply to an actor both to reprove the actor (an interaction) and to show the rest of the cast that he, the director, means business (a performance). Most conversations between three people generally take the form of a series of duologues, or interactions between two of the participants who are simultaneously "performing" for the third. Sincerity, candor, honesty; these are not necessarily at issue in "performing"; neither, necessarily, are hypocrisy, artifice, or contrivance.

Plays, which represent human interactions, also frequently represent human "performances" in exactly this sense. In *Hamlet*, for example, Ophelia converses with Hamlet while knowing that Claudius and Polonius are eavesdropping behind her; she is portrayed as engaging in interaction and performance simultaneously. Amanda, in *The Glass Menagerie*, pretends to drop a handkerchief so she can stoop and pick it up in front of Laura—a "piece of acting" on her part, says Williams' stage direction.

Performance, then, is not wholly separate from nor contrary to the normal interactions and communications among people. Performance and audiences are very much a part of our everyday life, irrespective of whether or not we live that life honestly, sincerely, or affectedly. That an actress playing Amanda, for example, is both interacting and performing at the same time is not a contradiction; these are, rather, two levels of behavior—communication—in which she is simultaneously engaged.

Now, of course plays have "real" audiences as well. Ophelia is performing for Claudius, and Amanda for Laura, but both are also performing to a group of public observers sitting in the "house." This, naturally, adds new levels to the problems of acting, but they are not wholly separate ones. Performing simultaneously to an onstage audience (the other characters) and performing to the audience "in the house" are not contradictory or antagonistic acts. They can be integrated, and for the finest actors, they are integrated.

THE INTEGRATED ACTOR

When he gets onstage, the actor faces a great many levels of awareness. He must interact and he must perform. He must relate in some way to a text, a theatre, an audience, scenery pieces, costumes, props, the demands of his director, the behavior of his fellow actors, the actions of the stage crew. He must also deal with potential distractions: the inevitable awareness of the potential presence of critics, of the state of his own career, of the offstage relationships he maintains—or wishes to maintain—with his fellow performers. The actor must deal with the anxieties of stage fright, vocal tension, physical clumsiness, the terror of forgetting his lines, of drying up emotionally, and—worst of all—of letting his confidence sag. He must be spontaneous without thinking about being spontaneous, and without appearing to try to be spontaneous. He must work within a fixed text, and yet make the words emanate from himself. He must create the play's character, and yet be personal and idiosyncratic enough to be humanly alive. He must fit into the play's style without losing a sense of humanity. He must be credible and he must be, in the best sense of the word, theatrical. These are, quite obviously, hard tasks.

Of course there are many actors who can "pull together" the various demands of acting quite naturally and unconsciously. At least there are many who claim to. John Wayne, the film actor, once boasted "I've never had a goddamn artistic problem in my life. I read what's in the script and then I go out there and deliver my lines." Certainly there are gifts which, at the very least, place individual actors at different starting points.

But the importance of "natural talent" and "born knacks" can be exaggerated. In the first place, it's quite appealing for the successful actor to portray his art as a matter of talent rather than developed craft; it makes him seem casual and effortless in his artistry. In the second place, the spontaneous talent that Wayne suggests for himself might also be the reason why Wayne, and actors like him, are often limited to a tiny range, modest in subtlety or brilliance. For most actors, success is achieved through study, struggle, preparation, infinite trial and error, training, discipline, experience, and work.

Much of that work is on the actor's body and on the voice. This is work done with an experienced teacher, and sometimes a good book. Several such books are mentioned in the Bibliography to this volume.

And much of the work is on the actor's mind. That is the subject of *this* book.

It is the mind, in its conscious and unconscious workings, that initiates all our actions—and our acting. It is the mind which controls the actor's concentration, his pursuit of intentions, his portrayal of character, his adoption of style, his performance within the theatrical context. It is the mind which integrates the actor's tasks, which integrates the actor himself.

There are two kinds of thinking that are important for every actor. There is the preparation and rehearsal thinking which the actor undertakes while working up his role. And there is in-performance thinking. The two are totally different processes. The first can be, depending on the actor's own preparation techniques, analytical, psychological, philosophical, literary, or theatrical. In-performance thinking can be none of these, not directly. In-performance thinking is spontaneous, free-wheeling, and creative, even in the most rigid of plays and dramatic styles and characterizations. It is forward-looking, purposeful, and bright-eyed. It is an exciting, often thrilling mental activity.

"Everything you do on the stage has to come from your mind."

—*Jason Robards*

When there are fundamental problems in acting—problems such as self-consciousness, distraction, dropping out of character or out of style, listening to oneself, failures of projection, of understanding, of emotional responsiveness—these problems are caused by unaligned, disordered, confused thinking. By the actor's trying to think about too many things at the same time—too many *contradictory* things. In order to combat this type of unaligned thinking, many actors try "not to think," and coaches the world over instruct them "Don't think! Just do!" But the human being simply cannot *not* think—anymore than he can willfully not hear, or not feel a pinprick. The fact is that people think continuously, and actors are people. The problems of acting do not require that actors stop thinking, but that they find out what to think about.

Properly aligned thinking must be the goal of every actor. When the actor's thinking is properly aligned, situation, character, style, and

---

"[In learning acting] It's not the emotional resources . . .
it's the brains. I find it's the brains that are the most
important thing, I really do. . . . It's a matter of thinking.
Really, it's a matter of learning a thinking process.
It's a matter of becoming aware of what it is you're
doing, of what it is you're feeling, and then it's a matter
of controlling it any way you want with your brain."

—Anne Bancroft

"I might say that an actor's business in his art is to
learn to use his self-consciousness as he uses any
other part of himself."

—Stark Young

---

performance are all part of the same thought process, all part of the same "think." If the actor's thinking is properly aligned, his tasks are integrated. He can perform singlemindedly and with total commitment in plays that are highly complex, characters that are highly unique, and styles that range from the most natural to the most abstract. Properly aligned thinking can release an actor into absolute spontaneity, and can reveal his personal wholeness. Finally, properly aligned thinking can provide the actor with his most effective and affecting instrument: acting power.

Acting power. It is the power to move, to dazzle, to entertain, to charm, to astonish, to frighten, to delight, and to engage an audience totally. It is "strength," of course, but it is also wit, grace, depth, and openness. It is the basis of true relaxation. It is the title and quest of this book.

CHAPTER 1

PLAYING THE SITUATION: OUT OF THE SELF

"I feel I am who I am playing. . . . You must somehow *be* that man—not just the part that shows in the role, but the whole of the man, his whole mind. . . . Oh God, yes, you have to feel it to do it. If you do it right, you do feel it. The suffering, the passion, the bitterness, you've got to feel them. And it takes something out of you and puts something in, as all emotional experiences do."

—*Laurence Olivier*

Philosophers have debated for many centuries whether a person's character shapes his situation, or whether his situation determines his character. It is sort of a chicken-or-egg debate, but one whose moral implications have important real-world results in the arenas of criminal justice and international diplomacy.

For the actor, fortunately, there need be no debate. *From the actor's viewpoint, it is his situation, not his character, which is dominant.* This is true for one powerful reason: *all people, and all characters in plays, think about their situation more than about their own personality or character.* We do not walk around in daily life concentrating on our characters, we concentrate on our situations: what time does the bus arrive,

17

what is this person trying to say to me, who is that over there, what does this mean, and so forth. In order for the actor to bring his character to life, he must act like the living person his character represents, and to do that he must concentrate on his character's situation, and not simply on his character's personality. Like his character, the actor must look outward and forward, not inward and back.

An interesting experiment in social psychology makes this particularly clear. Professors Edward Jones and Richard Nisbett, in 1971, invited a number of subjects to "rate" various individuals according to a standard scale of character traits: strong-willed to lenient, aggressive to mild-mannered, and so forth. The individuals they were asked to rate included their fathers, their friends, Walter Cronkite, and themselves. They could also, if they wished, make the response "depends on situation" for any particular pairing of person and character trait. The results showed something very interesting: the subjects, to an extraordinary degree, used the "depends on situation" option *only for themselves*, while for their friends, their fathers, and Mr. Cronkite, they were able to find fixed character attributes. The professors concluded that the human being is peculiarly egocentric in this regard: we all believe, they suggest, that "personality traits are things *other* people have." Conversely, from our own perspective, we find ourselves fluid, natural spirits whose behavior springs not from any rigid personality attribute, but which "depends on our situation." Other people are the "characters" in our lives.

In playing a character who is a human being, therefore, the actor must play *the character's own egocentricity*. He must play the character *from the character's point of view*, not from his own point of view. He must be the one person in the play who does *not* think of himself as a "character," but rather thinks of his behavior as being essentially a response to a situation. He must, in short, concentrate fully on his character's situation; this will become the focus of all of the actor's work. The development of character, style, and the techniques of performance, which are discussed later on, are all developments that will derive from this focus on situation; they are not things that can be tacked on to it.

To this end, we must limit ourselves in this section to examining interactions without regard to character traits, stylistic necessities, or the obligations of performance. We shall explore only those ways in which the actor lives life onstage. We must not, of course, ever take the part for the whole, and say (as have some of the most idealistic devotees of Stanislavski) that this is the sum of acting; rather we should see it as the basis on which performance is built. Because until the actor can effectively represent a person onstage, he can never represent a character, nor create a style, nor electrify an audience in performance.

SITUATION AND CONTEXT

The situation of the play is the situation existing among the play's characters. That situation, however, exists within the theatrical context, which is a higher-level framework. The context may be the theatre, with its proscenium, scenery, lights, text, and audience; or it might be any other medium of theatrical art.

In order for the actor to concentrate fully on his character's situation, he must find a way not to concentrate *directly* on his theatrical context. This is perhaps the most basic concern of the actor, and it is a mental concern.

Consider the sportsman—the baseball player, for example. His two worlds are quite distinct. His context is the world of baseball; where three strikes make an out, a ball over the fence constitutes a home run, a successful season means a renewed contract for next year, a good rapport with the "fans" means negotiating points towards a raise in pay. This information is all true, but the player cannot directly think about all of it while he is up at bat. It must be suppressed from consciousness, and driven into deeper areas of the mind.

This is done by a conscious effort known as *concentration.* The concentration of the ballplayer is entirely on *situational* rather than contextual factors. In baseball, the situation includes the number of outs, the men on base, who's pitching, what's the score, what's the inning, and so forth. In addition there are a number of intangible factors that describe the situation: the feel of the air, the sense of morale (teammates and opposition), the dampness of the ground, the fatigue, the drive, and the apparent strategies of the other players. The player's concentration on these situational aspects of the game is total, at least as total as is humanly possible. It is this complete *absorption* into situation which creates the excitement and the very reason for athletic competition.*

It is noteworthy, and important, that the ballplayer will win his *contextual* goals as a by-product of his total concentration on the situational ones. If his concentration is absolute, and his power and talents come to his aid, he will gain the following of the spectators and the appreciation of his employers, even if his team loses from time to time. If he goes after those contextual rewards *directly*, however, he is accused of grandstanding, publicity-seeking, and show-boating; he rarely lasts in the business.

Situational involvement is the *only way* to suppress contextual awareness. This is one of the great ironies of consciousness: that it is impossible, on strict command, to *not think* of something. If we are told "Do not think of a purple giraffe," we cannot *not* think of it, because we first have to think about what we are not to think about. Psychologists call this a "double-bind." If we are told "don't try to do anything," we can only follow the command by doing something (trying not to try), thus we are bound to failure. "Relax!" is a common double-bind, because relaxing means not trying to do anything at all, but the command to relax requires an effort—which is the opposite of relaxation. "Don't follow this command" is the ultimate double-bind; "Act your age," as a little contemplation makes clear, is a clever variation of it.†

*It is this total immersion of the athlete into his game, interestingly enough, which has been given by the ancient Greek historian, Herodotus, as the reason games were invented in the first place. Herodotus attributes the invention of games to the Lydians, who were visited by a great famine. He reports: "For a time the people lived on as patiently as they could, but later, when there was no improvement, they began to look for something to alleviate their misery. Various expedients were devised: for instance, the invention of dice, knuckle-bones, and ball-games. . . . The way they used these inventions to help them endure their hunger was to eat and play on alternate days— one day playing so continuously that they had no time to think of food, and eating on the next without playing at all. They managed to live like this for eighteen years." *The Histories*, Book One, translated by Aubrey de Selincourt (1954), pp. 52–53.

†The double-bind theory was first proposed by Gregory Bateson and others in 1956. Bateson holds that the double-bind is pathogenic, and is one of the main causes of schizophrenia—as when a mother continually double-binds a child, forcing him or her into crooked and stultified ways of thinking. Shakespeare, however, was familiar with the concept, as we see from Claudius' remark, in *Hamlet:* "like a man to double business bound, I stand in pause where I shall first begin, and both neglect" (III, iii, 42–44). See Bateson, *Steps to an Ecology of Mind* (New York: 1972), esp. pp. 201–278.

The only way to suppress contextual awareness is to fill the mind with something else. In concentrating on the past few sentences, the reader has forgotten the purple giraffe, although that could not have been done by forgetting alone. The mind can only deal with one thing at a time; the mind's eye must have a single focus.

This is not at all to say that the actor is unaware of contextual matters—that would be as undesirable as it is impossible—but only that he does not concentrate on them in performance. In Chapter Five we will see how contextual considerations, driven into deeper areas of the mind, come forth at the proper time to inspire performance to its highest potential. But this can happen only when the situation is fully realized and can be fully played. Even then, the actor's concentration, his conscious in-performance thinking, is strictly devoted to the successful outcome of his character's situation—that is, to *winning*.

WINNING

Situations are not static, they are dynamic. All life is fluid and relative; even in the world of science, since Einstein, we are given to understand that the concept of "a moment in time" is a useless one.

The situation of the ballplayer, as he comes to bat, is a mobile and dynamic integration of moods, feelings, perceptions, contingencies, and ideas. These are *events*—hypothesized, feared, expected, or intended—which come together in the player's mind. They would be absolutely chaotic if they were not organized into some sort of useful structure—and they are. That structure is *winning*. Winning—the lust for victory—is the mind-set which determines the way the player sees his situation, and how he acts upon it. For the professional player there is no need to dwell on the focus on victory, which has been immortalized by football coach Vince Lombardi into the professional athlete's credo: "Winning isn't the most important thing. It's the *only* thing." It is the athlete's concentration on winning which structures both the athlete's absorption and the spectator's fascination; if the fans feel the athlete is not trying to win, they become not only uninterested but angry.

Of course, with the sportsman, the "win" is a quantitative victory, with the rules of the game awarding so many points for such and such behavior. Also in sports, one person's victory is usually another person's defeat; in these ways sports remain an imperfect metaphor for life, and for the theatre. But the primary parallel remains: in acting, as in sports, *situations become dynamic when a victory is sought,* when the actor pursues *winning.*

Winning in life, or winning on the stage, does not necessarily mean making someone else lose; it simply means gaining the fulfillment of some self-designated goal. The goals stem from the basic human instincts: survival, love, happiness, and validation. All human beings direct their actions, sometimes effectively and sometimes not effectively, toward goals drawn from those general human instincts.

The universal foundation of a credible performance—and this holds true in any character, in any play, in any style of performance— is the accurate rendition of a character who, like any human being, is *trying to win* goals; who is trying to achieve something for himself, some fulfillment, some satisfaction, some happiness. He may not know exactly what it is, he may be as inarticulate as a Bedlam Beggar, he may be psychotic, perverse, misguided, or bizarre, but he is after something that represents, to him, a victory.

The character may not ever get his victory, of course. That is something the playwright will probably determine, or the director. It may even be better to say that the audience will determine it; and even beyond that, it may be better to say that nobody will ever determine it. In the objective analysis, "victory" is an abstract and perhaps ultimately elusive concept. "Classifying people as successes or failures is looking at human nature from a narrow biased point of view," observed Chekhov. "Are you a success or not? Am I? What about Napoleon? And your servant Vassily?" The actor cannot *determine* that his character shall win. All he can do, in enacting his character, is to *try to win.* And that is because the character himself, seen as a real person, is trying to win.

This means that "getting into a character's situation" is a dynamic and focused concentration, with the focus on the character's long-range and short-range victories. The actor, in getting into the character's situation, focuses on *improving* his character's situation. His goal is not analysis but action, not understanding but winning. This is what people's lives are all about, what characters' lives are all about, and what the actors must portray. The actor who shows a character not trying to win in a life situation will be as successful with the public as a boxer who throws fights.

"You are the spokesman for your character, you put
his case. Are you going to win or lose? There'll be
no Drama if you look like a loser at the outset."

—*Clive Swift*

There are cases in which this is not obvious as it may seem here.
There are characters in the dramatic literature of all periods who seem
confused and defeated by life, bored, disgusted, against happiness,
against love, and generally nihilistic. Inexperienced actors frequently
jump to nihilistic interpretations of characters, because they are easy
and personally unthreatening to play. But the deeper, positive victories are there to be played. The most disillusioned character has deep
longings for joy; the most anti-romantic has deep needs for validation;
the most confused has a passion for clarity. The refusal to take one's
life is, in itself, an ultimately positive act which confirms that the
quest for victory remains an active one. The goal of the actor is to find
just what kind of victory can be wished, what kind of situational improvement can be sought, what kind of winning can be pursued.

INTENTIONS

The importance of this can hardly be overstressed. The most common
term for the character's drive to victory is *intention* (occasionally "objective"), and virtually all schools of thought about acting agree on
three principles:

1. The actor must play intentions, not attitudes or indications.

2. There is a hierarchy of intentions, including large intentions (superintentions) and small, moment-to-moment intentions (subintentions).
3. Intentions are only positive. "You cannot play a negative intention."

Intentions, of course, are *character intentions;* they are situational, not contextual. Principle one, above, means that the actor must concentrate on improving his character's situation, rather than attitudinizing, posturing, or indicating to the audience that he is the character. The baseball player, for example, plays baseball; he does not try to look like a baseball player. Hamlet tries to improve his situation vis-à-vis Claudius, he does not go around trying to look like a melancholy Dane. Principle two implies that some victories are more long-range and general than others; the need for love, for example, might dictate a drive to wed Juliet, which might dictate a wish to awaken Friar Lawrence. The first is a superintention, the last a subintention, in this hierarchy. And principle three indicates that intentions should all be phrased in their positive aspects—in terms of things the character wants to do, rather than things the character wants not to do. This is simply a matter of perspective. If a person wants to avoid the cold, we can also say that he wants to find warmth. Both are correct, in analytical terms, but only the latter can be *played* with requisite power and intensity.

At this point it might be wise to ponder some examples and exercises involving situations, contexts, winning, and intentions.

EXERCISE: REMOVING THE AUDIENCE

Take a naturalistic scene that has been memorized, rehearsed, and presented before an audience, preferably in an acting class. Restage the scene as taking place in public; in a campus dining hall, for example, or in the bleachers at a sporting event or a band concert. Then have the "audience" take the part of other members of the public, sharing the same space with the actors. Some audience members can be designated as friends of one of the actors, some of the other, some of both, and some of neither. Let everyone in the audience participate— including the instructor if it is an acting class—as "characters" in the restaged scene. Then have the characters re-enact the scene without regard to any theatrical presentation whatsoever, responding to whatever stimuli their new surroundings provide. Repeat several times.

Removing the audience is often the only way an actor can be made fully aware of all the performance "tricks" that *automatically* pop up every time he appears on stage—on *any* stage, even an acting class platform. We are familiar with stage technique from earliest childhood; we see it not only on the stage, but in television commercials, lecture platforms, and political appeals. It is hard to gain self-awareness of our own overexposure, hard not to pick it up and use it. When it is pointed out to us, we tend to deny it. (In our minds, if not in our words, we are all capable of saying "please give me some criticism of my acting," and then rejecting in our minds everything we are told.)

Exercises, such as the one above, are far better than criticism in showing us, both as participants and observers, the tremendous difference between interacting and performing, the tremendous *theatricality* of interacting without performance "tricks," and the huge unwanted baggage of poorly developed, immature "performance techniques" we have picked up unconsciously, and which we automatically thrust between ourselves and our most effective performance ability.

GAMES AND META-GAMES: IMPROVISATIONS

Games are another means of removing the performance context from "acting" behavior, since they involve the actor in situational interactions. While games have been particularly popular in acting training since the landmark publication of Viola Spolin's *Improvisation for the Theatre* (1963), they are not exactly a new development. Jacques Copeau used them in company training exercises for the Theatre du Vieux Colombier in 1913, and one can easily imagine their frequent use in the days of commedia dell'arte and before. Games, of course, are essentially systems which are highly improvisational, and in which the ending—unlike a play—is unscripted. Because of this, games are easier to play than scripted roles, since the player's ignorance of the future is genuine, and his involvement consequently is more freely and fully entered into. Games and improvisations are frequently used by directors and acting coaches to draw actors into deeper situational involvements than they are reaching in scripted scenes or plays. This can have a profound teaching effect, if the game involvement can then be transferred to a scripted involvement.

EXERCISE: GAME-PLAYING

Memorize and rehearse, with a partner, a short naturalistic scene involving verbal (but not physical) conflict, such as an argument between father and son, husband and wife, or two sisters. If this exercise is done in an acting class, the entire class can divide into partners and similarly prepare scenes. Perform the scenes.

Now play a physical game, either one-to-one (such as table tennis, arm wrestling, foot-racing) or a team game (such as "Red Rover" or "Streets and Alleys"). Analyze the energy level in the scene against that of the game. Was the game more intense? Did it involve more "caring" from the participants? Did it create more emotional excitement? Was the conflict sharper, more precise, more "real?" The answer to some of these questions will ordinarily be "yes."

If this exercise is in an acting class, try this experiment. Go outdoors on a pleasant day and find a large vacant area near where other people are passing. There, perform three or four of the scenes without specifically trying to attract an audience. Then play a vigorous game of "Red Rover." Which activity spontaneously draws the largest number of casual spectators? In the cases where this experiment has occurred, the game attracts many more spectators than the scenes. As the game seems to involve more energy, more caring, and more intensity on the part of the participants, so it creates more fascination for passing (and remaining) spectators. In short, sheer physical and emotional energy is, by itself, "theatrical," even in the form of a simple children's game.

Now, *make the game playing and the acted scene fuse, by engaging in both at the same time.* Actors who are paired in a scene are now paired in a game which is to be played simultaneously. For example, the father and son scene is performed with the actors playing table tennis at the same time. The husband and wife play their marital discord while arm wrestling (preferably, in this case, the standing version in which the opponents try, while shaking hands, to force the other off balance). The sisters argue while running a race.

In this exercise, do not rehearse the game itself, or try to orchestrate the scene to it; rather, simply *try to win the argument and the game at the same time.* Try to make your winning within the game aid you in winning within the scene; and try to make your winning within the scene aid your winning the game.

The concentration on the game situation, and the intention of winning, lends a depth to the interaction and distracts the actor-player from contextual awareness, bringing out greater and greater personal energies. The combination of game-playing and situation-playing is, as a result, an intense theatrical mechanism, which many playwrights and screenwriters have taken advantage of. The first act climax of Arthur Miller's *A View from the Bridge* is a noteworthy example, in which Marco and Eddie engage in a weightlifting contest (lifting a chair by one leg) while inwardly contesting the right to control a family situation. *Hamlet,* of course, concludes a host of inner conflicts with a dueling game. Films have frequently featured their climactic moments occurring in the prizefight ring, or at the poker table, or in the pool hall, or even in a hot pepper eating contest. Directors also add game situations or game interpretations into scenes of theatrical conflict, often by suggesting that the characters are "sparring," "fencing," "jousting," or "scoring" with each other. Actors should recognize, and use, the possibilities of games and game-like competition in liberating their strongest energies.

A META-GAME: GAME-FIXING

A meta-game is, literally, a "game about a game." It provides a fascinating exercise for a group of actors, an exercise called "game fixing."

In Game Fixing, a group leader establishes a basic one-against-one game such as those mentioned in the previous exercise, preferably a short game that can easily be played by everybody. Then the leader divides the group into pairs of opponents who are reasonably equal in their skill at playing the game. Each pair of opponents will then be matched, one at a time, against each other with this proviso: the group leader will first privately instruct each pair of opponents as to whether their match will be "honest" or "fixed." If they are to play an "honest" match, both opponents simply play all out for victory as they would ordinarily do. If they are to play a "fixed" match, they *pretend* to play an honest match, but must reach the prearranged score as instructed by the group leader. Everyone then watches the series of matches, and votes as to which matches were "honest" and which were "fixed." After a round of matches, the meta-game is then repeated two or three times, with new instructions from the group leader. Winning the meta-game, therefore, consists of convincing the spectators that both your honest and your fixed matches were honest— while also seeing through the dishonesty of the others.

This game can be scored, if you wish. Give yourself one point for each time you correctly "vote" as to whether the matches you watch are fixed or honest, and one point for every time another player votes your match as being "honest." Notice that you get the same points for having your honest matches voted honest as your dishonest ones; the appearance of honesty is equally essential for honest and fixed matches.

Playing a fixed game, and convincing the observers that it was an honest one, is structurally identical to acting a part in a play; in fact those who participate in fixed sporting events, such as professional wrestlers, are widely considered to be actors, not athletes. The theme of the fixed sporting event is fairly common in the theatre (for example, *The Great White Hope*), partly because of the Pirandellian aspects of an actor playing a player acting.

It is interesting that in game-fixing it is not at all unusual for "honest" players to be judged "dishonest" by observers. This results from the implicit double-bind of the requirement to "appear honest." To try to "appear honest," one must think about what it takes to "appear honest"; yet one of the most important characteristics of the truly honest person is that he is oblivious to the need to appear honest. He simply *is* honest; he needn't think about it at all. To "not think about it" is, of course, an impossible command if one follows it directly; here is a fine opportunity for the actor-player to test how well he can throw himself into a situation, and drive contextual considerations out of his consciousness. Everyone who takes part in the game-fixing exercise should have an opportunity to play both "honest" and "fixed" games in the meta-game.

WINNING: THE PRESENT AND THE FUTURE

Winning is *enjoyed* in the present. It is *pursued* in the future. Both enjoyment and pursuit are vital aspects of acting performances.

We don't think about this often, but most of our wakeful moments are winning ones; little (or big) victories that occasion at least a flash of joy. We smile at someone and they smile back at us: we have "won" something very pleasant, and we take joy in that victory. We feel like sitting down, we *want* to sit down, so we find a place to sit down and we *enjoy* sitting. Another little victory with its accompanying dollop of pleasure.

We enter a conversation because it interests us; when it stops interesting us we find a way out of the conversation, and then enjoy the silence. In sports, winning all too often necessitates another's losing, but in life we can win entirely on our own. For most of us, *the majority of our daily moments are victories.* Certainly the "big wins" may be far beyond our grasp (or what's a heaven for? as Browning asked) and days and weeks may go by with depression sinking into depression; the fact remains that we daily engage in literally thousands of win-directed, purposeful activities in which we generally do in fact win. And when we win, we experience at least a momentary happiness; a fleeting, evanescent joy.

Therefore it is one of the most important aspects of acting to experience, along with your character, the joy of these victories, the relish of the moment. And this joy is *immediate;* it is what we mean by "acting in the here and now," in the phrase popularized by the psychologist Fritz Perls. *There can be no great performance without a quality of pure relish.* It permeates the behavior of all dramatic characters, whether great heroes, great villains, or all the more ordinary figures. Naturally we must see the quality of relish in Hamlet; but we must also see it in Claudius, Ophelia, Osric, and the Second Gravedigger. We must see it in the pathetic Laura of *The Glass Menagerie*, not only in the grand moment when she dances with Jim O'Conner, but in the plainer moment when her mother drops the subject of her leaving the secretarial school. To the world, Laura may be a failure for dropping out of the school, but the actress playing Laura must see her not with the world's eyes, but with her own—Laura's—eyes. To Laura, she *wanted* to drop out of school, she's *happy* that she did it, and she's absolutely *ecstatic* that she's going to get away with doing it.

Essentially, characters (like people in the world) are who they are because they *want* to be who they are; they do what they do because they *like* doing what they do. If a character is melancholic, it is because he or she prefers melancholy to gregarious stridency. Characters, like people, may be presumed to have created their own personality; from their point of view (if not from their psychoanalyst's or dramaturgical analyst's), they are acting in pursuit of pleasurable ends and relishing their victories when they happen. This is not to deny that life—for people as well as characters—presents us over and over with its big failures, tragic disappointments, appalling circumstances, outrageous deprivations, and catastrophic reversals. It *is* to say that from moment to moment, in the here and now of human behavior, we are who we want to be, doing what we want to be doing, and taking a delight in it all. To lack that delight in performance is to fail to create the life of your character.

EXERCISE: RELISHING MOMENTS

1. Decide to enter a (real or imaginary) room. Enter it. Delight in entering it. Look for a chair to sit in. Find the chair. Exult inwardly at finding a chair not already taken. Sit in the chair. Relish sitting in the chair. Take a breath. Taste the air. Relish the air you breathe. Gorge yourself with it.

2. Close your eyes. Relish the freedom that permits you to close your eyes. Relish the fact that you will be able to open them again at will, but choose to keep them closed. Run your tongue around the inside of your mouth. Enjoy the feel of your gums, your teeth, the shape of your jaw. Relish your saliva.

3. Reach your arms out. Enjoy your health. Appreciate your size, appreciate the space you can fill.

4. Look around you. Find something to look at and enjoy looking at it. Let the joy reach delight, even ecstasy. Make no effort to show your feeling, but make no effort to hide it either.

5. Look around you. Find a person to look at, and enjoy looking at him or her. Find something very wonderful about the person. Make no effort to show (or hide) your feeling, but indulge in it freely, fully. Relish the air, too; your position in the chair, your freedom to observe, your attractiveness, your secret worth.

6. The following is the first stage direction from the play called *Butley,* by Simon Gray. Using a combination of real, makeshift, and imaginary props and furniture, go through the following pantomime relishing every moment in your own way:

"An Office in a College of London University. Two desks, opposite each other, each with a swivel chair. Ben enters, in a plastic raincoat, which he takes off and throws into his chair. He has a lump of cotton wool on his chin, from a particularly nasty shaving cut. He goes to his chair, sits down, looks around as if searching for something, shifts uncomfortably, pulls the plastic macintosh out from under him, searches through its pockets, takes out half a banana, a bit squashed, then throws the raincoat over to Joey's desk. He takes a bite from the banana, removes it from the peel and drops the last piece onto his desk. Then he throws the peel onto Joey's desk. Then he touches the cotton wool and tries to pull it off. He lets out an exclamation. Touches his chin, looks at his finger, mutters "Bugger!" He gets up, looks under his desk, drags out a bulging briefcase from which he pulls an opened bag of cotton wool. He delves into his briefcase again and takes out a tin of Nescafe. He shines the base on his sleeve, then holds it to his chin as if it were a mirror. He tries to put the cotton wool on. He shoves the Nescafe tin back into his briefcase and stuffs the cotton wool into his jacket pocket. He goes across to the main switch and flicks it on. The strip lighting flickers into brilliance. He checks the cotton wool using the glass door of his bookcase as a mirror, then, unable to bear the striplight, flicks it off again. He goes across to Joey's desk and tries the lamp. It comes on. He wipes stray wisps of cotton wool from his fingers with the banana skin, then drops it into the clean ashtray on Joey's desk. He switches off Joey's lamp and carries it to his desk."

THE FUTURE

Lovely as the present is, and wonderful as it is to drink it in, the present is also, by itself, elusive. While the past yawns darkly behind us, and the future limitlessly ahead, the present is but a single line of vague dimension separating those two vaster infinities. And it is a moving line at that, impossible to catch. The very moments that we taste disappear as we taste them; the sentence you just read is already in the past, so is the one you are reading now . . . or *were* reading then. . . .

The point is that we can only fully experience the present by being in it, and being in it means looking at the *future*. For that is what we continually face; the next moment, the next hour, the next day, and the lengthening futures beyond. Ahead is where the victories lie, the fantasies, the intentions to be realized, the situation to be improved. And it is all there in the future, although visualized at the moment. As football coach George Allen says, "The future is now."

When we analyze a character, as a psychiatrist might, it is customary to explore his past to find motivating and determining influences. The actor does this as part of his homework in characterization, as discussed in a later chapter. *But at the moment of performance, the actor rarely thinks of the character's past and never concentrates on it.* This is because the character doesn't, because people don't. This is perhaps the greatest difference between analyzing a character and playing a character: the actor must think from the character's viewpoint,

---

"The actor is an artist, not a critic. His job is not to explain a text, but to bring a character to life. To understand as an intelligent man and to understand as an artist are two completely different things, and it is only by being absolutely clear about their relative importance that an actor can build up his part."

—*Paul Claudel*

---

not from his own. He must look actively into the future, not retrospectively and meditatively into the past. Even Hamlet's famous retrospective meditations are culled up as the bases for what should (or might) become future actions.

In his in-performance thinking, the actor must treat his character as *self*, not as other nor as object. The actor should work to see through his character's purposeful and win-directed eyes, not through his actor's analyzing ones; he should see what the character sees, and just as important, remain ignorant of what the character does not see. He should adopt his character's thinking, including the character's mindsets, thinking channels, and moment-to-moment thoughts. He should, finally, develop the same self-centeredness as his character. It is for these reasons that the actor must act from intention rather than motivation.

INTENTION VERSUS MOTIVATION: CYBERNETIC ANALYSIS

We must clearly understand that motivations and intentions, far from being synonymous terms, are in fact opposite viewpoints. Both are interpretations of behavior, "motivation" from the past and "intention" from the future perspectives. Our interest in motivation is a result of deterministic thinking, which holds that every action (or "effect") is the result of a preceding action (or "cause"). There is nothing specifically *wrong* with deterministic thinking, which is at the heart of Newton's physics, Pasteur's medicine, and Freud's psychology; but newer thinking systems, taking into account Einstein's physics, intracellular biology, and post-Freudian psychology, tend to dispense with the deterministic perspectives and replace them with future-oriented cybernetic ones. Cybernetic thinking tends to be more accurate in complex systems (of which the human personality is surely one) and it is more useful in living, ongoing systems which cannot be fixed and frozen for analysis (as on a psychiatrist's couch) without severe alteration. The trend toward conjoint analysis and reality therapies is a mark not only of changing thoughts about psychotherapy, but changing thoughts about thinking.

Cybernetic analysis is based on feedback from the future rather than cause from the past. It is the best kind of analysis for the actor, because it is closer to the analysis that his character makes, and that we make daily. This may be made entirely clear by an illustration:

What we have here can be described essentially in two ways. We can say, deterministically, that we have a man running away from the bear. The bear is the "cause" and the "effect" is the running away. Because we are outsiders looking at this drawing, this is the most usual first-reaction description we would give to this scene.

If we were the man running, however, we would almost certainly think this: this is me running toward a safe haven. The man in question, at the moment of running, is not thinking about how he happened to be where he is, or how the bear happened to be where the bear is. The man is concentrating totally on how he can get to the door safely, how he will open it, how he can increase his speed, how he can take the best path to the door, and so forth. He is planning his immediate future—the next ten seconds of it—and probably making contingency plans as well ("if the door is locked, I will climb on the roof"). He is looking ahead, imagining possible and contingent futures, developing subintentions out of his superintention, and reaching out for any information (feedback) which can help him fulfill his intentions. He is thinking cybernetically at the moment, not deterministically. The actor *playing* that man should think cybernetically as well.

The reorientation from deterministic to cybernetic thinking is absolutely vital for the actor to make, for it is the central mechanism by which he moves from understanding a character to playing the character and bringing him to life. It is the process by which the actor enters into the character's mind, and sees with the character's eyes. Three key reminders will focus the actor's attention on this reorientation:

1. Seek the purposes rather than the causes of your character's behavior.
2. Do not ask "Why." Ask "What for?"
3. The character is "pulled" by the future, not "pushed" by the past.

Why do we say "purposes"? It is, of course, frequently comfortable in life to say that we have no purposes. Purposes often threaten others, and are confused with ambitions and schemes. It is certainly more pleasant to think of one's crying as "caused" by hurt feelings than "intended" to induce guilt. But the actor will always be better off by exploring, with a great deal of frankness, the intentional and purposeful nature of his character's acts—even the most unconscious and seemingly innocent actions of sympathetic and innocent characters.

"What for?" is not at all a synonym of "Why?" even though most people use the two terms interchangeably. "What for" asks in terms of the future, and in terms of an intended result. "What did you do this for" means "for what intention, for what anticipated result, did you do this?" "Why" relates to the past and to determinism. "Why did you do this" invites answers of prior motivation and causes.

Why did the chicken cross the road? Because his mother made him.

What did the chicken cross the road *for?* To get to the other side. The whole point of the old joke is that the deterministic question (why?) is given a cybernetic answer (to get to the other side—a result, not a motivation).

"Why" has, of course, a reputation for being the world's greatest question. We needn't quarrel with its importance to philosophers or to deterministic psychiatrists, and there will be times that we will use it as actors. But in the onstage moment to moment investigation of behavior, "what for?" is a far more useful and important area of examination.

The character is pulled, not by any external force, but by the intended results he imagines or sees ahead of him. This is a metaphor, of course; the running man is not truly "pulled" by the cabin door, and the man who is "called" into the priesthood may in fact be called merely by a projection of his own desires; nonetheless that pulling has the character of an outside force if only because, *from the subjective viewpoint*, it is perceived by the character "pulled" as being such. One of the greatest advantages of seeing action as being "pulled" rather than "pushed," is that pulling is a far more accurate process, as any child with a toy wagon knows. Accuracy in pushing depends on the interrelated assortment of many different vectors: in order to push a wagon (with freely rotating axles) it is necessary to push from at least two vantages with each force precisely counterbalancing the others; to pull the wagon requires a single rope and no counterbalancing at all. In analyzing behavior in terms of the "pushing" of past motivational causes we are forced to reckon with the literally billions of incidents, traumas, memories, pushes, and shoves the flesh is heir to; this makes any interpretation, in all but a handful of cases, mired in excess data. As Professor Paul Watzlawick reports, "the search for causes in the past is notoriously unreliable . . . the most appropriate strategy . . . is a search for pattern in the here and now rather than for symbolic meaning, past causes, or motivation." Looking at behavior from the intentional, or "pulling" perspective, we can frequently isolate the significant forces with great accuracy.

FEEDBACK AND FEEDBACK LOOP

Feedback is the governing principle of cybernetic systems and of the actor-character's behavior when viewed cybernetically. Feedback, essentially, is the information we seek out to guide us in pursuit of our intentions; it is our radar. A common example of feedback in a cybernetic system is the thermostat on a regulated furnace; the furnace is a cybernetic system calibrated to go on when feedback reveals the room temperature is too low, and to go off when feedback reveals the opposite. The cybernetic system, therefore, is a self-correcting system rather than a continuously correct one. "Smart bombs" and guided missiles are similarly self-correcting cybernetic systems rather than perfectly aimed projectiles, and they depend on feedback from their sensing instruments to reach their targets. Physiologists, particularly in the Soviet Union, have explored feedback principles in all animal behavior, even at the cellular level.

The feedback loop is simply the cycle of information in any communication system, or any interaction. When two people talk, a simple feedback loop is engaged, in which both people are receiving and sending out information to and from each other. Both of them, following their intentions, seek the information which will guide them in im-

"There's a physical law called Kirchoff's Law of
Radiation, which states that the best absorbers are the
best emitters. Actors are in the business of emitting,
of giving out, but they can only give out what they've
managed to take in and absorb."

—*Hume Cronyn*

proving bad situations—and in maintaining or improving good ones.

A feedback loop is *always engaged* when people are conscious of
each other's existence. One cannot *not* communicate. To remain "un-
communicative" is to communicate dislike, disapproval, or a variety
of other feelings and informational bits. In the feedback of a common
interaction, an ordinary conversation for example, thousands of signals are transmitted and received every minute, from conscious verbal
dialogue, to conscious non-verbal signals (shrugs, winks, gestures), to
the unconscious and autonomic behaviors of our physiology, behaviors
of which we are all skilled observers and interpreters. We all know, for
example, how to understand the way another person's breathing shifts
when they are enraged with us in an affair (political, business, or romantic); we know how to read the hesitations, grimaces, nervous
laughs, studious looks, eyebrow archings, flesh reddenings, eye moist-
enings, nostril flarings, and chin juttings of our friends, rivals, parents,
and real or imagined lovers. Whether these behaviors are consciously
or unconsciously generated may be a subject of great controversy case-
by-case; that they are all part of the feedback of information which
makes us adjust our behavior toward the satisfaction of our intentions—and sometimes to adjust our intentions as well—is quite
certain.

The actor who gets into his character's situation, therefore, gets
into his character's feedback loop. Like the character he plays, he both
sends and receives a great spectrum of information which guides him
toward the fulfillment of his intentions and superintentions. This is

essentially what Stanislavski meant by the actor "living the part," which could be perhaps more specifically described as "living the character's life," or experiencing the character's interaction. The mechanism for doing this may be called making contact.

MAKING CONTACT

Making contact is a fairly obvious process; it becomes important only when attempted at depth. In making contact, *the actor experiences his character's interactions by the simple means of interacting with the other actors;* it is with them that he makes contact and with whom he exchanges information. In this way acting is an entirely real behavior.

Making contact, on the surface level, is or can be physical. Touching is the most obvious form of contact; looking into the other actor-character's eyes (eye contact) is equally direct. But indirect contacts are quite as real: listening, feeling, sensing, and evaluating.

"The people who talk about the Method at great length are the people who are involved—for the most part— in what I call the abuse of the Method. They're the people who look for the sickness in a role, not for the health, and this is not what sick people do; sick people look for the health. Right now I'm playing Ben Franklin as a sixty-nine year-old man, but I'm not thinking him old because Ben thought young. Now, he moves a little more slowly than Harold Hill did, but his mind is just as young as Harold's was, so you put on the accoutrements of age but you think young."

—*Robert Preston*

"Actors are in the highest degree in *connection* with
each other. And this they are without strain, by no
overt means. . . . Their emotions simply occur, easily,
abundantly. They overflow in action; action, considered
as an expression of the *energy* between the Self and
Object, an 'oscillating' character—back and forth,
back and forth. It is a matter of many levels."

—*Morris Carnovski*

EXERCISE: THE MIRROR

One of the most common theatre-training games is the mirror
exercise, and it is an example of a pure feedback contact
between two people. In the basic mirror exercise, two actors
face each other and mirror each other's movement. Neither is
designated as a leader; both simply watch and follow each
other. "Thinking" need play no part in the mirror exercise,
because the cybernetic principles work unconsciously; a left-
ward movement stimulates a rightward (mirroring) movement
in the person opposite; this occurs at the instinctual level. In
the purest sense, mirror exercises draw their structure unconsciously, and are naturally choreographed by the subtlest
intentions and mind-sets of the participants.

Variations on the mirror exercise are these: (1) A mirror to
music: mirror exercises performed to recorded or live music,
or to randomly played piano chords. The music enters into the
feedback loop and induces new directions in the movement.
(2) A vocal mirror: the addition of sounds and words, which
must be acoustically mirrored (repeated) by the person opposite.
(3) Three or four way mirrors, or more: additional people in the
exercise. (4) One way mirror: with a real mirror.

The reason why mirror exercises are so effective, and so universally in use, is that they force a total situational concentration; a total concentration on the *other* person rather than the self, and a total concentration on the future (what is the other person about to do?) rather than the past. These concentrations are strong enough to drive out all contextual awarenesses (such as the presence of an instructor or fellow classmembers) and therefore provide a useful example of complete situational involvement.

Obviously, the prime requisite for making contact is the *total immersion into perceiving the other*. An actor who does not do this is simply not living his character's life, and therefore not living at all; he is simply presenting the audience with a series of actions (movements, gestures, and lines) which are out of the human context and therefore lifeless. Receiving information is as important as presenting information; we only do either one in concert with the other. An actor who does not listen, does not observe, does not sense his situational opportunities, is only playing one half of his part and is only representing one-half of a human being. This can hardly be overstressed.

THE ACTOR AS OBSERVER

The actor's responsibility as an observer is a keen one. While it may seem at first to be less showy than line delivery or balletic movement (which will be discussed later), observing is one of the most powerful stage actions that can be performed. It is also one of the most riveting. The mirror exercises can be immensely theatrical to spectators, when situational concentration and observation are total. A boxing match, ping-pong game, or other sporting competition is fascinating when seen as a battle of observations; the players are ferreting out each other's possible weaknesses through a microscopic examination of their moment-to-moment actions and changes. The concentration of the actor on his situation interests us as much as anything he *does*; lacking that concentration, we are hard put to be interested in anything he otherwise presents us. Almost every bad performance can be distinguished by the glassy, unseeing eyes of the bad performer, and his apparent disinterest in everything but making a good impression to the audience. One of the criteria for judging players in the game-fixing exercise (earlier in this

"Every night when I go out onstage, I remind myself to keep my responses fluid, to keep them really moving. Whatever is said to me, I can really respond. . . . Although I never push my responses, I do try to coax them."

—*Anthony Perkins*

chapter) is how much they seem to be observing their opponent rather than posturing in a competitive attitude.

EXERCISE: THE FISHERMAN

Playing a fisherman is a good exercise to test observation in an actor, for fishing is a subtle example of a feedback situation.

When asked to play a fisherman, virtually everybody who knows anything about fishing will be able to put an imaginary hook on an imaginary line, and cast the line into an imaginary river.

What distinguishes the fine actor in this exercise is that he will, in addition, wait for a fish to bite! He will receive imaginary tugs on his imaginary line, and adjust his line in conjunction with the information fed back to him from the situation he initiated. In short, he will be seen to *want* fish—like a fisherman! He will be playing an intention (to catch fish) rather than just demonstrating fishing techniques. For him the situation will be lived, not merely described.

This fishing metaphor has a great many applications. We often think of certain things we say as "fishing" comments; that we are "fishing" for a compliment, or for a clue, for example. To an extent that we are seldom aware of, however, all of our communications "fish" for some sort of response. Many scene acting problems can be solved by the coach, or director, simply asking the actor to play his scene, or

"Dancing is, for me, beyond a series of steps, or the
reproduction of a story, or the expression of a
mood or feeling, or the visual display of music, an
amplification of our energies in a way special to it.
Sports also are an amplification of energy, and there
are many similarities: baseball, football, gymnastics—
yet dancing is different. It has its own quality; it is its
own necessity, and unlike sports, there is no goal,
nobody wins, or rather each dancer has the chance to
win at any moment over the course of the performance."

—*Merce Cunningham*

line, as if he were "fishing for" something rather than "declaring"
something. This returns the actor to the ever-present intention, away
from motive or attitude.

VULNERABILITY

It could be thought that making contact is easy to do, since it begins
with observation, which is a natural human act. It is not easy to do for
most of us, however. There is a reason for all the glassy stares and stiff
acting we see in the beginner (and all too frequently in the veteran):
it is because nature has provided us with defenses against adversity.
Stiffness makes us more formidable; glassy stares make us more frightening, labored breathing makes us more awesome. This has been true
biologically for many thousands of years, and it is hard to shake off
now—particularly in the potentially threatening context of the theatre,
with its audience, friends, critics, and employers. Concentrating thoroughly on another, of course, means dropping one's concentration on

"Olivier is a great actor partly because he shows us so
much of himself in all his performances, partly because
he is unafraid to reveal those elements in his personality
that most of us are trained to keep hidden. Men are
taught from childhood to be ashamed of their femininity:
Olivier exploits his brilliantly and therefore enables
all of us to come to terms with a part of ourselves."

—*Michael Billington*

oneself, and that risks a dangerous exposure to the person who is sensitive to real or imagined vulnerabilities. As British stage director Patrick Garland says, "All human beings surround themselves with layers of protection to prevent exposure, and yet actors are in part required and impelled to reveal themselves all the time." One of the hardest things for an actor to learn is the mechanism for allowing his vulnerabilities to breathe, and to break down his emotional rigidities.

These rigidities are like flags, which the actor holds up as if to say, "this isn't me." Nowhere is the flag more evident than in a heavily "dramatic" scene, where the character is seen to cry, scream, shout, and groan in utter despair. All too often the actor gives us, instead of his own despair, a grand, cruel, *magnificent* despair drawn from his theatrical imagination. In brief, while he is pretending to be in despair, he is presenting us with what he thinks of as magnificence; what we see is not his agony but his (unfounded) exaltation. This is all a sham performance, and the audience, of course, sees right through it. Invulnerability is invariably covered over by the most obvious sort of overacting—what the audience refers to as "ham acting."

What the actor must do is be able to get down to an essential rawness in which his vulnerabilities are neither defended nor hidden. This does not mean, however, that they are necessarily put on the table for everyone to chop at. While it has become common in recent years for group therapy or self-revelation sessions to replace all or part of re-

---

"One of the things I like about my profession, and that I find healthy, is that one constantly has to break oneself to pieces."

—Liv Ullmann

"I doubt myself the way everybody else does. The thing I loved about doing Hummel was this kid was inept at everything but he had this great hope. He had hope and I loved him for it. I loved to show that desire."

—Al Pacino

---

hearsals for certain plays, these practices are probably overrated. A sense of trusting within the acting company is the most productive environment for this rawness, as is the ambience created by a sensitive and skilled director. Yet the actor must always be on the alert for techniques to develop his own freedom from invulnerabilities, and his own capability for healthy exposure.

EXERCISE: I CAN BE HURT BY YOU

One fundamental exercise for developing emotional vulnerability is an absolutely simple one: two participants face each other and say, in alternation, "I can be hurt by you." This can be repeated on deeper and deeper levels by a sensitive coach, who first asks the two people just to *say* the sentence, then to *mean* the sentence, then to "make the other person *know* you mean it." This simple exercise is one of the most powerful devices for drastically deepening the situational involvement of actors in an intimate scene.

Intrinsic to the success of the "I can be hurt by you" exercise is the absolute fact that, regardless of the people involved, *the statement is true.* What is more, it is *known* to be true. Everybody has the power of hurting everybody else, and while those hurts are not of equal degree, none of them are inconsiderable. We are all hopeful of the respect, admiration, and friendship and perhaps even love of everybody, and therefore anyone has the power to hurt us by withholding themselves. So the exchange of sentences is simply an exchange of known facts; but they are *facts that are never said or implied in ordinary discourse.* Quite the opposite, virtually all our daily and moment-to-moment communications convey just the opposite: that we are powerful and invulnerable people who cannot be hurt by anyone! Social conditioning that transcends generations and lifestyles has made us try to appear practical rather than emotional, realistic rather than dreamy, knowing rather than naive, enigmatic rather than having our hearts on our sleeve. A few bad life-experiences—romantic failures, emotional rejections, losses and disillusionments—and our exteriors harden further yet. But this hardness is tenuous; it is postured rather than felt. Far from making us truly powerful, the effort to cover our vulnerabilities makes us apprehensive and wary. The posturings of the actor afraid of self-exposure are usually pathetically unsuccessful.

The simple and pure conveyance of the "I can be hurt by you" message, therefore, lifts a huge burden from the actor's shoulders. It is a public admission of his most secret vulnerability; once he has admitted it, and been seen to admit it, he has little left to fear, and little left to hide. Then he is free to build a truer power base, one which derives from his own feelings about himself rather than a desperate need to hide behind some sort of artificial posturing in the name of characterization or stylization. The frank, shared confession of vulnerability is a first step toward acting with commanding power.

EXPECTATION

Vulnerability liberates acting; expectation provides the driving force. Expectation is itself a powerful mover of men. Maxwell Maltz, in an all-time bestseller entitled *Psycho/Cybernetics,* shows how improving one's expectations ineluctably leads to an improvement of one's fortunes; this is also the basic theme of the popular self-improvement doctrines of Dale Carnegie and Robert Ringer. In a series of celebrated experiments on classroom education, scientists observed that students who were privately designated to their teachers as "potentially high achievers" became high achievers *in fact,* even though the original designation was utterly false (the students had been randomly selected). Sports figures universally report that expectations of victory are essential if victory is to be achieved; expectation is a self-fulfilling prophecy, a service in its own behalf.

The actor making contact with his situation should do so *always with the expectation of winning.* This is true even when the character, as determined by the script, will eventually lose. It is true even when that expectation can be considered hopelessly unrealistic. It is true because it echoes the behavior of people in life.

Let us look at some examples. The man running from the bear, we understand, is concentrating on the haven of the cabin door. He expects to reach it. That expectation may not be very realistic, but if he didn't expect to reach it—didn't at all—he wouldn't be going toward it.

In *The Glass Menagerie,* Laura, as it turns out, does not win the love of Jim O'Conner. But she intends to win it and she expects to win it. It is Laura's *expectation* which is the most appealing and enchanting aspect of her character, and it is the failure of that expectation to be fulfilled that gives the play's final scenes their great poignancy. A performance of that play that did not give the audience the whole portrayal of a girl's (dashed) expectations would be emotionally sterile.

Therefore the actor should not simply look to the future; *he should lean into it.* His concentration should be active and positive—expectant. The American Conservatory Theatre of San Francisco uses the verb "positate" to describe this "positive concentration," and this is a good motto to follow. In a play where all the actor-characters are playing to win, and expecting to win, the action is going to be dynamic and engaging. Where they have already given up without a fight, the action is perfunctory and futile, despite the possible brilliance of the line readings and the scenery.

EXERCISE: EXPECTANCIES

Take a character and write up his expectancies. Visualize him having everything he wants. Visualize a day in his life one year from now, with all his expectancies fulfilled. What does he hope other people (in the play, or in the world of the play) will become? What does he hope will happen to them? In short, give a complete description, in words, drawings, or discussion (or a combination), of the *ideal future* that the character himself perceives and works toward. Create several ideal futures for the character at different points in the future—for tomorrow, for next week, and for five years from now. Create *contingent* ideal futures for the character; that is, futures that can be expected or fantasized if a certain event comes about. In all these imaginary exercises, do not be constrained by realistic considerations. Fantasize freely on behalf of your character, and let your imagination soar! Remember Liza Doolittle, the flowergirl:

> One day I'll be famous! I'll be proper and prim
> Go to St. James so often I will call it St. Jim!
> One evening the King will say: "Oh Liza, old thing,
> I want all of England your praises to sing.
> Next week on the twentieth of May
> I will proclaim Liza Doolittle Day!
> All the people will celebrate the glory of you,
> And whatever you wish and want I gladly will do."
> "Thanks a lot, King," says I, in a manner well-bred;
> "But all I want is 'enry 'iggins' ead!"

The expectations of Liza, unrealistic and displaced as they are, provide her (as well as the actress playing her) with the momentum of power.

IDEAL FUTURES: SUMMARY

The ideal future is an effective summary concept, embracing all of the topics discussed earlier in this chapter. When the actor plots out the ideal future of his character, he is making situational discoveries, he is adopting the character's viewpoint, he is defining the intentions which are to be won in the future, and he is creating the expectations that provide sufficient hope and drive to empower the performance. He is also setting himself up for a fall, which becomes the source for his vulnerability, and opening himself up for feedback, which becomes the source for a change in direction. The concept of the ideal future, since it contains the unknowns of the future, is a device which can set the actor into the *flux* of the character, the improvisational nature of human acts even within a scripted play. It creates, for the actor, a context in which he is dynamically, purposefully, and powerfully moving through a play, rather than placidly reiterating foreign lines in an alien environment. It makes acting a *process* rather than a result. The specifics of that process are discussed in the following chapter.

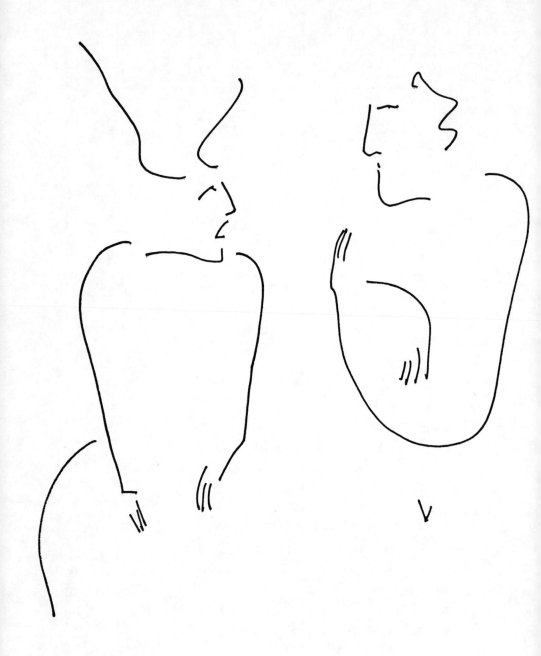

mani

CHAPTER 2

PLAYING THE SITUATION: INTO THE OTHER

"The closest thing to acting is bullfighting or boxing.
It's a matter of adjusting to the other man's blows.
You're so busy adjusting it's difficult to think of anything
else."

—Anthony Quinn

Playing the situation, or being involved in a situation, means interacting with other people. Interacting takes place along a feedback loop, where every word, gesture, breath, glance, and physiological act communicates meaning. Behavior, then, is a process of communicating: receiving and emitting signals. In acting, the actor *communicates* with his fellow actors, just as in the play the characters communicate with each other.

Communication and interaction are both ongoing systems, not single events. The feedback loop is always engaged when people are conscious of each other's presence (or suspicious of each other's presence); when the loop exists, the interaction and communication are continuous, both at the conscious and unconscious levels.

Communication has two basic modes, and they occur simultaneously. Communications theory has labeled these the *content* and *relationship* modes of communication.

Content and relationship modes were first described when it became necessary to develop computer languages. It was found at that time that computers needed to be fed information at two entirely distinct levels: (1) data for processing, and (2) instructions on *how to process* the data. The "how to" instructions became a sort of meta-information which provided a context for the basic information.

In ordinary human conversation, the same two-fold nature of communication takes place. On the first level, we transmit a certain specific content; on the second, we proffer a relationship between ourself and the other person, a relationship that will suggest to him how our content should be received.

For example, a college professor, in a lecture, says, "Shakespeare was born in 1564." That Shakespeare was born in 1564 is the content of the communication, but it is not the whole communication. That the professor stands while the class sits, that he speaks in complete and formal sentences instead of colloquial fragments, that he speaks unquerulously, wears pressed trousers, a shirt and a tie, that he reads from notes and carries a briefcase: these all communicate too, conveying the relationship message that says "I want you to know that the sentence I just spoke is correct, supported by evidence, accepted by all authorities—of which I am one—and you are to write it down and memorize it forthwith." This "relationship message" qualifies the content and directs how it should be received. If the professor dressed himself in a clown suit, moved like a gorilla, and spoke like a baby, it is certain that the content would not be received in the same way, and the whole communication would be vastly altered. Relationship communication is the foundation of all communication—of all conversation and interaction—because while relationship messages may be exchanged without content (as with a smile), content is meaningless without a relationship.

The communication of relationship is not limited to speakers. In the same example, students of the professor will be communicating relationship messages to him: by the way they nod (or refuse to nod) at his remarks, chuckle at his witticisms, write down his summarizing epigrams, and smile at him when he looks their way. It is vital to realize that at every moment we participate in relationship-mode communications with everyone of whose presence we are aware. We cannot *not* do this.

Relationship-mode communications are not statements; they are *invocations.* One person cannot define a relationship, he can only suggest how he would like it to be defined, and suggest it in such powerful terms that the other person will accept that definition. Communicating a relationship is like the fisherman throwing a baited hook into the sea; it is an incomplete act until a bite is felt at the other end. This completes the loop and the communication.

Since communication is a continuous, ongoing event, we may say that the relationship mode of communicating is a process of the *continual redefining* of a relationship. Every character in every play is engaged in that process; every character continually redefines his relationship with every other character. Obviously this ongoing redefinition is of more dramatic importance when it is seen to occur between Hamlet and Gertrude, for example, than between Hamlet and Horatio— but it takes place in every relationship, and it must be seen to be taking place in every staged relationship.

The responses to relationship invocations can take any of three basic forms: confirmations, rejections, or disconfirmations. The student who nods brightly at the professor's remarks obviously confirms the relationship the professor is trying to establish; so, in a more modest way, is the student who simply sits and listens. The student who makes scowling faces, on the other hand, or raises his hand in objection, or creates a class disturbance, is expressing rejection. But the harshest response to a relationship communication is disconfirmation, as by the student who reads a newspaper during the lecture, or engages in extraneous gossiping. The disconfirming response conveys the message "I have no interest in how our relationship is to be defined—you do not exist for me." It is through the ongoing exchange of relationship invocations and their various responses—which themselves can then become relationship invocations—that human relationships grow, develop, change, and (although certainly not always) decay.

RELACOM

The importance of relationship-communication is so wide-ranging as to be unavoidable in the study of acting, but our awareness of it is so new that we lack a suitable term for it in theatrical parlance. "Subtext," a term developed by Stanislavski, refers to relationship communication but to a good deal else besides; "subtext," which means, literally, "under the text" or "between the lines," is essentially a literary term referring to the "real" meaning of a line. Relationship communication however, may be conveyed *by* the line as well as under it, and it may be totally irrespective of the lines. Relationship communication occurs without a text, and is best not considered as tied to it—even by opposition.

Therefore, we have little choice but to refer to relationship communication by its own name, or by the "coined" term *relacom*. Relacom:

(a) is the short form of "relationship communication."
(b) is always the invocation of a relationship, not the announcement of one.
(c) is not necessarily communicated consciously, and in fact is usually an unconscious communication.
(d) creates the basis for communicating content.
(e) always exists when people are in contact, even without an accompanying content communication.
(f) is most usually nonverbal, and may not necessarily be closely definable at the verbal level.

Relacom, although a newly defined term, points to what are *far and away the most important and significant parts of most day-to-day interactions*. If we study the tape recordings of ordinary conversations, we will find that most of them are trivial at the content level, but rich at the level of relacom. Apparent content questions like "How are you doing?" are, of course, not content questions at all, and no one expects a content answer. Content is often an icebreaker; we say "Nice day, isn't it," in order to find, through nonverbal cues, how the other person will relate to us this morning. Eric Berne has called these "stroking" communications, because their effect is to induce a verbal caress akin to a mother's stroking of her infant; Berne has shown how predominant these stroking communications are in everyday life. Another psychologist has claimed that "all messages when viewed at their highest abstraction level, can be characterized as 'Validate me' messages." Naturally this invocation of validation, or of love, respect, admiration, or trust, is not a conscious or deliberate, focused communication. *The relationship mode of communication is not one of which we are fully aware most of the time.* The professor is not consciously invoking respect, and the student is not consciously pulling for a good grade. But

---

"Acting doesn't have anything to do with listening to
the words. (As you're first told in high school plays—
'Listen, don't just wait for your cue, listen to what the
other person is saying.') We never really listen, in
general conversation, to what another person is saying.
We listen to what they *mean*. And what they mean is
often quite apart from the words. When you see a scene
between two actors that really comes off you can
be damned sure they're not listening to each other—
they're feeling what the other person is trying to get at.
Know what I mean?"

—*Jack Lemmon*

---

these things happen, and they can be seen to happen, and they constitute
the inner action of every play. They must be played with the same
intensity they have in life.

EXERCISE: THE CONTENTLESS SCENE

Memorize, with a partner, the following lines of dialogue:

A: Hi!
B: Hello. *Howare you* 7
Sure, works. A: What'd you do last night?
B: Oh, not much. How about you?
A: Oh, watched a little T.V.
B: Anything good?
A: Well, no. Not really.
yeah, well B: See you later.
A: OK.

Then play the scene as if it is occurring in the following circumstances:

1. A casual pick up.
2. Husband and wife meeting the night after a trial separation.
3. Father and daughter at breakfast after she's been out late.
4. High school girls meeting after each suspects the other of dating a mutual boyfriend.
5. A homosexual pick up attempt.
6. A rejection of friendship.
7. Lovers unable to meet except for a few moments.
8. Any of the above as a telephone call.
9. Any other situation suggested by the group.

This exercise may be performed by a large group, with A's pairing off with B's serially.

When the exercise is performed, it becomes clear that the content mode of the dialogue becomes relatively insignificant, and that the relacom becomes virtually the "whole" scene, without changing a word of the text. It can also show how riveting a contentless scene may be when strong relacom is established by the performers.

RELACOM VICTORIES

In the previous chapter we discussed the general victories that each character, like each person in life, seeks. Victories essentially derive from very basic and biological drives, toward survival, security, power, love, and validation. But they also have highly specific subgoals. These subgoals can all be viewed as relationship victories; or more simply as relacom victories. This is because it is *from, with, and for other people that our life-victories are to be won*. We do not act in the abstract; we act in the context of our world. For the most part, that context is human. Man is a social animal. Most of the victories we expect will be gained through our relationships with other people.

In a relacom victory, we try to favorably redefine our relationship with another person in a specific way. Insofar as we can verbalize this process, we usually do it by characterizing the person as having a functional relationship to ourselves. "My wife," for example, defines an individual person as a function of "me" rather than as an entity in her own right. Persistently we tend to think of people, at least privately, as "my lover," "my friend," "my enemy," "my colleague," "my roommate," and so forth. Socially, we may find this tendency to treat other people as functions of ourselves rather reprehensible; psychologically, however, it is ingrained, because it develops in earliest infancy. Specialists in infant psychology can demonstrate that the child's first impression of reality is wholly self-centered; the child believes that his mother, for example, is a part of him, and in no way sees reality as having a separate existence. The child's first intellectual task is to distinguish himself from his mother; to discover her as a separate person living a separate life. This task is never entirely completed, not at the deepest levels; all adult life, it is possible to say, is in part an effort to come to terms with the separateness of others.

Relacom victories, therefore, are highly private adventures, frequently immature and often antisocial, but always present in the deeper levels of psychological reality and human intercourse. We see people, in part, as being functions of ourselves, and we also seek to redefine that function favorably to ourselves. We may feel, for example, "Alice is my friend, but I want her to become my lover." This is an intention toward a relacom victory. "I want him to be my employer," "I want him to be my idolator,"—these are other intended relacom victories, expressed in the "functional" manner.

To be effective in performance, relacom victories should be specified as narrowly as possible. What kind of "friend?" What kind of "lover," "employer," or "idolator?" Consider the following expanded list of possible "relacom victories":

procurer	stooge	abductor	old lady
apprentice	pacifier	doctor	mistress
interpreter	rationalizer	admirer	jester
debtor	defender	king	cleanser
voyeur	yes man	subject	whore
playmate	no man	punisher	stud
recorder	doer	victim	defiler
torturer	nurse	eulogizer	hatchet man
imitator	inspirer	angel	leader

soldier	coach	slave	worshipper
manipulator	historian	sister	killer
child	catalyst	comrade	pimp
fan	savior	colleague	pal
stepping stone	valet	teacher	nemesis
damsel	quickie	rival	first lay
eunuch	critic	god	executioner
mouthpiece	mystic	corrupter	protege
footlicker	maker	confessor	redeemer
big brother	abuser	confidante	cannibal
puppet	pet	buddy	rapist
guinea pig	pastor	doll	bean bag
supplier	analyst	beast	boss
moulder	tease	sodomist	fairy princess
pusher	icon	flagellator	

Relacom victories consist of pursuing these specific intentions (as designated by the text, by the director, or by the actor in his homework on the script) within the confines of the dialogue and action of the play; using the dialogue and the action, as well as the actor's own personal gifts, as tools to achieve the relacom victory so chosen.

EXERCISES: PLAYING RELACOM

1. Take the memorized contentless scene, and play it with a partner after having selected one of the specific relacom victories listed above. After the scene, have observers try to guess which relacom victory each actor was playing for.

2. Take the following scene from *Woyzeck*, a nineteenth-century German play, and, with a partner, memorize the parts. Then play it, choosing one of the specific relacom victories to win during the scene.

> WOYZECK: The pistol's too much.
> JEW: So, are you buying or not buying. Make up your mind.
> WOYZECK: How much was the knife?
> JEW: It's good and sharp. Going to cut your throat with it? Make up your mind. I'm giving it to you cheap as anybody. You can die cheap, but not for nothing.
> WOYZECK: It'll cut more than bread . . .
> JEW: Two groschen.

WOYZECK: Here! *(Goes out.)*
JEW: Here! Like it was nothing. And it's good money.
    The pig!

After the scene, have observers try to guess which relacom
victories were sought.

3. With a group of actors, take either the contentless scene
or the *Woyzeck* scene, and have half the group learn one part,
half the other. Then, pairing A's with B's, or Woyzecks with
Jews, perform the scenes between pairs simultaneously, with
each actor engaging in a relacom of his own choosing. At the
end of the round of scenes, exchange partners and repeat.
Notice how the relacom determines the action and characterizations of each scene, and how the personalities of the
individual actors, as well as their conscious choices, can affect
the relacom that is played.

4. With a partner, play any scene from any play, already
memorized, with a specific relacom victory chosen from the
above list which is not necessarily pertinent to the scene as you
have previously understood it. Have observers try, as before,
to guess the relacom victory that is pursued, and the change
in the scene from when it had been performed previously, if
that had been the case.

5. Play any unstructured improvisation with selected relacom
victories in mind, but avoid any direct content expression
pertinent to the relacom.

EXERCISE: ANALYZING RELACOM

Take a well-known play and analyze the possible relacom in
terms of the above list, being bold and imaginative in your
choices. What could be the relacom, for example, between
Hamlet and Gertrude? Hamlet and Claudius? Claudius and
Gertrude? Hamlet and Horatio? Hamlet and Ophelia? Ophelia
and Laertes? and so forth.

In exploring and defining the relacom victories sought by his
character, the actor must allow himself abandon, not restraint, for
timidity will only lead to stereotyped and passionless performances.

Unfortunately, we are socially conditioned to have a horror of ambition, or at least of admitting our ambition, and we have a great deal of reluctance to picture ourselves as anything like grasping, climbing, plotting, or designing people, particularly insofar as we may have "designs" on the lives of others and fantasies about them. But we do, and characters in plays do; we mustn't shrink from the reality of the character's plans, hopes, and fantasies. The speculation of the character's wished-for relacom victories should be penetrating, incisive, potent, and subtle. It should involve self-analysis, for that is where the most unique and idiosyncratic—and therefore the most unexpected and theatrical—fantasies and ambitions will be found. It should dig and it should reveal; probably nothing so regularly typifies dull and deadly theatre as the actors who insist—usually passionately—that their characters wanted nothing but modest goals, pleasantly pursued. On the contrary, most plays if not most lives are lived on the expectation of the great lures of carnality and power-lust, and to ignore that is to opt, in the theatre, for a genteel and quite unlife-like banality.

How do you play relacom? Since it is largely unconscious, it cannot easily be simulated consciously. Fortunately, the theatre provides the perfect and complete mechanism for playing relacom: *the actor plays it with the other actors.* While we must be dubious about any

---

"Most actors' problems, professional or amateur, deal with tension. In a very professional actor, someone like Bruce Dern or Karen Black, the tension is because they haven't made a choice that has taken enough of their mental interest. In other words, they haven't made a vital enough choice; it's not up to a level that will engage their imagination and get them into pretending unselfconsciously."

—*Jack Nicholson*

---

single statement claimed to be "the secret of acting," there is some reason to think that if there were a secret, that would be it.

In short, if John, playing Othello, decides that Othello's relacom
victory at a certain moment was to make Brabantio, played by Joe, into
Othello's footlicker, the task for John is to make Joe become John's footlicker. If John-Romeo wants to make Jane-Juliet his lover, then John,
while acting Romeo's lines, tries to make Jane fall in love with him.

At the level of relacom, the actor and the character are indistinguishable from each other; they are merged. This is why acting is *acting*.
This is why it engages, not only the consciousness of body and voice,
but the entire human organism: the autonomic nervous system, the
sweat glands, the emotions, the tear ducts, and the thousands of hidden
processes which control intonation, resonance, movement, flickerings,
heartbeat, and respiration.

The relacom of a scene is not necessarily for actors to discuss during rehearsal, and it is not something that they mutually "agree to play."
The relacom victories characters seek with regard to other characters
are pursued publicly but articulated privately. They do not stem from
any mutual agreement; in fact they evolve from disagreement, or dissonance, between one's self and another. Relacom exists because there
is tension between people that needs to be bridged, behavior that needs
to be adjusted, relationships that need to be redefined. If the actors are
forced to articulate publicly, or agree publicly, to the relacom of the
scene, they will often retreat to a simple and bland analysis of the potential relacom victories ahead of them—ones they will not be embarrassed to admit and to be seen to play.

For there should be no mistaking the fact that playing relacom
means *private fantasizing* among the actors in a play—fantasizing with
respect to each other. From the viewpoint of Jane-Juliet, after all, John-
Romeo is simply and singly one person. She sees one body and hears
one voice; her relacom response is to that body and that voice, and not
to an abstract name that is either "John" or "Romeo." "What's in a
name?" she might well ask, for names are irrelevant to relacom. She
simply projects her relacom victories, intended, fantasized, and expected, onto that human being across from her—and she works to win
those victories. Relacom takes place between *bodies*, not "names," or
"identities," or "characters."

We must understand that most people will have a certain reluctance if not an outright unwillingness to project what might or might
not be their own fantasies and wishes upon their fellow-actors. Many

---

"An actor must interpret life, and in order to do so he must be willing to accept all experiences that life can offer."

—*Marlon Brando*

---

people consider a good number of fantasies distasteful and therefore unimaginable. A person concerned about his own possible latent homosexuality, for example, could easily feel threatened by the instruction to fantasize himself in love with another person of his own sex—and even more threatened to realize that he must play that fantasy fully to the other actor. This sort of reluctance or refusal usually leads to caricatured portrayals, where the actor, as mentioned earlier, holds a figurative flag in the air proclaiming "this character is not me!" Nothing could be more debilitating to a performance. *To the actor, nothing must be unimaginable; nothing must be unplayable.* What the actor does in his private life is, of course, his own business; what he allows himself to dream on in the theatre is the theatre's business. An actor who is mentally inhibited from playing for relacom victories which, in life, are repugnant to him, is an actor whose range is critically limited both emotionally and behaviorally. The actor must have full freedom in his own mind, and not shrink from imagining, and imagining *expectantly,* the relacom victories which are theatrically engaging.

EXERCISE: FANTASIZING FREELY

By yourself, fantasize freely about a fellow actor while looking at him or her. Without revealing or trying to reveal anything yourself, think these thoughts about and "to" the other person:

> I would like to love you.
> I would like to kill you.
> I would like to torture you.

I would like to explore your body.
I would like to explore your mind.
I would like you to be my _____.

What happens to your mind when you do this? What inhibitions interfere with your following these instructions?

Variation: Fantasize freely about your partner when performing the mirror exercise. How does the fantasy affect the movement? How does the movement affect the fantasy? In a feedback loop, remember, there is no cause and effect; every element "pulls along" every other one.

Variation: A group of people are asked, by their leader, to fantasize freely about each other while performing mirror

_____

"The better I get as an actress, the freer I feel. Actresses have to exhibit themselves, to hang themselves up on a clothesline. Onstage, you often find that you're free to do what you can't do in real life. . . . In my own life, I was brought up to be well-mannered, no matter where I was or what I was doing. . . . Onstage, I found . . . I was free to reveal exactly what I felt."

—Jane Fonda

"An actor can't be a prude or a moralist. If he is, he shuts his eyes to the possibilities of feeling for or with another kind of human being. . . . [The actor's] job is to portray his character with the greatest sympathy and understanding."

—Melvyn Douglas

exercises. They are instructed not to reveal, or try to reveal, anything whatever of themselves, and not to discuss the exercise afterwards. Does this exercise make you nervous? Why? Don't you realize people fantasize about you anyway? And that they know you fantasize about them? When this exercise is used during the rehearsal of a play, it can dramatically deepen the relacom of the play's interactions, and the intensity of its emotions.

EMOTION

Playing relacom with another actor brings out the actor's own emotion. This is vital for his performance, because it is only the actor's own emotion which is usable on stage.

We are conditioned by life to show little or no emotion, just as we are conditioned to project images of invulnerability. This conditioning causes a wide spectrum of acting problems. For the rankest beginner, it usually means passionless and placid line readings, feeble movements, and vapid interactions. For the second-stage beginner, it all too frequently occasions great histrionics—simulated but quite

---

"When you start to rehearse with other people something begins to happen. What it is exactly I don't know, and don't even want to know. I'm all for mystery there. Most of what happens as you develop your part is unconscious, most of it is underwater. . . . you get taken over by some force outside yourself. Something happens."

—*Kim Stanley*

---

artificial emotional posturings. Both of these manifestations are refusals, conscious or otherwise, to allow the audience (or anyone) to see our *own* anger, lust, or romantic longings. This is theatrically unacceptable, even if it is covered by an imitation of Al Pacino's anger, Glenda Jackson's lust, or Liv Ullman's romantic longings.

What is most important about the actor's own emotions is that they are unique to him and they are idiosyncratic to his personality (as are Al Pacino's to Al Pacino), and as a result they contain the breath of life. Moreover, they stimulate or catalyze the body's autonomic systems, and lead to the otherwise consciously uncontrollable endocrine reactions: increased heartbeat and blood pressure, dilation of the pupils and bronchi, adrenalin and sugar release in the bloodstream, contraction of the spleen, and so forth.

The engagement of the body's physiology is an adjunct of emotional involvement, and it cannot be faked.* In the close-up acting of films, the physiological behavior of the actor can be quite directly observed; even in stage performances, however, the audience is quite aware of major physiological processes going on before their eyes. In a celebrated example, the fine American actor Hume Cronyn could be seen from every seat in the house to blush a fiery red during a climactic moment in *Noel Coward in Two Keys.* The moment occurred when Cronyn read his past letters from a former (homosexual) lover; Cronyn reported that his "technique" was simply to allow himself to be deeply involved in the situation, and release the emotions which naturally flowed from that involvement.

A more complex problem regarding emotion arises when the actor uses his own emotion, but plays it directly, or "pushes" it. Emotion cannot be consciously played. An actor who tries to "show fear" only "shows showing," which is showing-off. This is contextual performing, and it is frequently called *indulgence.* One of the first mechanisms developed by Stanislavski was his "emotional recall" or "affective memory," in which an actor recalled a situation in his own life to stim-

---

*There is a long-standing controversy among acting theorists as to whether emotion causes physiological response or physiological behavior causes an emotional response. Common sense has traditionally supported the first view; the so-called James-Lange theory (after its separate discoverers) suggests the second. Most contemporary psychologists consider the controversy to be irrelevant, and use instead a cybernetic feedback model which dispenses with cause and effect, and considers emotion and physiological change interrelated, with neither having primacy over the other. See "Failure of the James-Lange Theory" in Jeffrey A. Gray, *The Psychology of Fear and Stress* (1971).

"Should the actor work out the details of his part in
personal terms, should he succeed in engaging his own
secret anxieties and enjoyments—his private beliefs,
his dream-life characteristics, should he then insinuate
these secrets into the ebbing and flowing of the play,
he will be inevitably swept into the main lines of the
action—he will be forced unconsciously from point
to point in his performance."

—William Redfield

"The actor lives uniquely in the present; he is
continually jumping from one present to the next. In
the course of these successive presents he executes
a series of actions which deposit upon him a sort of
sweat which is nothing else but the state of emotion.
This sweat is to his acting what juice is to fruit. But
once he starts perceiving and taking cognizance of
his state of emotion, the sweat evaporates forthwith,
the emotion disappears and the acting dries up."

—Jean-Louis Barrault

---

ulate an emotional display during the course of his performance. Stanislavski dropped emotional recall in later life, but many actors continue
to draw up and push out their emotions in this way. Few actors are
comfortable with the practice, however, and it is more often harmful
than helpful.

How then should emotions enter into the playing of a part? Jean
Louis Barrault, the great French actor, mimist, and director, uses a sublime metaphor for emotion in performance: Berrault compares it to
the sweat of a long-distance runner. Run hard, suggests Barrault, and
the sweat will form. Try to sweat (try to "show that you are running

hard"), and you will fail to concentrate on running, and fail to sweat. The drive toward relacom victories will draw forth the actor's own emotion as surely as the drive toward the finish line will draw forth the half-miler's sweat. Emotion, the perspiration, must be *drawn* from the body; it simply cannot be pushed out.

The problem of creating emotion honestly and idiosyncratically does not, of course, end with the understanding of Barrault's metaphor. Understanding emotion and creating it are two different things. Every actor at one time or another will face the stage direction "breaks into tears and sobs helplessly." Without a satisfactory mechanism to turn on one's own tear systems, the actor is forced to rely on fakery or gimmickry. Several of these mechanisms are a matter of characterization, and are discussed in Chapter Three. One which is presentable here is the actor's playing *to suppress the physiology of the emotion.* This is sometimes called "playing the opposite," or "playing against the emotion." Essentially, the actor first contemplates all the physiological symptoms associated with the emotional state the script dictates him to play; then he tries consciously to suppress them in himself. If the script asks him to sob helplessly, for example, the actor tries to imagine all the symptoms that that act would bring forth: tears, of course, and perhaps a churning of the stomach, a shortness of breath, a weakness of the arms and knees, a looseness of the bowels, perspiration on the soles of the feet, and so forth—whatever the actor imagines would happen to *him.* Then he tries to *suppress* all of these imagined physiological changes; to tighten his bowels, relax his lungs, steady his stomach, embolden his limbs, and dry his soles! If he makes this conscious effort, and goes back into playing the relacom of his scene, the emotions are likely to arise spontaneously. We might say that this is a case of double-binding the self, or "fooling" one's own body; it "works" because our body is familiar with suppressing the manifestations of emotion, and finding those suppressive functions at work, the "body" comes up with the emotion to justify it! Stimulus-response theories find this difficult to explain, but it is a very simple outgrowth of cybernetic and double-bind systems.

Playing the opposite draws emotion from the actor through real, personal, and situational means, for playing the opposite is nothing more than engaging in the character's own behavior. It is the *character* who tries to suppress emotional displays which threaten his posture of invulnerability. When the actor engages in this character intention— when he tries to tighten his own (and the character's) bowels, breathe normally, and stop the sweat he feels beading on his palms, the actor is simply doing what the character would be doing, and his emotions will be forthcoming as a reaction to the character's intentions, not as a direct and conscious result of them.

EXERCISE: PLAYING THE OPPOSITE

1. Play a drunkard by trying to walk a straight line with absolute precision. (This is a classic example. The drunkard is not identifiable because he cannot walk a straight line, but because he tries so hard to suppress his fear of being unable to do so.)

2. Play a son grieving for his mother's death by trying to laugh at a joke told by your well-meaning but insensitive uncle.

3. Play a wife who is fearful of dying from cancer by bravely giving your husband instructions on having the house cleaned before you return from the hospital after surgery.

4. Play a love-torn fiance by coldly describing your lover's desertion of you for another.

5. Deny that you hate someone.

In all of these exercises, you need not "protest too much"; simply "enough" will do. Concentrate simply on *doing the exercise* rather than making the exercise work. The exercise cannot be pushed or it becomes exactly what it has been created to overcome. You cannot yourself judge if the exercise has worked (although you can certainly tell when it doesn't): better let an outside observer judge the exercise while you concentrate on doing it.

TACTICS

Tactics are the means by which we win, or seek to win, our ideal futures. They are the conscious and unconscious strategies of relacom.

It will seem at first glance, most likely, rather offensive to discuss behavior in terms of tactics. Most of us pride ourselves on behaving naturally and spontaneously without any thought of tactically manipulating our environment, or other people. The idea that man has tactics is particularly loathsome in most contemporary religious, moral, and social thinking, which holds spirituality as the virtual opposite of tactical plotting and planning. A recent book and film which suggested that Jesus Christ acted tactically in the development of Christianity was universally interpreted as being an attack on Christ—by non-Christians as well as Christians—on the underlying assumption that tactical behavior is *on its face* immoral, regardless of the worth of its consequences. Added to this, knowledge of the tactical basis of our victories often takes much of the relish away from them; it is all the more pleasing to think that we have "won" something without having sullied ourselves by tactically "going for it." Therefore we all have many built-in inhibitions against examining the tactics of our behavior, or the tactics of our character's behavior.

These viewpoints cannot be disputed morally, and of course there is much human behavior that clearly is spontaneous and non-tactical. A baby's cry as it leaves the womb cannot appropriately be described in tactical terms, for example. The fact remains, however, that if we are candid enough to examine behavior closely, we can see that most of it is, at least in part, tactically designed—consciously or unconsciously—to aid us in achieving our ideal futures and our relacom vic-

---

"People hearing about [Georgy Girl] would say, Oh, that's about a girl who has problems. Georgy Girl to me was a very different person, very ruthless. Most people saw her as a sweet softie. I don't think she was a softie at all. She was manipulating and very shrewd. People loved her, I think, because they recognized their own terrible faults and were glad to see them put up on the screen. I think she was quite ruthless. That's not to say that I disliked her. I liked her for all that. I have to find likeable things about the bad things [my characters] do."

—Lynn Redgrave

---

tories. People use tactics, characters that represent those people must be seen to use tactics, and actors who play those characters must use those tactics. This is therefore a necessary field for the actor to study, and to study closely.

Tactics may be roughly grouped into two major categories: those that *threaten* and those that *induce* ("induction" tactics). The former are "I win, you lose" in nature; the latter, which are much more common, are tactics aimed toward mutual satisfaction, mutual victories. Both kinds of tactics can work, both can fail, and both can be used in a myriad of combinations. Together they create an actor's power and his electricity on stage, threat tactics being primarily responsible for the actor's forcefulness, and induction tactics giving the actor his charm. "Charm" here is used not in the debased sense of "charm school" behavior, but in the more evocative sense of a person's capacity to draw pleasure from another aɪd share it—as a snake charmer pleases himself, his snake, and his audience. It is an infectiousness, in other words, which is transmissible.

Let us always remember, in this discussion, that most tactics are entirely unconscious and spontaneous. Raising one's voice to win an argument (a threatening tactic) is most usually automatic and natural, but it is still *intentional* (deriving from an intention), and it is tactically directed toward victory at both the content and the relacom levels. That is, when the person (character, actor) raises his voice in this way, he is using a tactic both to win the subject (content) of the argument and to redefine his relationship with the other person (I want you to be my student). This may be subtle, even undetectable. But it happens.

We must also remember that there is nothing necessarily malicious, unkind, or cynical about tactics. Smiling to receive a smile in

---

"Power lies in the logic, the coherence of what you are saying."

—*Constantin Stanislavski*

return (an induction tactic) is a universal and usually spontaneous act of human kindness. And yet it is also a purposeful communicational signal. We don't, in fact, ordinarily smile in the privacy of our rooms; rather, we smile *in order to* create a climate that is desirable for us to inhabit. Whether the smile is "genuine" or "fake" is perhaps ambivalent, and is certainly irrelevant to its tactical usefulness.

Finally, we must remember that most tactics are not in the least devious, but on the contrary are right out in the open (which is why the actor must particularly be aware of them). The two examples above—raising the voice and smiling—are wholly observable tactics. Tactics only become devious and hypocritical when they are covered by a meta-tactic (a tactic to hide tactics) which attempts to deny them.

THE META-TACTIC OF DECEPTION

The meta-tactic is an attempt to deny that tactics are being involved. Meta-tactics can be entirely direct, as exemplified by a former President of the United States who repeatedly declared that he wanted only to make things "perfectly clear," and that he was "not a crook." More often meta-tactics take the form of voice tones, postures, expressions, and grimaces that indicate obliviousness to tactical pursuits. The sanctimonious tone, the pious stare, the aloof carriage, and the bland, quizzical expression are all characteristics of the meta-tactic of deception. Actors must be able to spot these and to play them as well.

THREAT TACTICS

Threat tactics do not necessarily imply a direct and immediate physical assault; they simply convey the message, "I am stronger than you are, and you would be mistaken to try and cross me." Threat tactics are largely implicit, and almost always subtle and indirect. Even the feeblest of dramatic characters can be shown to employ some of them, though not necessarily with any great success, and most dramatic characters can be shown to attempt to use all of them from time to time. Threat tactics are those by which the character seeks to dominate a situation by intimidating, frightening, or overcoming others. They should be explored by the actor in playing every role, as a means of developing the character's full range of action. Several are identified in the following paragraphs.

Taking charge   The basic threat tactic is simply to dominate a situation by confidently and assuredly issuing commands. There is a familiar (true) story about a frail lady schoolteacher in New York who was taking a class of third-graders to the Museum of Natural History on the subway. When she arrived at the appropriate station she stood and declared to her charges, "Everybody out!" To her astonishment, the entire contingent of passengers—commuters, shoppers, and tourists—rose and meekly followed her and her third graders out of the subway car and onto the platform. Sudden, unexpected, and seemingly determined action frightens people and tends to make them subservient and obedient. It is astonishing how much "power" is simply available for the seizing; a good offense with positive expectations and a take-charge attitude is a strong and useful acting tactic.

Overpowering   Mere size, and the brandishing of size, is a threat tactic of equally high utility. Raising the volume of your voice has a frightening, and sometimes a paralyzing effect. A whole host of predominantly male behaviors—huffing and puffing, setting the jaw, narrowing the eyebrows, curling the lip, flaring the nostrils, drawing up to one's full height—have been labeled "flexing" tactics by many social scientists, who claim they play a function in the control of women by men. Much of this behavior is biological, and can be seen in animals: the roar of the lion as well as the arching and hair-raising of the kitten are both instinctual tactics to appear powerful.

Observing intently   The investigative power is an intimidating and threatening force, and investigative agencies, regardless of constitutional restrictions that are placed upon them, quite frequently become bastions of might. Tom Wolfe reports the brilliant tactic of Ken Kesey, whose itinerant bus crew was frequently subjected to police raids. Kesey bought movie cameras, and countered the police investigators by filming them with his cameras; the police quickly panicked and went away. Lie detector tests, which depend on the subject's fear of exposure, can be defeated if the subject becomes an investigator himself, and simply observes his "investigator" for clues as to, for example, the investigator's family life. To be able to see without being seen (to be invisible), of course, is one of the great power fantasies of small children and not a few adults.

Conclusiveness   A forceful person does not willingly prolong discussions, he concludes them to his benefit. Effective speaking, then, requires conclusiveness; the gesture, expression, or tone which conveys the tactical message "and that is all there is to be said about it." To be conclusive, say your lines as though they were curtain lines, as though they ended an argument rather than continued it. Conclusiveness compels silent attention, respectfulness, and adherence.

Attack   While usually used to denote the technical need in speech and singing to "hit" hard on the first word of a sentence or a lyric, the actor's attack is, in fact, an echo of his character's tactic. For while a play arranges dialogue in the form of alternating speeches, in life one is not ordinarily handed the opening to speak—one must make it. Conversational analysts call this "turn-taking"; essentially, in order to talk, one must make everybody else listen (or at least agree not to talk). The actor must not assume that he has an unchallenged right to speak just because the playwright has given him a line to say, nor the unchallenged right to continue speaking just because he hasn't finished his scripted speech. He must earn that right to speak and keep speaking. He must seize the floor, as it were, or take the stage within the stage. He can do this by hemming or grunting, of course, which is an invocation for everybody to shut up. This was an early and much-abused technique of the Actor's Studio in their quest to duplicate the give-and-take of everyday life. Or the actor can attack his speeches strongly by declaring, in his manner and vocal tone, situational intent in the very first syllable. Playwrights, if they are good, will help this out. More than 90 percent of the first words of most Shakespearian speeches are only one syllable words, which are easy to attack; many of the words which are more than one syllable are the names of the person addressed, repeated words, or commands like "listen," all of these being themselves effective turn-takers.

Follow-through   This, too, is commonly considered simply a matter of acting "technique," and countless actors have been instructed, rather routinely, not to "drop the ends of their sentences." What happens when an actor does drop the ends of his sentences is usually that he is making a contextual signal; he is letting the other actors know he is at the end of his scripted speech. In the process, the tactics of his speech are utterly disregarded.

Most frequently, it is at the end of a speech that the most significant tactical communication resides. The end of the speech usually contains the hook of the invocation; the implied or stated question that demands a response to the relacom. Speeches ordinarily are not dropped, they are *tendered.* The French often say "n'est-ce pas?" ("isn't that right?" or "don't you agree?") at the end of their declarative statements; in English we convey the message nonverbally, but we convey it just the same. Concluding a speech and demanding a response is just as tactical, and can be just as much of a threat tactic, as beginning a speech: giving up the floor and observing the person who takes it can be a powerful act. Follow-through, then, is an important *practical* action for the actor-character.

Implying a hidden arsenal   The threat of hidden weaponry—physical or psychological—can be implied by various behaviors to strengthen a character's relacom position. A simple exercise demonstrates this: in a weakly played scene, have the most offending actor pretend to hold an imaginary club behind his back. The repeated scene will be emboldened and better for it, regardless, ordinarily, of what the scene is about. The hidden weapon can also be information—something you know that the other character does not—or the awareness of a special talent. Imagine, for example, that you are a karate champion.

Screaming   The scream conveys that the screamer is beyond rational control, and therefore beyond the restraints of reason. When added to the others, screaming is a very effective threat tactic, and it is used quite often in the theatre as well as elsewhere. It is obvious that Adolf Hitler perfected the tactical use of screaming, and was able to gain control of the masses, the army, the generals, and most of the intellectuals by his supreme capability of seeming to totter on the brink of madness. Tantrums, recklessness, and gestures of indiscriminate violence can add to the tactical effect.

This is a short list of the threat tactics used in everyday life, in character interactions, and in the actor's portrayal of character interactions. As has been suggested, they are essential in developing the force of an actor's performance. But force is only half of power; the other half is charm, or magnetism. These attributes are created through the actor's use of induction tactics.

INDUCTION

A feedback loop is a circuit, and information which flows between people in a feedback loop is like the electricity which flows in a wiring circuit. When we speak of "electricity" existing between two people, it is the electricity of feedback; the constant flow of "vibrations" that is mutually emanated and supported.

Electricity can be created by a massive chemical or atomic discharge, but it is more commonly created by a process known as *induction*, in which an electrical circuit (a coil, actually) is rotated in a magnetic field. It is convenient, if not actually precise, to think of the electrons as *pulled* along by the induction, as contrasted to being pushed, as by the chemical discharge. Induction works similarly in a feedback flow of information. An *inducing* individual guides and directs the other person with whom he is engaged. This is far and away the most powerful force we have in creating attitude change in others.

The inducement of induction is essentially *ourselves.* Induction tactics are not used in win-lose situations but in situations capable of mutual victory.* Love is an obvious example of a goal which can be reached only through induction. The basis for induction, and for its success, lies in the pronounced human tendency—if not the human instinct—toward social conformity. We are not ordinarily aware of this tendency, because adult life makes us more conscious of our individuality than our shared social characteristics, but a little reflection will reveal that in our day-to-day and daily routines, we are far more similar to our fellows than different from them. This is a biological or sociobiological necessity; we, as a species, seek security in numbers, in being one of many, being part of a larger and stronger society than we can create on our own. In the long run, anthropologically, social conformity provides social protection, and we seek to insure that our uniqueness never becomes so eccentric as to ostracize us entirely from our race. Teenagers, entering adult society for the first time, acutely experience this instinct toward conformity. Whether we like it or not, admit it or not, we are *joiners.*

Joining takes the form of imitation. If we see someone smiling, we tend to smile. If we are in an audience, and the audience applauds, we tend to applaud. If they laugh, we tend to laugh. If we are amidst glum faces at a funeral, we turn glum. We tend to dress, speak, and gesture as our fellows do—or certainly as those do whom we would like to *think* of as our fellows. We join a society, or a social class, by imitating the behavior of those already in it. To the extent that we do this with

*Game-theory specialists call win-lose situations "zero-sum-games," meaning that for every point won, another player must have a point lost; therefore the "sum" of the player's scores would be zero. Mutual victory situations are called, in this terminology, "non-zero-sum-games."

a group of people, it gives us a sense of social belonging, class status, and a group identity. To the extent that we do it with a single person, it becomes individual fusion, family, and love. It also becomes our escape from loneliness, isolation, and alienation. As such, it is one of the highest goals of man; according to Erich Fromm, an important psychiatric analyst, the fundamental goal of living is "the achievement of interpersonal union, of fusion with another person, in love." This is "joining" at its most powerful; obviously tactics which rely on this human tendency or instinct will be mighty indeed.

INDUCTION TACTICS

Induction tactics involve, primarily, *projecting onto the other person the same behavior you wish him to adopt.* The instinct for joining takes care of the rest, if nothing interferes. Smile and you induce smiling in others. Put out a hand and someone will shake it with their own. Look serious and your friends look serious in return. Talk quietly and those around will lower their voices. A doctor's "bedside manner" is pure induction; by projecting calm assurance the doctor induces his patient to be calm, and to be assured. You cannot induce a person negatively, of course; you can only induce him to engage in what seems to him like pleasurable behavior, behavior he would like to join (and with you, a person whom he would like to join). "Laugh and the world laughs with you, cry and you cry alone."

More complex uses of induction involve the figurative "getting inside the skin" of other persons. In the induction of smiling, you virtually climb right inside them and smile for them, until they cannot help themselves but smile. In this manner induction becomes more like its sister, *seduction.* Stanislavski had a marvelous sense of this. "Infect your partner," he suggested. "Infect the person you are concentrating on! Insinuate yourself into his very soul, and you will find yourself the more infected for doing so. And if you are infected, everyone else will be more infected." Getting inside the skin means, above all, *understanding* the other and figuring out his mind-sets; drawing the other person out, getting in synchronization with the other, "walking in his moccasins," as the Indian proverb suggests. An actor who makes full use of his observation of others, and can project himself into other actors, *infect* them in Stanislavski's sense, is an actor who has charm, magnetism, and most importantly stage presence. His stage power will stimulate intense audience interest. Some of the basic induction tactics which have universal utility are these:

Confirming Nodding, smiling, and diminutive "um-hmm"-ing is more prevalent in conversation than we usually think. These confirmations of the other person's relacom work like a magnet to draw him out and to draw him in a specific direction, much like the children's game of hot and cold where the "leader" says "you're getting warmer!" Nodding with someone indicates intellectual (content) agreement; smiling with someone conveys the impression that you share a sense of humor with them. Laughing at a friend's joke not only confirms *it* but confirms *him:* it conveys not just "What you say is funny," but "I find you an amusing person."

Disarming The handshake developed among medieval knights as a gesture that precluded a reaching for one's sword. Induction tactics involve the projection of visages of openness and harmlessness; the bowed head of the suppliant, the bended knee of the suitor, the helpless shrug of the negotiator, and the sloe-eyed look of the courtesan.

Lulling Soothing by gentle sound or motion, lulling harmonizes with the body's alpha-wave systems and quiets the body's defense and attack systems. It is used to put babies to sleep, as in lullabyes, and to allay anxieties in adults. Soft music, euphonious sounds, and the "love hum" of people who make soft sounds when they kiss or caress are all lulling activities which, however spontaneous, do have tactical results.

Amusing Wit, joking, and engaging in humorous interplay are among the most wonderful induction tactics possible, since they connote a sharing of values (an agreement on what is funny) and a childlike playfulness in which union is both possible and desirable. Many of our most ordinary and clichéd "stroke" confirmations are based on something that was at least once whimsical: "How's it going?" "Can't complain." "Think the rain'll hurt the rhubarb?"

Inspiring Although it is not easy to achieve, an inspiring appeal— a call to arms, an appeal to pursue a profound, greater-than-personal goal—sets apart not only the political leader but often the successful salesman, teacher, lover, or friend. That an inspirational tone may be tactical does not at all mean that it must be insincere; on the contrary, it is the sincerest of inspirational messages and tones that are almost always the most effective tactically. The expression of wonder—at life, love, the theatre, the universe—and the commitment to values, ideals, causes, and people, can be used to inspire feelings in the hearts and minds of all who come in contact with them.

Flattering The word "flattery" originally meant a smoothing and gentle touch. While frankly deceitful flattery may be pernicious, flattery itself is an entirely benign and gentle act which simply means discovering the best parts of someone else and singling them out for a little praise. Flattery is rarely completely untruthful in any event. In Jean Giraudoux's marvelous play *The Apollo of Bellac*, Apollo advises Agnes to tell men that they are beautiful. "Even the ugly ones?" she asks. "All of them. In the depth of their hearts, even the ugly ones know that they are beautiful," replies Apollo. And when Agnes tells the ugly ones that they are beautiful, they *become* beautiful, much as students who are designated as high achievers become high achievers when they are treated as such. Flattery gives the recipient an expectation of improvement, and an identity to live up to. Agnes, in flattering men, liberates them.

Frankness Frankness is a special kind of flattery; it conveys the impression that the speaker means "you are my equal if not my superior, I have to level with you about this matter, you must be treated with importance." Creating the image of frankness is a high priority task of politicians in America; no presidential candidate can afford not to cultivate it. Frankness is a confirmation of another's adulthood and intelligence.

Seduction Seduction is simply biological induction, and it is of considerable importance in the theatre because so many plays deal with it, either explicitly or implicitly. In seduction, the inducements are sexual, and the mechanisms for stimulating sexual arousal are

---

"You must have a twinkle in your eye, a naughtiness— and the audience must realize your mind is working faster than your words."

—*Jeremy Brett*

---

well enough reported in anthropological and sociological literature that they needn't be detailed here, except to say that seduction, as an inductive process, involves the projection of the physical self into the other—the imitating of the kind of physical behavior you want another person to adopt. Therefore seductive behavior usually takes the physical forms of the various mating rituals and body language cuing— the winks, wriggles, gasps, croons, whispers, smackings, pinchings, tiltings; the movements of the tongue, the eyebrows, the mouth, the lips, the hips, the eyes, the thighs, the pelvis, the fingers, and the feet— which from time immemorial have catalyzed desire.

Playing these inductive tactics, then, requires that the actor take an active part in *leading* and *guiding* the attitudes and responses of the other actors. The magnetic actor is magnetic not because he makes eyes at the audience, but because he dazzles, delights, and infects the other actors with his presence, his concerns, and his whole being. He makes them smile, he makes them laugh, he makes their bodies do strange things, he makes their juices flow. Fine actors working inductively with each other develop rapport and ensemble; they develop a shared mutuality which is love itself. It was Sir Laurence Olivier who said, "actors must understand each other, know each other, help each other, absolutely love each other: must, absolutely must." This love comes out of the electricity of interaction in inductive feedback; it comes from acting with purpose and with tactical strategy.

PLAYING TACTICS

The tactics that have been described are part of the basis of moment-to-moment behavior in daily life; when they are played on stage they bring added life to the characters, and give energy and power to the character interactions.

In playing tactics on stage, you *actually use the tactic on the other actor.* If you, Tybalt, are designated to threaten John-Romeo, you must *actually threaten John.* If you, Romeo, are designated to seduce Jane-Juliet, you must *actually seduce Jane.* You must try to win, and use the best tactics in that struggle. The consensus of pretenses which is a play permits you to do this; the need for brilliance and intensity in a theatrical performance *requires* that you do it. Whether or not you succeed

"Actors work on each other's emotions."

—*Eileen Heckart*

in that struggle is not important—it is determined by the play and by the other actors in any event—what is essential is genuineness of your attempt, and the strength and power you throw into it. As the great mile runner Roger Bannister reports, "Failure is as exciting to watch as success, provided the effort is absolutely genuine and complete." And what applies here to foot-racing applies equally well to acting.

Tactics should be directed not so much toward the other actor's mind as toward his body. The strongest relacom signals are given not in words but in physiological signals, hums, grunts, eyelid flickers, palpitations, and the rest. Tactics of threatening and inducing are rarely performed consciously or received consciously; they should be addressed to the fluids of the body, to the muscles, and to the glands. *The actor should play tactics strongly enough to create visible changes in the other actor's autonomic systems.*

Tactics should be played *creatively*, not merely selected from a chosen list. You have your own tactics, those that you use spontaneously; these should be the basis for many that you will use onstage, and they will be just as spontaneous onstage as they are in your life, if you are pursuing intentions while you act. But you also have an imagination to draw upon. What can *you* do? What *can* you do? What *could* you do if only . . . ?

Tactics may be played with your heightened and acute observation of other people, and adjusted according to the findings of that observation. The depth of your relationship to the other actors is crucial. Study your partner: his face, his eyes, his body. Look for cues in his observable physiological behavior. Study *his* tactics. Observe what is really there before you. Unmask him. Undress him. Perceive him. Investigate him. Try to imagine *his* fantasies; the way he sees you as a function of *his* life. Get inside him. Evaluate the effectiveness of your tactics as you go along. Those that seem to work: intensify. Those that seem to fail: adjust. *Work.* Try for your victory, *really* try. Get it!

Is this, one might ask, a bit dangerous? Does it threaten the possibility of ensemble? As to the first question, yes, it is a bit dangerous, but a certain edge of danger is an inescapable ingredient of the highest levels of any endeavor, whether in athletics or in art. But it is certainly not unfairly, unwarrantedly, nor unexpectedly dangerous; the other actors in the play are acting too—they are trying to do the same thing you are, and they can only be fed by your efforts. Your use of real tactics actually *dignifies* the other actors and their own work on their roles. By *really* trying to seduce Jane-Juliet, you are helping her become Juliet. By *really* trying to threaten John-Romeo, you aid him in becoming Romeo. As for the possibility of ensemble, the interplay of real people playing real tactics in a scripted "play" situation, far from threatening the ensemble, absolutely creates it. It is maximum *sharing;* the actors implicitly agree to believe in the reality of each other as characters, and by so doing they reveal their own personalities as they seek real victories, both personal and mutual.

EXERCISES: PLAYING TACTICS

Take any scripted scene from a modern realistic play, and analyze it for tactics. Go through it three times, listing first the tactics implied by the author's stage directions (for example, "shouts"), second the tactics implied by the dialogue, and third the tactics which you imagine to be appropriate to the situation. Be bold in defining the tactics, and use a good mix of both threats and inductions. Then play the scene.

Take the contentless scene from the beginning of this chapter and play it using *one* of the tactics listed above for each character. Play the scene again with different tactics. See if you can use them all, in successive re-enactments.

Enlarge the list of tactics by your own analysis.

Videotape a real-life situation and analyze the taped interaction for the tactics used. Do the same with a videotape of a TV talk show or a good TV soap opera.

Analyze your own behavior in terms of your personal tactics. Be frank with yourself. Analyze the tactics of people you know well, of members of your family. This, of course, becomes a splendid background for developing characterizations.

Improvise scenes between characters who are designated by their social standing, situation, and tactics. Make these unexpected; try playing a seductive Nazi general or a bullying paraplegic, for example.

DANGER AND THE UNKNOWN: THE DOWNHILL SKIER

When asked if they enjoy acting, many young actors reply, "yes, if I know exactly what I'm doing." It may be foolish to take issue with such a lightly asked and lightly answered question, but it is worth considering that this attitude will make the actor both safe and sorry.

Confusion is the natural state of man. We exist in flux, in process, and neither our identities nor our personalities are fixed. Obscurity is at the heart of our actions: the obscurity of the unconscious, of our instincts, and of our carnality. Like Oedipus, we are always pulled forward by a future that is as mysterious as it is compelling. The Greeks called it Fate, the Elizabethans called it Fortune, the existentialists call

---

"If I'm reading the script and am held by the story and
by the character, and do *not* know how to play it,
then I'm pretty well convinced that it is a good part.
When I say 'don't know how to play it' that is 100
percent right. I don't think any actor knows how to
play a really good part. . . . The better a part is written,
the less clear it is."

—*Jack Lemmon*

"I was getting successful and very confident, and that's exactly the quality that Elia Kazan [the director] didn't want (in *Sweet Bird of Youth*). And the thing that I give him points for in terms of the play is the way he handled me. He'd come over to Geraldine Page and she'd say, 'What if I try this?' and he'd say, 'Try it.' Or he'd go over and say, 'Geraldine, why don't you try this?' And so we would play the scene, and then we would separate, and I would hear him go over to Geraldine and say, 'Ah, right on!' I'd say, 'God, I thought she was really off a little bit, that's not what I expected her to do.' Then he would always walk over to me and say, 'Ah, try it again.' He was chopping me down. By opening night, it was marvelous. I really didn't have any security in the part at all. And that's precisely what he wanted."

—*Paul Newman*

---

it the absurd: it is our target, always beckoning, always eluding complete apprehension, always causing confusion and uncertainty. At lucid moments we feel on the verge of grasping it; we are poised, expectant of some final understanding; these are moments that the psychologist Abraham Maslow calls "peak experiences." And although the grasp fails, *the poise, the verge, the expectancy remains. This poise, this expectancy, this "playing at the edge," is the true dynamic of the actor.* It is this that gives acting its excitement.

Nietzsche said that "understanding precludes acting." He did not mean stage acting, but he might as well have. The merely good, "safe" actor contents himself with "understanding" his role objectively. That sort of understanding can be comprehensive and exact, but it stultifies rather than stimulates great acting because of its very objectivity. It is deadening because it means thinking of the character as an *object* instead of as the self, because it means "understanding" what the character cannot understand, what is unknown and unknowable, mysterious and subversive. The actor must face his character's unknown future; he must share his character's consequent *danger,* and he must risk being overwhelmed. He must let himself go; poised not only for a victory, but poised on the edge of uncertainty, the verge of uncontrol.

The downhill skier is, perhaps, a good analogue of an actor getting into a staged situation. His situational involvement is absolutely intense, total. See him poised at the very moment between resting on the hilltop and beginning his descent. His weight is forward; he is leaning into a future which he cannot absolutely control. He cannot stop himself at will. His actual course is unknown and dangerous; he must observe thousands of individual and discrete pieces of information at every moment—each rock, tree, hillock, patch of ice or powder, each crevice, each skier, each gust of wind. The finish line is his goal; he is induced by gravity and by his will to win, and he adjusts his direction according to the information he receives. There is danger, and because of the danger there is exhilaration, both on his part, and on the part of those who watch him. If he were mechanically glided down a track, there would be no interest: the interest comes in the fact that he is *thinking* as well as skiing. He is, at the moment we see him, the complete actor in a situation. He is an intensely theatrical figure.

SUMMARY: TACTICAL RELACOM

Tactics and the playing of relacom are the guts of interaction in life and on the stage. The actor who defines and seeks ideal futures, and who plays tactical relacom in their pursuit, is an actor who is visibly *working.* If he is going to perform the passion of Lear, the fervor of Juliet, the mirth of Arlecchino, or the sarcasm of Archie Bunker, he cannot get away with mere shadows of passion, fervor, mirth, or sarcasm; he must give us their real presence. The actor must be seen to be seeing, thinking, planning, working, and acting. And he must be seen to be doing all these things not in the context of the theatre, but in the situation which he shares with his fellow actors on stage. He must be continually redefining his relationship with them, and he must be seen, because of his positive and expectant communication of that relationship, or relacom, as striving for higher things. Only if this happens will the actor be able to create his own life on stage, and only if he can do that can he possibly create the life of a character other than himself.

CHAPTER 3

PLAYING CHARACTER

"If you can legitimately bend a character, if you can make him behave in a certain way, as long as it's logical that he could behave that way, and if that way is dramatically or comically more exciting than a standard behavior pattern, then I say bend that character. It's the actor's duty to find out the most exciting way a role should be played, then to play that role to the hilt. This could mean bits of business, it could be underplaying, it could be climbing up and down the walls, it could be chewing up the scenery, but if he doesn't give it hell, make his characterization as complete and compelling as possible, he isn't fulfilling his function as an actor."

—*Jack Lemmon*

Much that passes for character acting, among beginning actors, is really a form of character assassination. There is an obvious reason why this is so; having gradually evolved our own personalities after many years of conditioning, we have a natural and innate, unconscious feeling that we are already the best "characters" that we could possibly become, and to play any character significantly different from ourselves is to "take a step down." For this reason young actors frequently turn immediately to stereotype and parody when asked to play a person of the opposite sex, or a person of notably different sexual, racial, generational, or political orientation. They *compete* with their characters at the personal level, and make clear their own superiority to the characters they presume to represent.

CHARACTERIZATION: CHARACTER EGOCENTRICITY

Playing a character means, however, playing the character *from the character's point of view*, not from your own. It means adopting the character's egocentricity (literally, "self-centeredness"), the character's feeling that he (not you) is at the center of the universe, and that the other characters are simply functions of himself. Horatio, for example, must think "Hamlet's my friend," not "I'm Hamlet's friend." The basic principle of character egocentricity is that the actor playing a character thinks of himself as a *subject*, not as an *object*. He sees himself in the center of his environment—even if he is only a minor character in the play.

That is not to say that a character is egotistical, or that the actor must take an egotistical approach. Egotistical and egocentric are, in fact, *opposite* perspectives. The wholly egotistical person can think of nothing but himself. The wholly egocentric person cannot think of himself at all: he can only see the world around him, being in the center of it. The egocentric person lives, as it were, behind his own eyeballs, and sees the universe as his very special, personal environment. Jean Piaget, the child psychologist, explains that the child is "totally egocentric—meaning not that he thinks selfishly only about himself, but to the contrary, that he is incapable of thinking about himself. The egocentric child is unable to differentiate himself from the rest of the world; he has not separated himself out from others or from objects. . . . The whole course of human development can be viewed as a continuing decline in egocentrism, until death or senility occurs." It is precisely the childlike, self-centered perspective—a foundation of each character's personality—that an actor must find and explore in the quest for effective characterization.

We might recall the Jones and Nisbett experiments mentioned in Chapter One, which showed that people think of themselves as "responding to situation," and other people as having fixed personalities. This is a form of the same egocentricity, by which we all think of our-

how we know things
reference pts.

selves as exemplifying the "norm" of behavior, and everybody else as being "characterized" by their deviations from that norm. It is not that we think this consciously and rationally so much as that we think it innately and instinctually; this sort of thinking is part of our episte-mological machinery, the mind-sets we have derived from infancy. Characters in plays have the same egocentricity and the same self-centering epistemological machinery. *Characters, in other words, do not think of themselves as characters,* any more than we do. They think of *other* people as characters—they think of themselves as, quite simply, themselves. Therefore the actor's performance as a "character" must be seen to emanate from a self-centered mind. The actor plays situation *out of himself,* and he plays character out of himself. This is, and must be, a binding principle.

Still, we know quite well that actors play characters who behave very differently than the actors behave in life—even differently than the actor would behave in the character's situation in life. This is obvi-ous. Naturally, then, the playing of "character" involves a certain *transformation,* and this too goes without question. How does the actor make the transformation into Othello, for example, and still play out of himself?

SUBJECTIVE TRANSFORMATIONS

The resolution of this problem hinges on this principle: *the basic trans-formation the actor makes in playing "character" is not a transfor-mation of what he plays out of, but what he plays into, or toward.* In playing a character different from himself, the actor imaginatively transforms, not himself, but *the events and the actor-characters in front of him.* These transformations are contrived for *dramatizing* purposes. They are *subjective transformations*—transformations of what the character sees rather than what the character is—and be-cause they are subjective the actor sees them from his own perspective rather than from an "objective" one. The character can then retain the idiosyncratic uniqueness of the actor himself, the intensity of his situational concentration and the power of his pursuit of victory; char-acterization is *drawn from* the actor rather than *added on,* and can be played with urgency rather than caricature or parody.

"When I played a detective in *Twilight Walk*, I played
him as a human being who just happened to be a
detective. . . . Most actors play detectives the way
they've seen other actors play detectives. I like to
think I don't do that kind of imitation."

—*Walter Matthau*

Example: Playing the paranoid   This can be made clearer by example.
Imagine the task of playing the paranoid. To go about it *objectively*,
you would research paranoid behavior in textbooks, observe paranoid
behaviors in a mental institution, and make a transformation of yourself by imitating the behavior you saw. This technique is objective because you retain your "objective" feelings and knowledge about paranoia as you yourself know it, and then simply mimic the outward
manifestations of paranoia as you perceive it in others.

The converse or *subjective* method is to research and discover not
the paranoid's behavior but the paranoid's *vision*. You would not seek
to make a transformation of the paranoid as seen by the world, but
would create instead a transformation of the world as seen by the paranoid. In the simplest version of this, we know that a paranoid "sees"
evil and danger lurking in the minds of other people; this then becomes
the contrived transformation for the actor playing the paranoid; he
"sees," in his imagination, the other actor-characters as being a vicious
pack of would-be killers. Making and then responding to this imagining,
the actor need do nothing else to "play the paranoid," for he will *be*
a paranoid; moreover, he will be *his own kind of paranoid*, and will be
that paranoid for the duration of his mental transformation. He need
have no concentration on himself, no concentration on whether or not
he is effectively "being" anything. His concentration is completely
on the outside world, on the pack of killers, and his "characterization"
is simply a response to that world as he sees it. The actor is not thinking
about a paranoid, he is thinking *as* a paranoid. This is a subjective transformation; the basis for characterization.

Subjective characterization demands the planting of certain pre-

*Must think as character
on stage; think
about character at
home.*

"The actor must not only 'do his job' in a conscientious manner, which is what anyone must do; he must also trap his unconscious (a neat trick) and he must trap it *on cue* (a neater trick)."

—*William Redfield*

---

conditions that will later govern the conscious and unconscious directions of a performance. It allows the actor, in the words of that fine performer William Redfield, to "trap his unconscious," and even to "trap it *on cue.*" To do this means a certain amount of double thinking, to be sure, about character as well as about situation, but it is important to realize that the thinking is on different levels, and takes place at different times. The thinking about character (I am a paranoid) takes place during the actor's homework. The thinking about situation (these people are trying to kill me) takes place during the moment of performance.

The difference in levels of these thoughts—and the difference in the time that they are engaged—may be further illustrated by this analogy:

Example: The skier and the slalom It has already been pointed out that the actor, in playing a situation, resembles a downhill skier, racing to the finish line with total concentration and tactical absorption in his search for victory. But the downhill race is only one event in a skiing competition; another is the more sophisticated slalom race, in which the skier must circumnavigate a series of flags in a preconceived order while still trying to reach the finish line in the fastest possible time. The slalom course is *designed* by a slalom designer, and the skier, in negotiating the designed slalom course, traces a path which turns out to be quite elegant in its complex combination of curves, sweeps, turns, and eventual straightaways.

The elegance and beauty of the slalom race is achieved by the joint effort of the slalom designer and the skier, but the joint effort is not at all one of ordinary collaboration. *At the moment of the race, it is a confrontation.* The slalom designer's flags are the skier's obstacles.

The slalom designer's goals are to create demanding challenges; the skier's goal is to surmount them. The slalom designer contrives his course in such a way as to elicit graceful turns and exciting contours; to have the skier leave, as it were, an elegant track in the snow. The skier, however, is not in the least interested in being graceful, exciting, or elegant, or in leaving a track in the snow; he is trying to get to the bottom of the hill as fast as he can without breaking the rules (going on the wrong side of the flag). Elegance, excitement, grace, and beauty are *unconscious by-products* of his race. Like the downhill skier, the slalom racer concentrates fully and solely on the contingencies ahead, and on the processing of information in the mental calculus which will draw him toward the fastest, truest path to the finish line. Although his task is more complex, the slalom racer's pursuit of victory is no less single-minded, ferocious, and absolute than the downhill racer's.

CHARACTERIZATION PLANTS

Characterization is approached in the way of the slalom race, not the downhill. In developing effective characterization, the actor, using cues provided him by the playwright, the director, the designers, and by his own imagination and research, "plants" those slalom flags along the path of his own intended victory. He does this as the skier might go up the hill the morning before a race and plant his own flags. But also like the skier, he does not plant the flags while racing—he does it as part of his preparation, part of his homework. From that point on, during the performance (or race) itself, he plays against those flags; against, in the paranoid's example, the terror of menacing adversaries. Just as the skier does not need to make a conscious effort to look graceful, elegant, or exciting, so the actor need make no conscious effort to appear to *be* the character he portrays. Characterization, in this sense, will be not so much a matter of the actor "playing character" as of the audience *inferring* character from the actor's behavior.

The basic mechanics, then, for characterizing a person is to examine his possible world, his vision and understandings, and then to play *as yourself* into, with, and against *that world*. It is as though *you* saw what he saw, thought what he thought, wanted what he wanted, and feared what he feared. Whether you remain *you*, in an objective sense, is not relevant; you *are* you to yourself, subjectively, and capable of acting with your own power to win situational victories. You retain the self-centeredness, the egocentricity, and the personality of a live human being. You can then bring that life into the character you play—a far more important goal of the actor than presenting an objectified, well-dissected puppet or corpse.

The following techniques, or methods of playing character, use the basic mechanism just described. In each case, "character" comes from the pursuit of situational goals from the viewpoint of a character's transformed vision of the world. Each technique is accompanied by exercises which both illustrate and teach the techniques.

RELACOM VICTORIES AND PLANTED OBSTACLES

The parallel between the slalom racer and the actor-character is essentially this: both seek to achieve victories while having to negotiate a path through or around planted obstacles. These obstacles can be

---

"To me, the ultimate idea is total concentration, to eliminate all impeding outside ideas and thoughts. So the moment I step on stage, I have a straight line of concentration. From then on, everything is spontaneous, a conditioned reflex. You can't think your way through a performance. When I have those fantastic moments, when all is happening right, it's so easy. I say to myself, My God, it's so easy."

—Edward Villella,
premier ballet dancer
and collegiate boxing champion

---

planted physically on stage. Play directors often stage slaloms of their own, as by making an actor enter down a winding staircase; the actor simply plays "I've got to get down this staircase to tell John such and such," whereas the director, by designing a spiraling obstacle to his direct path, creates an interesting contour showing off the actor's cos-tume, and perhaps also showing the idiosyncratic way the actor stumbles while trying to spiral and talk to John at the same time. The actor, given his situational involvement, will always take the straightest line to the victory; it is necessary for the director (or the actor in his homework) to plant obstacles which will give his action some contour, and bring out some "characterizing" details. Obstacles are not necessarily physical. Most often, in the creation of character, they are psychological. These lie at the very heart of most dramatic structures, of most plays. Hamlet, for example, vows in Act One, to revenge his father's murder, but he does not complete the deed until Act Five; the nature of the obstacle which occasions this delay is a matter of choice, of interpretation, and it determines not only "what happens in *Hamlet*," but what is the *character* of Hamlet. This is a famous example, but all plays involve obstacles to the fulfillment of situational victories; this is what makes plays play. In *Death of a Salesman*, Willy Loman is offered a job by a kindly neighbor. If he took it, he would not commit suicide, and there would be no more death, no more salesman; the play absolutely depends on an obstacle, psychological in that case, preventing Willy from taking the easy (and non-dramatic) way out. If Romeo persisted in refusing to duel Tybalt, if Peter (in *The Zoo Story*) left his bench and went home, if Laura (*The Glass Menagerie*) wasn't crippled and Jim wasn't engaged, these dramas would simply cease to exist, because the characters' dramas would fail to exist. The traditional dramatic structure of "boy meets girl, boy loses girl, boy gets girl" is worthless without the middle, muddling event.

It is the interpretation—the choosing, identifying, and planting—of these obstacles, together with the determination and specification of relacom victories which determines the "character" of the characters. Relacom victories, covered in the previous chapters, are frequently obvious, explicit in the script and derived from the most basic of compelling instincts: survival, affection, security, validation. Obstacles are much murkier and lend themselves to complex and often varied interpretations. Let us look more closely at the possibilities inherent in the example of Hamlet.

Example: Hamlet The psychological "obstacle" which causes

Hamlet's delay has been subjected to a great many interpretations throughout the controversial literary history of that play. Many of these interpretations have a playing validity and have given rise to exciting "interpretive" productions of Hamlet.* For example:

> Hamlet is deeply frightened of killing his father figure and loving his mother, therefore we have the Oedipal Hamlet.

> Hamlet is deeply frightened of becoming an adult, therefore we have the arrested-development Hamlet.

> Hamlet is deeply frightened of his feelings for men, therefore we have the latent homosexual Hamlet.

> Hamlet is deeply frightened of his instincts, therefore we have the over-intellectual Hamlet.

> Hamlet is deeply frightened of dying, therefore we have the pragmatic Hamlet.

> Hamlet is deeply afraid of offending the gods, therefore we have the spiritual Hamlet.

> Hamlet is deeply afraid of chaotic emotional situations, therefore we have the rationalizing Hamlet.

> Hamlet is deeply afraid of ambiguities, therefore we have the passionate Hamlet.

In every case (and of course they are simplifications in the extreme), we see that Hamlet's "delay" is caused by a certain deep, psychological, probably unconscious, fear which induces a certain hesitation between the act and its execution, which in turn makes us— the audience—deduce a certain "character" from the actor's consequent behavior.

Example: Benjamin   Let us take another example, one that is fixed on celluloid in this case: the character of Benjamin in the celebrated

---

*Literary critics tend to argue in favor of their interpretations as being "right." In the theatre of the twentieth century, however, interpretations are suggested more with the idea that they may be stimulating, exciting, fascinating, or simply theatrical. This has caused, unquestionably, a certain amount of ill will between literary critics and play directors; it should be remembered, however, that the interpretation used by the play director must stand the immediate test of the audience's sense of plausibility on a line-by-line as well as an overall basis. Literary critics, on the other hand, can afford a certain gratuitousness.

Mike Nichols film, *The Graduate*. Benjamin is a young college graduate, played in the film by Dustin Hoffman, who is seduced by Mrs.
Robinson, an older married woman played by Anne Bancroft. If Benjamin could respond boldly and debonairly to the first seductive remarks, there would have been no comedy to the film, and virtually no
story to the film. On the contrary, director Nichols placed every
imaginable obstacle in Benjamin's way: physically, by providing suspicious hotel clerks, overly friendly partygoers, a bleak hotel room, and
an outrageously forward Mrs. Robinson. But beyond even these obstacles which the screenwriter, the director, and the set designer provided, are the psychological obstacles that Dustin Hoffman played.
These included a deep fear of sexual inadequacy, of being seen naked,
and of being seen looking at the naked genital area of a woman. It was
Hoffman's desperate, anguished playing through and around those
(imaginary) psychological obstacles which created the hilarity and
poignancy of the role. In sum, and at the risk of a slight simplification:
Hoffman's playing toward the relacom victory "I want you to be my
lover" created the situation; Hoffman's planting and playing around
the obstacles of feared sexual inadequacy created the character. And
since both victory and obstacle could be "located" in the same specific
area, Anne Bancroft's loins, Hoffman's point of concentration was
single-minded, direct and entire.

It is clear from these examples that, as the excitement of the
slalom racer derives from the *confrontation* between the skier and the
slalom course, so *the excitement of a theatrical performance derives
from the confrontation of the character's ideal future and his obstacle,*
and the path the actor takes to achieve the one around the other. Hamlet's tragic action is the confrontation between his situational drive to
revenge his father, and the dramatically chosen obstacle which im-
pedes him; Benjamin's comic action is to surmount his feelings of
inadequacy and win a sexual victory. This confrontation provides the
tension in a role, the inner conflict which is the mark of the human
being in a dramatic situation.

We have spoken of obstacles as psychological. There are physiological obstacles as well, and these may eventually become psychophysiological. Laura's crippled limbs, for example, in the *The Glass
Menagerie,* is a physical obstacle; and because it creates psychological
obstacles as well, it is therefore psychophysiological. The poignancy
and pathos of Laura's character stem from the conflict between her

"Peter Palitzsch, a German director, taught me that everything we portray on stage ought to be shown from two sides. When I smile, I must also show the grimace behind it. Try to depict the countermovement— the counter-emotion. I remember the opening scene of *The Chalk Circle.* At the first reading I thought I was to play a woman in a heroic situation. Her name was Grusha. Revolution had come to the village where she lived in poverty. While she was running away she found an infant abandoned by its mother. My interpretation was to sit down and look tenderly and softly at the baby. Sing to it, pick it up, and then take it with me.

"'Think a bit deeper,' the director said. 'Show her doubts, surely she must have had some? Her cowardice: don't you feel it? And what about her ambivalence in the face of this new responsibility? The audience will sympathize with you anyway, they will recognize you as acting in a way they themselves might have acted. No spontaneous nobility. Not necessarily symbolizing goodness all the time.'

"My interpretation became this: The woman is sitting with the baby, but puts it down as she realizes what a hindrance it will be on her flight. She stands up and walks away. Stops. Doubt. Turns back. Reluctantly sits down again. Looks at the little bundle. Then, finally, she picks it up with a gesture of resignation and runs on. Without joy and without any great emotions, she starts a new life with the child. Rebukes it for the difficulties it has caused her. Laughs at its pitifulness and helplessness. Her maternal feelings are not immediately aroused; are not given any romantic expression. Only then, when no situation or character is obviously good or evil, is it truly interesting to act."

—*Liv Ullmann*

purposed victories and these obstacles to them; her desire to dance against the physical malfunctioning of her limbs; her desire to win Jim against her feeling, induced by the physical defect, of unworthiness.

Place obstacles, then.
Then act around them.
Don't act them place.
Then place obstacles.

PLAYING AGAINST

In every case, whether the character's obstacles are physical impediments in the set, psychological anxieties, or physiological handicaps, they must be planted in advance, not during the moment of performance. *Obstacles are not played, they are played against.*

This means that the planting function and the playing function of acting are quite separate ones, and take place at separate times. Naturally the stage plants are, for the most part, imaginary; acting is more difficult, psychologically, than slalom racing. But the plants can be made, and made to stick, by the act of playing against them. *Playing against an obstacle confirms the obstacle.* This was demonstrated in the "Playing the Opposite" exercise in the previous chapter. Further exercises in this vein suggest a wide variety of character obstacles, physical and psychological, to play against.

EXERCISES: PLAYING AGAINST PHYSICAL OBSTACLES

1. The falling ceiling   The ceiling is being lowered down slowly on top of you. Struggle to push it back up. Lose the struggle; the ceiling is stronger than you.

2. The closing walls   The walls are slowly moving toward you by hydraulic pressure. Try to resist them. Fail. Like the falling ceiling, which you can do simultaneously, this is a standard exercise in mime. The act of pushing against the imaginary wall will "create the wall" in the mind of an observer.

3. Tug of war   With another actor, engage in a tug of war using an imaginary rope. Try to win, both of you.

4. Bucking the wind   Walk against an imaginary hurricane. Walk upstream on the bottom of an imaginary river (with imaginary diving equipment). Try to overcome the current's strength. Let yourself win. Let yourself fail.

"I love obstacles because on the simplest level you have to achieve certain things as an actor because they're written in, but now you try to put everything in the way of achieving what you must achieve, and you frustrate the character. The frustration does two things. It creates a higher level of energy and dramatic conflict within the scene, which therefore makes it more interesting. It gets empathy from the audience because they have frustrations and they tend to identify and so to understand and to care because of self-identification. A good example of this came in the introductory scene in *The Apartment*. Billy (Wilder) had to show that he had all these different people using the apartment, and he had them on the phone trying to juggle time. It was a long scene, about five pages of . . . necessary background to . . . the plot. But Billy did a beautiful thing. He gave the guy a cold, and the scene worked because the poor son of a bitch had a temperature and a cold and was perfectly miserable and the audience knew how goddam lousy he felt and they loved the scene."

—*Jack Lemmon*

5. *Talk with your mouth full* Imagine your mouth full of food. Try to talk. Close your mouth and imagine your lips permanently sealed. Try to speak distinctly. Try to make someone understand that you require an ambulance immediately to save a dying child.

6. *Hide your defect* Imagine you have a pronounced physical defect which inhibits movement. Try to move so that nobody will notice.

7. *Hide your pain*   Imagine enormous pain when you walk. Try to walk without showing it. Play, by this manner, a presidential candidate seriously in pain trying to hide the pain for political reasons. (This situation, common in recent years with John Kennedy and George Wallace, is used as the climactic moment of the play *Sunrise at Campobello* when Franklin Roosevelt, recovering from polio, makes his first public, political appearance.)

8. *Emphysema*   Imagine that you have very little available lung capacity, and can breathe in and out only a half-pint of air per breath. Perform an improvisation unconnected with that condition, and try to breathe and act normally.

9. *Lose your bowel function*   Imagine that you are losing your bowel functioning capability. Perform an improvisation unconnected with that condition, and try to act normally.

10. *Be blind*   Imagine that you have recently been blinded. With your eyes wide open, "try" to sense your position and the position of others. Perform an improvisation as a blind person, trying to hide from the others that you are blind.

EXERCISE: PLAYING AGAINST PSYCHOLOGICAL OBSTACLES

1. *Fear of falling*   Plant a dread of losing your balance, as after a long operation or confinement. Try to walk around the room without falling.

2. *Fear of flying*   Plant a dread of losing your emotional balance, as after a deeply unsettling death or divorce. Perform an otherwise unrelated improvisation and try to keep your emotions in control.

3. *Fear of death*   Plant twenty ways you could die in the next five minutes, and perform an improvisation which attempts to defy those fears.

4. *Fear of arousal*   Plant a fear of being sexually aroused, and of being seen to be sexually aroused, by a person with whom you are about to perform an improvisation. Perform the improvisation.

5. *Fear of becoming violent*   Plant a great temptation to do violence on someone, and then fight that temptation during an otherwise unrelated improvisation.

Scripted scenes may be substituted for improvisations in any of the above exercises; these exercises, when used as directorial suggestions during the rehearsals of plays, can be extremely effective devices for eliciting character and character behavior.

CHOOSING SPECIFIC OBSTACLES

The specificity of the posited obstacle is of vital importance; it determines the specificity of character, and makes the character unique and identifiable. It also lends itself to bold rather than timid characterizations. The exercises above tend toward the general, since they are not directed to any specific character but to the understanding of consciousness and "playing against." In creating characters that live in memory, it is necessary to create obstacles *specifically*.

Example: Hamlet   Let us return to the example of Hamlet to discuss the specific playing possibilities of a single moment of high conflict: the moment when Hamlet, having come upon Claudius at prayer and drawn his sword on him, decides not to kill him at this particular moment. This is a crucial scene in *Hamlet*, and is particularly revealing of Hamlet's character and the nature of his thinking.

Hamlet "explains" the moment to us in soliloquy: he hesitates, and then spurns his initial reaction (which had been "now I'll do't") on the grounds that killing Claudius at prayer would send him to heaven, not hell, and would be an inappropriate revenge. Given the liberty of the theatre, we need not necessarily accept this explanation as complete, or even as correct. Hamlet is, after all, only a character in the play; he is not necessarily the best judge of his own behavior or motives, and he may have a great many reasons for persuading himself (or us) that such a rational motivation is the real one. It could easily be a rationalization for a much deeper dread. The director and actor, therefore, have a variety of options in choosing how this scene will be played (what victories will be played for, what obstacles will be played against), and the choices they make will determine what kind of character we—the audience—will deduce that this Hamlet is. Several possibilities of specific obstacles might be suggested for this example:

Oedipal dread: Fear of drowning in Claudius's blood   This is a simple fantasy which could emanate from an Oedipal situation. Let us assume that Hamlet is terrified of killing Claudius because, at the unconscious level, that represents the acting-out of the tabooed Oedipal situation: a killing of the father-figure in order to conquer the affections of the mother-figure. In this case the Oedipal situation is intensified, because by killing Claudius, Hamlet figuratively "becomes" his father (the unconscious goal of the Oedipal fixation), carrying out his revenge, taking his throne, and even taking his name and title.* But this is tabooed, therefore it is deeply and unconsciously dreaded. Now, vivify that terror by this precise fantasy: imagine that stabbing Claudius will cause a jet of blood to stream into your open mouth; you will drown in Claudius's blood. Now try to stab Claudius; you will find yourself paralyzed in a double-bind. The harder you try to stab Claudius, the more you will gag. *Now* put up the sword and speak Hamlet's line: that it is rationalization will at once be clear with no further effort on your part. This is a highly emotional fantasy which can provoke a characterization detailed and powerful down to the smallest physiological detail.

Fear of exposure: Fantasy of nakedness This interpretation derives from Hamlet's own "chiefly loved" speech which describes Pyrrhus's first attempts to kill "the unnerved father" Priam. The speech tells how "(Pyrrhus's) sword, which was declining on the milky head/of reverend Priam, seemed i' th' air to stick./So as a painted tyrant Pyrrhus stood,/And like a neutral to his will and matter/did nothing." Imagine that as Hamlet's fantasy—as Hamlet might well imagine it— that if he raises his sword to kill Claudius his arm will freeze, he will become paralyzed, "neutral," and exposed as merely a "painted" revenger. Now vivify that terror with this fantasy: imagine that raising your sword will cause you to become suddenly naked and immobilized; your intentions totally exposed, yourself totally vulnerable to whatever torture or indignity that Claudius, turning and seeing all, may wish to inflict upon you. Now try to raise your sword; again you will be double-bound and paralyzed from doing so, and again that paralysis will seem, both to you and anyone watching you, physiologically accurate and psychologically engaging.

In both of these examples the Hamlet that we see could be considered aberrational or neurotic. To the actor, however, who has posited the appropriate fantasies in his mind, the behavior and its attendant

---

*This is, of course, a classical Freudian analysis of Hamlet, and while it is often made the subject of a great deal of scorn and amusement, it retains to this day a strong following among psychoanalytic critics. It can certainly provoke stimulating productions, and has done so often in the past. See Ernest Jones, *Hamlet and Oedipus* (1954).

physiological manifestations *is entirely logical* and follows from the very simple act of trying (and failing) to kill Claudius without drowning in his blood or freezing in his gaze. The fantasies may well be considered neurotic assumptions, but the actor playing *against them* does so with the full force of his own logic and his "normality." It is just that the fantasies are, in the end, insurmountable and the sword cannot be swung.

Hamlet's reason: Fantasy of a Claudius-God alliance   This interpretation is Hamlet's own, that the refusal to kill Claudius is a rational act designed to send Claudius to hell, not to heaven. Obviously, even with this interpretation we cannot simply consider this moment to be entirely reasoned and dispassionate; fantasies and projections, even if quite un-neurotic, are surely involved. Vivify this obstacle with fantasy: imagine that killing Claudius will send him immediately to God's dinner table. Imagine Claudius with God, Jesus, the Virgin Mary, and your mother and father sitting around the dinner table laughing and talking over a few glasses of ambrosia. If the fantasy makes you want to throw up, then it works in stimulating, again, a *physiological reality* to Hamlet's intellectual "decision," making the act—and the acting—visceral as well as cerebral.

EXERCISE: REFUSE TO KILL CLAUDIUS

As an exercise, learn Hamlet's speech in this scene (Hamlet III, iii, 73–95) and play it to an imaginary Claudius, and with a real or imaginary sword, planting each of these three obstacles. Play it to a real Claudius.

Create a fourth obstacle of your own invention, and play against that. Then ask an "audience" what kind of "character" your Hamlet was, in their opinion.

CHARACTERIZING OTHERS:
RECIPROCAL CHARACTERIZATION

Planting obstacles is a quite literal procedure for the actor, closely resembling the planting of props on stage before the curtain goes up. Planting means placing as well as inventing; specifically, *the actor*

"I don't act. I let the others do the acting. I just talk
to them."

—*Diana Ross*

plants his obstacles on the persons of the other characters in the play.
That is, the actor *characterizes the other actor-characters* in such a
way as to draw out his own characterization. This is a reciprocal process. We have seen it in one example already—the paranoid. The actor
who plays a paranoid does not try to "play paranoia" as such, or even
pretend to be a paranoid; what he does is to transform, in his imagination, the other actor-characters into devious, malicious, dangerous
antagonists. The "pretending" is done on them, not on himself; it is
directed outward rather than inward and on the projecting of characteristics onto other people rather than the playing of them oneself.
When the actor has characterized the other actor-characters in this
fashion, his own behavior will be drawn as in response to these characterizing assumptions; in this case the actor will give *unpremedi-
tated paranoid responses* (typical of a true paranoid) rather than
self-conscious imitations of a paranoid.

This is true to life. We recall from the Jones and Nisbett experiments described in Chapter Two that while people do not think of
themselves as having fixed characterizations, they do think of each
other as being "characterized." The actor characterizes other people
simply as a result of sharing his own character's egocentricity; the way
in which he characterizes them will direct the ways in which he will
interact with them thereafter. *Reciprocal characterization*, then, is
essentially a technique of characterization which is drawn from the
way we behave in life's interactions; like ourselves, our characters
should see themselves as relatively neutral and normal observers responding to the behaviors of unusual, "different," and frequently peculiar and incomprehensible "other" people.

A number of "characterizations" can be quite simply played by
this reciprocal technique of characterizing others instead of oneself.
For example:

Arrogance can be played by characterizing other people as fools, yokels, or weaklings.

Miserliness can be played by characterizing other people as greedy, grabby, and lurking.

Humility can be played by characterizing other people as powerful, brilliant, and knowing.

Bigotry can be played by characterizing other people of a suspected race or religion as being smelly, filthy, disease-ridden, immoral, and lascivious.

Apathy can be played by characterizing other people as insignificant, boring, having nothing to offer.

You can play geniality by making the reciprocal characterization that other people are lovable, funny, fun to be with, and fond of you.

You can play confidence by characterizing other people as admiring your qualities, approving your intentions, and supporting your actions.

And of course there are many others, ranging through the entire spectrum of general and specific characterizations. In each case, the actor need only plant the characterizing assumption on the other actor-character; on his body, in the arch of his eyebrows, the glare of his eyes, the set of his jaw, the suppression of his fist, the restlessness of his leg. The plant should be on the *person,* not simply on the "actor" or the "character" as abstractions, but on the physiology across the table that will inspire reciprocal interaction and reciprocal characterization. In that event there need be no difference between the physiological manifestations of characterized paranoia and real-life paranoia, for both should be the same until the fall of the curtain wipes out the consensus of pretenses, and the plants, on which the "acted" characterization is dependent.

THE "MAGIC IF" APPLIED TO THE OTHER

Reciprocal characterization has the enormous benefit of not reducing characterization to the level of "ordinary" human behavior, to the "lowest common denominator" kind of characterization which was a

well-noticed fault of the early American "method" actors and their
stuttering Caesars, hem-and-hawing Hamlets, and everyday Ophelias.
This tendency toward the humdrum derives from a misconstruction
of Stanislavski, and perhaps an ambiguity in Stanislavski himself.
Stanislavski says "Always and forever, when you are on stage, you
must play yourself." But playing yourself and playing *out of* yourself
are different things. Stanislavski, naturally, understood that the self
was the basis for acting, but that characterization also involved certain transformations. His key phrase for making the transformation
was the "magic if," by which the actor suggests to himself "If I were
in Othello's situation, what would I do?" Unfortunately this is too frequently shortened, with a catastrophic and unintended loss of meaning,
to "If I were Othello, what would I do?" This leads to objective, hind-
sight analyses of a fictional "Othello," and thus to imitative mimicry
rather than situational involvement.

The "magic if" should be applied to the *other* actors, not to the
self. The question the actor asks is not "What if I were Othello?" but
"What if she were Desdemona?" He goes on: "Is she trustworthy? What
can I expect from her? Will she support me in public? What do I need
to win her respect? Who are her friends? What does she really feel about
black people? How much does her father control her? Does she know
herself?" The answers that John-Othello draws or plants onto Jane-
Desdemona really will tell us—the audience—very little about Jane
or Desdemona. But they will tell us, during the course of the play, a
great deal about John-Othello.

EXERCISES IN CHARACTERIZING OTHERS

Perform a scene or improvisation with the following assumptions posited and fantasized onto the other participants in the
exercise:

a. They are stupid.	g. They are lovable.
b. They are dirty.	h. They are ridiculous.
c. They are evil.	i. They are devious.
d. They are brilliant.	j. They are dangerous.
e. They are gods.	k. They are beneath
f. They are leaderless.	contempt.

Perform a scene or improvisation with *one* other person, making
the following assumptions about that person:

a. He (or she) is adorable.
b. He is an undercover agent.
c. He is a fascist.
d. He is overly sentimental.
e. He is too serious.
f. He is smelly.

g. He makes $500,000 a year.
h. He wants your job or wife or girlfriend.
j. He has killed a man.
k. He has escaped from an asylum for the criminally insane.

Perform a scene or improvisation with one other person, transforming that person, in your mind:

a. Into a rattlesnake.
b. Into a sloth.
c. Into a gorilla.
d. Into a tree.
e. Into a brick wall.
f. Into Satan.
g. Into God.

h. Into a baby girl.
i. Into your father.
j. Into your worst enemy.
k. Into a sex object.
l. Into a diseased fingernail.
m. Into vomit.

In all of these exercises, do not try to *be* anything but yourself. Just respond *as if* the other people were as described; make all the transformations on them rather than on yourself.

PAST INTO FUTURE

Freudian psychology reports, axiomatically, that past experience dictates present behavior. Certain acute past experiences are called, by psychologists, "traumatic," and it is generally agreed that certain traumatic experiences can be said to cause current symptoms, even if the original experience is not consciously remembered. This is an absolute foundation of deterministic psychology, and actors who wish to explore the subtleties of their character have been urged, certainly since the time of Stanislavski (who was, of course, much indebted to Freud), to discover or fabricate their character's past life and experiences.

Cybernetic psychologies, however, focus on behavior as elicited by speculations about the future, rather than causes from the past. The difference is one of perspective rather than absolute correctness; while it is equally correct to say "water freezes at 32 degrees" and "ice liquefies at 32 degrees," we, living in warmer climates, are more likely to take the former perspective; the Eskimo is likely to take the latter. In the same way, the actor is more inclined to take a cybernetic and future-oriented perspective on behavior than a deterministic and past-caused one; this has the distinct advantage of allowing the actor to share his character's forward-looking thinking at the moment of action.

The distinction may be made clear by example. A man who, during childhood, was attacked by a barking dog (the traumatic experience), can be seen to jerk violently (the symptom) when a dog crosses his path. This cause-and-effect analysis is made by us—the observers. But the man himself does not think, upon seeing the dog, "that dog reminds me of the one I saw when I was a child"; rather, he thinks "that dog is going to attack me!" In other words, *the man himself, at the moment of confrontation, is not thinking of the past, he is projecting, or hypothesizing, about the future.* The actor playing the man will do the same thing.

An actor, therefore, studies the past of his character *only insofar as that past determines and shapes his thinking; only as it guides the fantasies, forecasts, hypotheses, and expectations that lie ahead of him.* The actor-character will look to the future and act toward it; obviously those characterizing contrivances which are dramatically useful to shape his characterization must be placed in front of him and not behind. Long and detailed exegeses about a character's past history do not reveal current thinking patterns, and are thus a rather useless diversion of the actor's homework; in fact, they are frequently harmful, because they allow the actor to presume to have a far more complex understanding of the character than will actually be presented.

The actor's homework, then, is concentrated on the task of *developing the character's past into a spectrum of fantasies and expectations of the character's future.* No doubt academic studies of psychology are useful to the actor, but so, unavoidably, are the actor's own well-earned understandings about human nature, gained through observation as well as by reading novels, biographies, histories, and plays which encapsulate the observations of others.

Putting the past into the future involves, among other things, characterizing others. The man who had the traumatic experience with a dog may well characterize dogs as dangerous beasts. If he had a traumatic experience with women, he may characterize women accordingly. The man who was raised in a black ghetto may well characterize whites as rich exploiters. The man who was educated in a rigid seminary may characterize young women as wanton voluptuaries. These characterizings do not *necessarily* follow, of course, but they are quite ordinary, and quite demonstrably effective in drawing out appropriately responsive behavior. In no case does that behavior depend on rational memory; it is embedded in the character's thinking, as a prejudice rather than as a thought.

EXERCISE: PAST INTO FUTURE

This is primarily a mental exercise; however, improvisations and scenes may be performed from it.

1. How would you characterize people, both generally and specific persons, if you had been raised:

a. In a convent?	g. By a tyrannical mother?
b. In a brothel?	h. By your next-door
c. In an army camp?	neighbor.
d. In a concentration camp?	i. In England?
e. During a civil war?	j. In China?
f. By homosexuals?	k. In a ghetto?

In each case, try to understand how this would affect your present-day thinking. Read stories or essays by people of the background you choose: how do they *see* things differently than you do?

2. Think about how much of your present thinking is shaped by your parents' thinking. Think about how many day-to-day behaviors you do which approximate theirs. Think how much you may resemble your parent of the same sex, and how you might be unconsciously adopting his or her characteristics, style of speaking, ethics, taste in recreation, and so forth. In each case that you spot a similarity, imagine what "you" would be like if you had had different parents.

3. Now think about ways in which your thinking or behavior is a specific conscious or unconscious *rejection* or repudiation of your parents' thinking or behavior. In what ways do you think of your parents as negative examples? In what ways are you trying to surpass them at their own game? Insofar as you are trying to do so, recognize the extent to which your behavior is still being determined by theirs—the extent to which they may have still determined the goals that you are striving for, even

by their negative example. In each case where you come up with something significant, imagine what you would be like if you had had different parents.

4. Do both exercises 3 and 4 from the point of view of a person with whom you are familiar.

5. Do exercises 3 and 4 from the point of view of a dramatic character with whom you are familiar.

We all think that we see clearly, and think clearly, and that our seeing and thinking is the objective "norm" from which other people's visions and insights differ; this is part of the universal egocentricity of perception and thought. These exercises make us realize that the way we think and the way we see are special, not universal; it helps us to move into new ways of seeing and thinking—into characterization— in the spirit of humility, not arrogance.

THE PRIVATE AUDIENCE

We have already seen that interaction becomes a performance when there is another person present to observe it. That "other person" becomes an "audience" to the interaction, and makes it communicational. In the presence of such an "audience," one cannot not communicate; a performance is automatically, if unconsciously, engaged. Thus far we have only spoken of this "audience" as it consists of "real" people whose presence is entirely physical.

Much of our daily behavior, however, consists of interactions with an audience which is not physically present. This is the "private audience," which is composed of all the people, real and imaginary, living or dead, whom we carry about in our heads as witnesses to our daily behavior, and for whom, in an ulterior sense, we frequently perform. Our private audience consists of all those "people" of whom we say "If only Harriet (or Mother, or Dr. Johnson) were here to see me now!" Parents, parent-figures, present and former teachers, siblings, lovers, relatives, and friends all figure prominently in our private audiences; so does anyone whose respect or love we ever sought successfully or unsuccessfully; anyone to whom we have ever felt the need, or the desire, to "prove" ourselves, anyone, in short, whose opinion we reckon into considerations of our "identity."

The private audience is not "real" in the ordinary sense, and it is not present in the physical sense, but nobody can doubt its influence—sometimes even its control—over much of our daily behavior. Often we find ourselves playing for the satisfaction of our private audience instead of for the real and immediate one beside us. Often we phrase our remarks in a way calculated to gain the respect of a private audience member—and no one else. Sometimes we are restrained from certain behaviors because of the feeling that we are being watched by members of our private audience—the "parents of our imagination," perhaps—and sometimes that feeling persists long after the person in question is out of our lives altogether, perhaps long after they are dead. Although the private audience may not be "real," its effects are certainly real enough, and it must not be looked upon as a purely mystical concoction; it is a part of the actor's psyche and of the character's psyche, and it has real consequences for both.

We interact with our private audience in a variety of ways. There are some members of our private audience we wish to make proud of us; their presence at our victorious moments will serve to validate our victories. Then there are those people we wish to make envy us, people we wish to show up or surpass; our rivals, perhaps, or our enemies, detractors, critics, and deserters. Who has not felt the urge, on occasion, to "prove oneself" in one's own mind to a departed lover, an estranged adversary? And then there are those whose disapproval we seek to avoid, and whose presence only serves to make us guilty, remembering past sins, failures, and omissions. A preponderance of supportive people in our private audience tends to make us buoyant, optimistic, and happy to "perform." A preponderance of detractors, disapprovers, and guilt-purveyors tends to make us depressed, morbid, tense, pathologically irrational. While introspection can confirm the existence, and to an extent the influence, of our own private audience, psychological analysis is required to uncover the phenomenon in its greater and more pervasive complexity. Here are a few examples of the private audience in our daily lives:

A young woman, accepting the proposal of marriage from a wealthy and handsome young man, a "good catch," pictures in her mind her proud mother, her envious girlfriend, her desolated former boyfriend with whom she recently quarreled. Later she will wonder why she accepted the proposal.

An actor, receiving a big Broadway role, gloats at seeing in his mind the astonishment of his former teachers and fellow-students, who have often derided his ambition.

A housewife, giving a dinner party, polishes the silver and crystal to the shine that would please her mother—who is not, however, one of the dinner guests that evening.

A professor gives a series of introductory lectures in a college course, but the lectures are too specialized for the freshman students. "I had the feeling," he later reports, "that the editorial board of the *PMLA* (a scholarly journal) was seated in the back row." His imaginary and private audience determined the nature of his lectures far more than his "real" audience.

A typist tenses every time she makes a minor error, even though her employer has never rebuked her for these mistakes. "It just seems that Dad's looking over my shoulder when I work," she reports.

Here are some cases in which the private audience is mentioned by characters in plays:

Tom, in *The Glass Menagerie*, concludes the play with a speech describing his recent life following the play's events: "I left Saint Louis. I descended the steps of this fire escape for the last time and followed, from then on, in my father's footsteps . . . but I was pursued by something. . . . Perhaps I am walking along a street at night. . . . Then, all at once my sister touches my shoulder. I turn around . . . Oh, Laura, Laura, I tried to leave you behind me, but I am more faithful than I intended to be!" Tom's action is ruled by two members of his mental, private audience: his father, whose footsteps he pursues, and Laura, to whom he remains faithful. Tom's inability to "play to" both of these "non-present" characters simultaneously causes an emotional paralysis.

Willy Loman, in *Death of a Salesman*, has actual dialogue with his brother Ben, whom he has not seen since he was three years old, and whom he "sees" now only in his imagination (although playwright Arthur Miller has allowed us to see Willy's imagination in this play, which was originally titled "The Inside of His Head"). Willy, whose only memory of his father is "a man with a big beard," has sought unsuccessfully to find, in his highly fantasized brother Ben, a father-figure who could validate his life; with Ben's failure to fill this function, Willy then turned to Dave Singleman, a "salesman in the Parker House," who is probably also somewhat fantasized in Willy's recollection. Willy's final inability to find, and relate to, an effectively supportive private audience occasions his son's comment after Willy's suicide: "He never knew who he was." To fail to grasp one's private audience is to experience an empty and insecure identity.

THE PRIVATE AUDIENCE AND ACTING

Private audience ties into acting as a transformation between the actor and the character; it is one of the techniques of reciprocal character-ization. The private audience of a character consists of those people, living or dead, real or imaginary, for whom the character ultimately performs; those whose respect he desires, whose envy he wishes, whose disapproval he tries to avoid. *The actor, in transforming into a charac-ter, creates and plants the character's private audience, and plays to it.* He does not do this simply by naming off the "people" that popu-late the character's private audience, but by actively imagining them with human characteristics, physical and emotional embodiments. Sometimes he will do this by substituting real people known to him, sometimes by imagining "people" in his own private audience that can be successfully, and appropriately, transferred to the character's private audience. He then imagines these people as invisible witnesses to his behavior, judges to his actions, silent commentators to his deeds. He does not play to them directly; he simply plays knowing that they are there around him and in him—his ministering angels, his haunting spirits, the personified voices of his conscience—and of his courage.

Example: Tom Wingfield Let us return to Tom Wingfield, in *The Glass Menagerie*, as an example of a character with a complex and important private audience which we have already seen in part. Tom knows the influence his father and sister hold over him in his mind, an influence which is no less strong for being irrational and unwise. But this is hardly the extent of his complete private audience. There is also his mother, more dominating than either of the other two, most probably, and the one we might imagine Tom more truthfully telling, at the end of the play, to blow out her candles. There is his friend, Jim O'Conner, to whom Tom is probably not as indifferent as he outwardly presumes to be, and Mr. Mendoza, whose disapproval hurts Tom, most likely, more than he lets Jim (or us) know. Then there is "Malvolio the Magician," whom Tom assists in a vaudeville act one night (or says he assists). Malvolio's influence is no less great if Tom simply made up the story; real or imaginary, his image exerts an influence on Tom, which is all that is important. Then there are the more shadowy figures; the co-workers at the shoe factory, the strangers on the street, the couples at the Paradise Dance Hall, the union officers at the merchant marines, and "the huge middle class of America . . . matriculating in a school for the blind," a generation with which Tom wishes to identify himself. Finally, there are four figures whose importance is inestimable, but who have no interactions with Tom (during the play) at all. The first is Clark Gable, who for Tom epitomizes "all those glamorous people—having adventures." The second is Shakespeare, whom Jim nicknames Tom after, and whom Tom implicitly accepts as a role model. The third is the idealized "Christian adult" that Amanda continually holds up to Tom as the proper model for his behavior. And the fourth is the high school English teacher, never mentioned, who we must presume lies somewhere behind Tom's sneaking off to write poetry. These figures filter through Tom's mind all the time; when he is out by himself on the balcony, when he is working at the shoe factory, when he is arguing with his mother, when he is joining the merchant marines, when he is following his father's footsteps. The task for the actor is to identify and characterize this private audience, to plant and personify it, and then to play the play's action in an attempt to win his private audience's respect, to prove himself to his private audience, to avoid his private audience's disapproval, and where necessary, to "show up" his private audience. The depth to which the actor can create and vivify Tom's varied private audience will be the measure of richness he can bring to his characterization.

THE PRIVATE AUDIENCE AND GOD

The presence of a character's private audience hovers over him and inside him. It is the "voices" of Shaw's St. Joan, the good and bad angels of Marlowe's Dr. Faustus, the Godot of Beckett's Vladimir, Estragon, and Pozzo. It is, one way or another, the "God" of many characters, and playing these characters means playing under the eyes of the character's God—and not the actor's God. *Characterizing God, then is a reciprocal technique for transforming into characterization.* The concept of God, which is a viable one with many dramatic characters, can in those instances become a useful summary concept of the private audience; God, for God-fearing characters, becomes the supreme being of the character's private audience, and the actor playing that character need only play to achieve the salvation, and avoid the damnation, of the *character's* precise vision of the Supreme Deity.

The characterizing, planting, and utilizing of a character's private audience creates some of the most powerful and intense characterizations. The more important and the more powerful the private audience, the more awesome the characterization might become. Private audiences that move into the divine or supernatural realms can be staggering; they are virtually required in dramas committed to ritual experience, and extremely exciting in dramas of deep spiritual, moral, or tragic import. How else can the actor even begin to play Antigone, or Sir Thomas More, or Orestes? Private audience is certainly a vital key to character, both in ourselves and in our characterizations.

EXERCISES IN CREATING, AND PLAYING TO, PRIVATE AUDIENCES

1. Discover your own private audience   You cannot very well create a private audience for your character until you have discovered and analyzed your own. Think of all the people who come into your mind in various situations. Think, particularly, of your parents and parent-figures, of your past and present teachers, professors, coaches, best friends, lovers, brothers, sisters, roommates, and rivals. Think, if applicable, of your God. Do you think of someone special when you answer a question in class? When you write a paper? When you tell a joke? When you are in a first-class restaurant? When you drive a car? When you are in a romantic situation? Do you ever behave in a way directed toward that nonpresent person? Is that person's "presence" supportive? Is it harmful? Would you rather drive that person out of your mind? Are there times that you try but fail to drive them out of your mind?*

*Most forms of psychodrama involve the patient's "acting out" of confrontation scenes (imaginary) between themselves and members of their private audience. The theory is that by making yourself aware of your private audience—making it, as it were, a public audience—you will become more free from its unconscious and often pathogenic control. Abreactive or cathartic therapies, which seek to induce the patient to throw off the pathogenic control of the private ("primal") audience, much as Aristotle said that a tragedy should induce us to throw off pity and terror, employ various psychodramatic techniques.

2. Discover, by analysis and creativity, a dramatic character's private audience   First, list:

    a. The other characters in the play known by him.
    b. Characters not in the play but mentioned by him.
    c. Unnamed characters known to be important in his past.
    d. People who might be presumed important in his past.
    e. The character's concept of God.

Rank these characters in order of their overall importance to him, and specify the situations in which each character might appear in his private audience. Then flesh these "characters" out in your own mind by visualizing them, imagining a conversation with them, putting words in their mouths, etcetera. Use people in your own private audience, if you wish, to embody people in the character's private audience.

3. Play to the private audience

    a. Memorize a speech of the character's, preferably a long speech that is particularly informative or characteristic. Recite the speech into a mirror, while imagining that the mirror image is not of you, but of an individual in your character's private audience. Repeat the speech, substituting another person in the private audience.

    b. Memorize, with a partner, any short scene from any play. Play the scene imagining that a member of your character's private audience is standing invisibly behind you. Repeat the scene, substituting another person in the private audience.

    c. Memorize Hamlet's soliloquy as he decides first to kill, and then not to kill, Claudius. Deliver the speech to the back of a chair, or to another actor, imagining a member of Hamlet's private audience standing behind you. Make that member of Hamlet's private audience your own father (representing Hamlet's father). Your own mother (representing Hamlet's mother). Your own uncle (representing Claudius). Your own English or Philosophy professor (representing Hamlet's tutor). Your own God (representing Hamlet's God). Make each of these people proud of you.

d. Memorize Tom's last soliloquy in *The Glass Menagerie.* Deliver it as if to any of the people in his private audience, as developed in the example above. Deliver it to your father (as his father); your mother (as his mother); your English teacher (as his English teacher); your God (as his God).

e. Play any scene, from any play, with one of the following people in your private audience:

Jesus Christ	The person who attracts
Richard Nixon	you most
Your hero	The person who embar-
Your God	rasses you most
Your favorite movie	Your worst enemy
star	Your severest critic
Your favorite singer	Your greatest admirer.

Since the person is not physically present, you cannot play *directly* for him or her; play entirely to your partner, but also play "for" the private audience that you postulate standing invisibly behind you.

Do not, in these exercises, make any effort to indicate the existence of a private audience; simply imagine its existence, plant it invisibly behind you or over you, play as though it were there, and notice whatever transformation takes place. These exercises cannot and should not be judged by anyone but you.

THE CHARACTER'S THINKING

In general, what we are pursuing in the study of characterization is this: *the adoption, by the actor, of the character's thinking and his thinking processes.* This does not simply mean the character's thoughts; it means, in addition, the way a character thinks. This can be called the character's personal epistemological machinery, or his mind-sets and thinking channels. The transformation of actor into character cannot be complete without this adoption. Edith Evans, the great British actress, reports that "by thinking you turn into the person, if you think it strongly enough." She continues "I think my (character's) thoughts when I'm playing a play that matters, because I am that woman all the time through." The way the actor characterizes the other people in the play, the way he fantasizes, hypothesizes, and plans around them, the way he sees them as obstacles or (in some cases) friends; this summarizes essentially as *what* the character thinks and *how* the character thinks. Dramatizing a character's situation—creating a "character"—must effectively rechannel or transform an actor's inner thinking as well as his outward behavior.

Thinking, of course, involves a great many things that are rather difficult to pin down. It involves perceiving information from the outside world, and choosing what information to seek out and perceive. It means locating obstacles and planning paths around them. It means characterizing other people and trying to figure out what they might do in given situations. It means making hypotheses and plans in the pursuit of desired and expected victories. It means *contingency* thinking: "what do I do if . . . ?" And it means playing out in one's mind various possible contingencies.

In a rather important phrase, Freud claimed that "Danken ist Porbearbeit." This translates as *"Thinking is trial work."* The eminent late psychiatrist Fritz Perls translates Freud's dictum more freely as "Thinking is rehearsing."* Characters as well as people "rehearse," in their minds, the contingencies of possible future interactions. This is not rehearsing as it is commonly known in the theatre, which is rehearsing a given script. Life's rehearsing is against unknown obstacles and fantasized futures. Ordinarily, *the character in the play "rehearses" events that are never to happen; actors playing those characters should make the same "rehearsal."* That is, Laura (in *The Glass Menagerie*) should rehearse her wedding with Jim. Macbeth should rehearse his destruction of MacDuff. Hamlet should rehearse assuming the throne. Juliet should rehearse married life in Verona. Arnolfe should rehearse his wedding with Agnes. These "rehearsals," these goings over in the actor's mind of actions which are not (it turns out) going to occur, are the mechanisms by which the actor thinks his character's thoughts, dreams his character's dreams, and lives his character's life.

---

*In *Gestalt Therapy Now,* ed. Joen Fagan and Irma Lee Shephard (1970), pp. 16–17. Perls continues, "Part of the reason why Freud could not follow up on this idea was because rehearsing is related to the future, and Freud was concerned only with the past." Freud, of course, was a determinist, and Perls was a cyberneticist.

EXERCISES: THINKING THE CHARACTER'S THOUGHTS

The following series of exercises asks you to think the thoughts of any character chosen by you from a play which you know well, perhaps a play and character that you are presently working on or have recently worked on.

1. Rehearse, in your mind, the events surrounding your character's greatest *possible* victory. Who will be there? What will they say and do? What will they look like? Rehearse an imaginary victory dance.

2. Rehearse, in your mind, the events which would accompany your character's *totally fantasized* (though practically impossible) victory.

3. Rehearse your character's most humiliating defeat.

4. Rehearse variations on your character's narrowly escaping from that humiliating defeat.

5. Rehearse your character's narrowly escaping the humiliating defeat and going on to achieve a sensational victory.

6. Think of each character to whom you relate in the play. From your own (character's) viewpoint, answer these questions about them:

    a. How would they react if you declared your love for them?
    b. How would they react if you tried to seduce them?
    c. How would they react in a natural crisis (such as a fire)?
    d. How would they react in an emotional crisis?
    e. What makes them nervous?
    f. What makes them frightened?
    g. What do they think about you?
    h. Do they care about you as much as they let on? Less?
    i. What do they feel about your race? Sex? Appearance?
    j. Describe them in a few words. In one word.

7. Give your *character* the following word-association test: from your character's viewpoint, what is the first word that comes to mind when you hear:

a. Hot	c. Hate	e. Kill
b. Mother	d. Justice	f. Struggle

g. I	m. Love	r. Important
h. Help	n. No	s. God
i. Useful	o. Next	t. Goal
j. Father	p. Why	u. Lust
k. Want	q. Duty	v. Against
l. If		

8. Take a walk in your neighborhood, and notice what your character would notice. Hear what he would hear. In what ways does the character perceive information differently than you do? In what ways does the character *want to* perceive differently than you do? In what ways does the character *fail to* perceive what you do?

9. Write a letter to the editor of your local newspaper in character. Sign the letter with your character's name.

10. Imagine your character had just become the President of the United States, either by election or by some extraordinary accident, depending on which of those is more plausible. Extemporize his first remarks to the nation.

TACTICAL SELF-CHARACTERIZING: MASKING

People do not characterize themselves to themselves, as we have seen, but *they do try to characterize themselves to others.* They try to project an image of themselves, in other words, for tactical purposes. Most of the tactics examined in the previous chapter would be carried out by a person's "trying to appear" one way or another to threaten or induce another party. This is called *masking.* No matter how honest, spontaneous and transparent we may claim to be, we all share this trait—it is biological—of adopting, in T. S. Eliot's sublime phrase, a "face to meet the faces that we meet." We talk and act a bit differently in bed than at work, or at a bar, or at a cocktail party, or at a P.T.A. meeting. The idea of "just being yourself" is, quite frankly, a total abstraction, for we are many selves and we wear many masks.

Much of our daily expression is assumed for tactical purposes. The serious look of the student, the sly look of the rogue, the sober look of the politician, the "hale-fellow" look of the Rotary greeter,

"Acting (and this is one difference between professional and amateur actors, though not every professional pays enough attention to it) is not a matter of assuming a fixed role but of showing how the character *acts*— that is, how he moves in and out of his repertory of roles; how he changes his disguise to meet every moment of the play, responding to changes in his situation and in the characters around him, revealing one thing and hiding another. . . . I can't think of better advice for a young actor than to remember that in any part he plays he must be changing masks from moment to moment. The life of any performance may be measured by the rate of change."

—*Michael Goldman*

the tight grin of the M.C., the frown of the librarian, the smile of the bashful girl, the grimace of the schoolboy called on to answer a question, the wink of the lover, the chuckle of the sycophant, the wide-eyed indignation of the overcharged customer, the menacing sneer of the linebacker, the coy fake-innocence of Muhammed Ali—these all are adopted visages calculated, usually unconsciously, to win some sort of victory or another. Even expressions which we ordinarily think are entirely spontaneous are frequently tactical: crying, for example, may spring initially from an automatic response (as a baby's crying springs from discomfort), but in the adult there is usually a moment when the person chooses *whether or not* to keep crying, whether or not to let the tears flow. At that moment, the crying becomes tactical— it is *intended:* to induce sympathy, guilt, pain, relief, or reconciliation. Frequently that moment of choice is very early in the crying sequence— even before the actual formation of tears. Crying, like the other masks above, is then often part of an interaction. It is not "pure behavior" when it carries the tactical purpose; it is *meant to* be observed, it is "acting for" the benefit of somebody else.

Characters, therefore, mask themselves to "act for" each other. Just like the people in real life whom they represent, characters may be seen to smile, laugh, cry, grimace, stare, wink, frown, glare, and smirk at each other to win some sort of situational victory or other. They may "try to appear" strong, wise, and knowing; or, on the other hand, they may try to appear naive, foolish, and helpless, all for tactical reasons. They may mask themselves in two ways: to hide certain features or feelings they do not want to have observed, and to project an image of themselves that is sufficient to gain them what they wish. In short, characters are as complex and as "hypocritical" as mankind is. The actors who play human beings must, of course, adopt their

---

"In any good play, the principal characters go beyond ordinary bounds in ways that remind us of acting. They are capable of some kind of seductive, hypnotic, or commanding expression, mixing aggression and exposure in a way for which the community . . . can scourge them. This is not only true of Tamburlaine and Blanche Dubois and Dionysius; even the thoroughly nice Rosalind of *As You Like It* is such a figure, with her boy's clothes and attacking wit, her power over those around her, her exposed position in the court, her unprotected flight to the forest, her danger and her energy and daring. . . . The characters of drama are actors. . . . And the actor's analysis of character will always benefit from thinking of the character as an actor—how does he read his audience? what is his repertory? what is the principle by which he changes his masks?"

—*Michael Goldman*

---

characters' masks and hypocrisies as well as their victories and their obstacles.

When an actor dons a tactical mask, therefore, he is "acting for" the other actor-characters. He is not "acting for" the audience! He is not trying to pretend to *be* his character, rather he is trying to *enact his character's pretending.* This is frequently a reciprocal of what we may think the character actually "is." The shy man pretends to be debonair. The actor playing the shy man pretends to be debonair. Since his obstacles are well planted, however, his pretending is going to turn out to be less than completely successful. The audience sees through it. They see a shy man. This, of course, is the way Dustin Hoffman played Benjamin—with a tremendous effort to wear masks of sexual prowess and savoir-faire. The audience saw through the masks, and in so doing, "discovered" Benjamin's true character, the character that Hoffman was so obviously trying to "hide" behind the mask.

MASKING A CHARACTER

The questions to ask with regard to masking a character are these: How does the character want to appear in general? How does he want to appear to the other characters? to each other character? How does he want to appear to strangers? How does he want to appear to himself? How does he want *not* to appear in general? What appearances must he avoid at all times and at all costs? What appearances must he avoid with each particular character?

The answers to these questions provide the shaping of the character's public behavior—what he tries to hide with his mask, and what he tries to show.

In the previous chapter we discussed some basic tactics that come into play because they are useful. In developing characterization, however, we must study the tactics that our characters use. These are not necessarily rational ones; they are chosen for subjective reasons, not objective ones, and they will not necessarily work. The subjectivity of tactical masking, of course, is the character's subjectivity.

Tactics usually come from the past. This is because they are learned, for the most part, unconsciously by trial and error. If the baby cries autonomically and spontaneously when he is born, he soon learns that crying leads to a removal of discomfort, and he quite unconsciously and unverbally learns the *tactic* of crying.

Because tactics are learned unconsciously, by the body as it were, they are unlearned unconsciously as well. Crying is unlearned when it is met, frequently enough, with indifference; crying is usually replaced, therefore, by tantrums, to which indifference can hardly be a long endurable response. So tantrums are unlearned, in many cases, by forced isolation or brutal punishment, depending on the culture. Then sulking takes over. Sulking is perhaps the commonest weapon of the five-year-old, for the reason that it carries behind it a five-year-old's strongest trump card; his power to withhold affection. To a guilty mother or father (guilty, perhaps, for having beaten the tantrums out of the child) this tactic is amazingly successful; as a result the child uses it well into adolescence and it becomes deeply ingrained. But

---

"I don't make decisions on how to play a part. I start off feeling wide open to the person I'm playing and to the people I'm playing with. I don't like to intellectualize about it. I try to feel my way. I try to react as well as act. When I was going to play Al Capone, I read his autobiography and the newspapers of his time. I asked myself, What did this man want? I decided he wanted to be respected. . . . He wanted recognition . . . the kid from the other side of the tracks who was always asking himself how to get where he wanted to be. One thing I did for Al Capone was to take out all small gestures. I played it pretty big—I wore my coat draped over my shoulders, and my hatbrim angled— because one thing I felt he wanted was to be big. I wanted the man's natural actions to declare themselves."

—*Rod Steiger*

---

that leads to a new problem; for sulking in adolescents, particularly when used as a tactic on anybody but their parents, is a notably impotent and futile tactic; when used by adults it is absolutely ridiculous. Sulking, therefore, is a tactic unconsciously used in childhood, confirmed by its success into a deeply ingrained habit, and carried unconsciously over into adulthood at great peril to the user.

The actor playing character, therefore, can find in the character's past a great source of masking possibilities. How did Hamlet, for example, get his way with his mother? With Polonius? With Ophelia? With his school friends? With Laertes? With the court in general? With the citizenry? With his father? What tactics did he use then, and which will he carry over now? What tactics did Amanda (in *The Glass Menagerie*) use when she was younger? What tactics toward men, her "gentlemen callers?" What tactics toward her children? How much of her handkerchief tactic (see p. 10), described by Williams as "a piece of acting" (for Laura), derives from the past? Does the tactic really work the way she would like it to? How long will she persist in using it?

The mask that characters wear, then, comes from their situational tactics and the activity stimulated by their quest for victory. It is not a reflection of how the *actor* wants to be seen, but of how the *character* wants to be seen. The choice of masks stems partly from the character's conscious choice of tactics, and partly from his unconscious carrying over of tactics that worked for him in the past. The way these are blended determines the specific configuration of the mask, and the way the audience will see through to the "character" who wears it.

TACTICAL EMOTION

We have spoken of emotion in the previous chapter as comparable, in the Barrault metaphor, to the sweat of the runner, autonomically induced by the act of running. There is also, however, the *display* of emotion as part of a tactical mask. We have already seen how, in life, crying may be stimulated autonomically but continued tactically. Even though the tactic may be futile, it may be pursued unconsciously as a carryover from the days when crying "worked." In the same way there are times when we may be stimulated into anger, and have then maintained (or increased) our display of rage purely for tactical purposes. People in supervisory positions (including play directors) have been known on occasion to feign anger in order to get more out of people than they are getting. Laughter is similarly feigned on many occasions, or at least exaggerated from an originally spontaneous chuckle.

Displaying emotion, then, has a function in human interactions, and as such it has a function on stage, *when done between characters.* If emotion is displayed by the actor to the audience it is called indicating, and there can be no place for this in the theatre; it is shallow and amateurish. But when done *between characters,* when exchanged as tactical relacom, the visible displaying of emotion is part of the character's mask, a tactical tool in his quest for victory.

As such, its "genuineness" is not at issue one way or the other. Tactical displays of emotion occur because they are useful, not because they are real. The emotion behind a tactical display can be congruent with the display (a smiler can be actually amused), or it can be opposite (a smiler can be profoundly unamused), or, as is often the case, the "real" emotion can be highly ambivalent or unknown. Tom, in *The Glass Menagerie,* for example, alternates between raging at his mother and making up to her, but it would be quite shallow to assume that he simply rages when he is angry and turns gentle when he is loving. In fact his emotions toward his mother are quite obviously very complexly intermingled and confused; often he is trying quite consciously to find the words that will express and clarify his emotional confusion, often he is displaying emotion as a "test" to see what kind of future relationship they might have if he behaved in a different way.

In the cases where "true" emotions are ambivalent or confused and uncertain, a display of emotion may well provoke the actual emotion corresponding to that displayed. Though now discredited as a general rule, the so-called James–Lange theory of emotion does apply in most of these circumstances; a person will tend to feel, and feel that he feels, what he projects as feeling. (This much is clear, if not from the James–Lange theory, from the research on cognitive dissonance.) Tom, while "acting out" his rage to his mother, may actually become enraged at her; the actor playing Tom, for his part, may actually become enraged at the actress playing Amanda. That "actual" emotion can often be registered in physiological tests; the autonomic nervous systems and endocrine systems can function in the appropriate ways even though the "emotion" began as something a character tactically chose to display.

The lesson is this: *while an actor should never indicate his emotion to the audience, there are many times when he will, as the actor-*

character, display certain emotions as part of the mask he adopts in situational interactions. That display may induce actual, physiological emotion. It may also induce a relacom response in the other actor which will intensify that actual emotion. The "emotional" involvement at the outset is not significant. It need not be pushed. It is enough, at the beginning certainly, and even sometimes at the end, that the emotion simply be tactically displayed.

This is obviously a useful device to counter the problem first discussed in the previous chapter—the problem of crying on stage. It can also be used for laughing on stage, or any other seemingly spontaneous emotional outbursts. Find the tactical reason for the character's display. Discover not "why" the character cries, but "what for." Find how the character *uses* crying, or tries to use crying, to solve situational difficulties and achieve situational victories. Then play the crying (or the laughing) for tactical, rather than emotional reasons.

Actors have always known this principle, of course. One of the sayings of the American Conservatory Theatre teachers is "perform the action, the feeling will follow." But actors have also been known to feel self-conscious and artistically "guilty" displaying emotions they do not feel, or do not feel that they feel. The guilt is unnecessary. *In displaying emotions for tactical reasons the actors are behaving exactly as their characters do; the actors are "in character" as long as they are acting for the other actor-characters and not for the audience.* Realizing this frees an actor from the self-consciousness of wondering about his feelings, from a self-consciousness which characters rarely have, and which usually prevents any spontaneous feelings at all. Tom, for example, when he yells at his mother, cannot simultaneously be asking himself whether this is "real" rage or "fake" rage; neither should the actor playing Tom.

Will real feeling follow? That depends on the play, the effectiveness of the tactic on the other actor-characters, and the actor. Perhaps the real feeling is not meant to follow; perhaps the character's display is only "a bit of acting," like Amanda's dropping the handkerchief. "Real" emotion, and more centrally our *awareness* of our emotions, is an intangible; its existence cannot be quantified or particularized, and in most cases it remains a rather mysterious presence, or process, even to ourselves. Displayed emotion, on the other hand, is part of tactical behavior in interpersonal interactions; it can be *played* in life and it can be acted by a player on stage, so long as it supports the overall drive of the actor—his *character's* ultimate victory.

It may very well be sufficient to let it go at that. For as enchanting

as the concept of "real emotion" may be, it remains determinedly in-
tractable in the pinning down. Thinking about emotion virtually precludes *emoting*. The concentration must be on victory, on the other
person, on the situation. The rest will follow—if it is supposed to.

EXERCISES: DISPLAYING EMOTIONS

These exercises are difficult to set up; they are self-conscious
if performed as assigned exercises, and genuinely immoral if
done in day-to-day life. It is best to try them on your own in
situationally appropriate rehearsals or improvisations with other
people; that is, within the context of stage-acting but without
specifically programming them with the persons you are acting
with. In each exercise you are asked to display a certain feeling;
in each case *try to make your partner believe that your feeling
is real.* Do not try to make the feeling real to yourself in any
way, but do not try *not* to either. After the exercise, note
whether your "real" emotions did become involved, and how.

1. Display anger. Within a scene, and where appropriate, assume
a mask of the greatest ferocity you can muster. Convince your
partner you are on the verge of losing control, that you will
squash him to a pulp. Make him shiver in fear. Go for his body;
make his spine cringe. If it is a scripted scene, make your
partner so frightened that he forgets his lines.

2. Display anguish. Try to make everybody feel your pain. If
they *really* feel it they will help you out of it, so make them
really feel it. Make their bodies sympathize with yours; curdle
their blood, make them gasp. Scream and cry—that will help.
Get inside their skin, make it crawl, make them help you.

3. Display hilarity. Make your partner feel that he is very
funny, and that everything he says is the wittiest thing you've
ever heard. Make him keep it up, infect him with his own
humor and your appreciation of it. Make it his happiest day
ever. *Roar* with laughter until neither he nor you can stop.

4. Display affection. (Please do this *only* in a rehearsal, and
only where it is feasible from the script to do so.) Make the
other person's heart beat faster, make him hold his breath,
make him feel you in the loins of his imagination. Convince
him of your longing, your need; make him sure of your devo-

tion. Make it clear to him that one step away from him your unhappiness begins. Make him *really* feel that. Make him wonder how you've managed to keep this all back before. Make him forget the rest of his lines. Make him want to ask you out after the rehearsal! (You had better be prepared to make clear, at a suitable time later, that you were "just acting" and doing what the playwright wanted you to.)

In each of these exercises, *the display of emotion is itself a real act, and will provoke a real relacom communication.* Let the communication go where it will; invariably it will intensify the levels of real emotion and idiosyncratic behavior of the acting on all parts.

PROPERTIES AND BUSINESS

Characterization is not simply a matter of the grand lines of perfor-mance, but of the multiple subtle and precise behaviors that combine to create, in the audience's mind, a sense of having observed a specific personality—a character. Many of these behaviors will arise spon-taneously in the actor's performance, since they derive from the actor's own unconscious ways of behaving. Many more will be specifically directed into the actor's performance by the director, or by the play-wright. But a whole host of individual behaviors—perhaps the most crucial of them—will be stimulated and evoked through the effec-tive selection of appropriate properties and stage business.

The importance of props and business is twofold. Most obviously, props and business are useful in conveying direct and immediate infor-mation to the audience. A character wearing a certain type of spectacles, for example, will be identified by the audience as a pedant; a character who is chain-smoking will be identified as hypertense, a character drinking to excess will be identified as burdened by a deep-seated anguish. Directors and playwrights often use props and business in this way, to create a shorthand and immediate characterization.

But props and business, if properly used, can also give the actor keys to more subtle and well-rounded characterizations, because they create meanings for the actor as well as for the audience, and stimu-late a whole range of unconsciously generated behaviors. These, too,

"I have never worked with anyone else who knows
how to use props the way that Geraldine (Page) can.
She can change a handkerchief or a broom, or a
tablecloth into her inner landscape. She can let you
know through these ordinary things her joy,
unhappiness, longing, and also those undefinable and
by no means ordinary mysteries hidden in all our
lives."

—*Jose Quintero*

"There are very successful mannerisms from certain
parts that stick to your own personality. It may be a
walk, it may be a way of listening to people, it may be
a story, it may be a way of sizing a person up. You
finally wind up as being half what you are yourself
and half fragmentations of the characters that you
play, not the unsuccessful characters but the successful
characters."

—*Paul Newman*

will communicate, because the audience is not merely observing *what*
business is done, but *how* the business is done. The manner in which
the actor responds to props and implements stage business creates the
specific contours of his character, and the richness of his characterization.

Consider, for example, the wealth of characterizing details that
are possible when an actor, while giving a speech, simultaneously mixes
himself a Manhattan cocktail and, at the conclusion of the speech,
drinks it. The actor must cross to the liquor cabinet (slowly? compul-
sively? nonchalantly? uncomfortably?), must pour from two different
bottles (carefully? sloppily? recklessly? craftily? looking at the glass?

looking at the person he's talking to? looking at the bottle to see how much is left?). The possibilities are endless. Does he take the time to recap the bottles? Does he offer the other person a drink too? Does he tease the other person with his offer? Does he brandish the bottle? Is he ashamed of drinking? Is he ashamed of the brand of liquor he is using? Do his hands tremble? Does he stir the drink or slosh it around? Does he omit the cherry? Does he plop the cherry in with greatly exaggerated pomp? Does he sip greedily? Nervously? Lustily? Defiantly? Tastefully? Desperately?

The answers to all these questions are rarely to be found in the text of the play; even the direction of pouring and sipping the drink is not necessarily in the actual playscript. But it is evident that the character portrayed during the sixty seconds or so that this behavior takes place will be shaped as much from the way in which the business is done and the properties handled as from the lines of dialogue which accompany the action.

Many playwrights are excellent at creating the kind of stage business that stimulates rich character performance. Chekhov's plays are notably detailed in behaviors; so are many of the plays of Eugene O'Neill and Tennessee Williams. Many directors, similarly, are very helpful in finding business and appropriate properties. Often, however, the actor is left to his own resources to develop business that will enrich his performance without detracting from its main line, or the main lines of the play. In these cases the actor should explore his own behavior and the real behavior of other people for possibilities, and see if these can be incorporated into his performance. Remember, it is not the business itself that is of immediate concern to the actor, but the way the business is performed. Making a Manhattan cocktail or opening

---

"Directing finally consists of turning Psychology into Behavior."

—Elia Kazan

---

an umbrella are very different activities, but if they are done in the same manner, they can serve the same purpose, and they can be used interchangeably to evoke—from actor and audience alike—a specific sense of character.

EXERCISE: CHARACTERIZATION THROUGH PROPERTIES AND STAGE BUSINESS

For this exercise, take a single memorized speech of about sixty seconds from any play, and perform it:

1. While mixing a Manhattan cocktail, as in the above example, sipping the cocktail at the speech's end. Do the exercise without planning beforehand how you will mix the cocktail; let your behavior come as a response to your feelings and purposes in the scene.

2. While (a) opening an umbrella indoors, and then (b) realizing that the umbrella, opened, will not fit through the door, and then (c) closing the umbrella sufficiently to let it get through the door, and then (d) going out the door with the umbrella, and then, at the end of the speech (e) opening the umbrella and closing the door behind you.

3. While taking off your outergarments and re-dressing yourself for some anticipated encounter.

4. While setting the table for a dinner party.

5. While trying to get comfortable in an underinflated inflatable chair, into which, during the speech, you accidentally drop and lose your wallet.

6. While sharpening a knife on a grindstone.

7. While watching, and pretending not to watch, the sexual provocations of the person in the scene with you.

THE CHARACTER RELISHES LIFE

We have, so far, discussed the character's intentions, his obstacles, his reciprocal characterizations, his past psychological history (giving rise to future projections), and the particular tactics and maskings he adopts to win his content and relacom victories. These all relate, one way or another, to the character's vision of the future.

Now we must explore the character in his present; most particularly, the character as he takes his fleeting delights in those victories he does manage to achieve.

What is the particular thrill experienced by Hamlet, for example, when he sees his father—not in his mind's eye but in a ghostly apparition? How does he experience seeing his old friends, Horatio and Marcellus? How does he relish his successful and "palpable" hits in the dueling scene? His beautifully sarcastic farewell to Claudius? His bewildering of old Polonius? His convincing of Gertrude? The particular joys of Hamlet are the apexes of his character, the peaks of his experience. In living through Hamlet's struggles, the actor must live (and enliven) Hamlet's joys and delights.

Albert Camus, the French playwright and philosopher, pointed out that an actor's life is one of the world's most ideal existences, because the actor gets to taste the joys of all his character's lives; to Camus, who believed that "the best living is the most living," it is easy to see why this career should in fact be ideal. All actors must be open to this, for the joy of acting is not simply the joy of being an actor, but the joy of being a *character:* you can experience the joys of living the character's life, and relishing his moments.

What, then, specifically defines a character's capability for joy? What past associations fill his memory, and are capable of being sounded? What private audiences beam at him from beyond? What sensory experiences fill him with delight? What smells make him happy? What sounds? What glances? What are his associations with twilight? With summer? With cold? How would he enjoy sitting on a a tractor seat driving down a dusty road? Or on a porch swing in Louisiana? Or on Claudius' throne?

Find, in each character, the thousands of moments to relish. The thousands of breaths that may be freely and fully taken in; the jokes laughed at and wit exchanged, the fluid and responsive pettings and strokings, the loving and interplaying. Find—and experience—the *playfulness* of your character; his joy in badinage and riposte, of gaminess and flirtation, of pillowfighting and shy sidewise glances.

Find the gentleness of each character; the grace, the affections, the quiet soundings, and play *with* them by playing them. Find, above all, the *positive* things about your character and the positive *specific* things about your character. Let yourself experience and enjoy these things. Indulge them. Remember, it is only when you are allowing yourself to wallow in the character's *despair* that you can be accused of "indulging in your role"—a rather stagey and ineffective practice. By indulging in the character's joys, and by relishing his victories— insofar, of course, as the script and the other character's actions will allow this—you are only engaging in the character's total life. And this, of course, will engage the audience.

If we look at this from an audience point of view, for a moment, we realize that we are never so filled with other people's presence as when we see them ecstatic. Who among us has not felt a great surge of feeling while watching an athlete win a great race, or a bride accept the ring at the altar, or a President get inaugurated? Moments of true joy, moments that are relished to the fullest, radiate a grand transmission of sympathetic feeling. They make the most disinterested observer glow with a sense of shared feeling. They can hush a crowd; they can inspire a populace.

Most beginning actors have a tendency to emphasize the pathos of their characters, perhaps feeling that self-pity is the best way of stimulating sympathy (from the other characters or from the audience). This is almost always as ineffective onstage as it is in life. Far more powerful emotional bonds are tied by the feeling of shared joys—no matter how trivial or slight they be—and with brimming happiness. Perhaps those joys are but moments in a long and dense tragedy. Perhaps, for Hamlet and for Laura, they seem insignificant episodes against weighty circumstances and tragic events. But they remain the sparks that tie the characters to the audience; the sparks, ultimately, that fire the will to live and life itself.

EXERCISES: RELISHING THE CHARACTER'S LIFE

1. Take any character and list *all* his or her victories in a single scene. Include such victories as

being left alone	being admired
being talked to	being befriended
greeting someone pleasant	being stroked
being challenged	being free

How does the character respond? Respond, in character.

2. What are the past associations of the character that would make him or her respond with relish to situations in the play? What memories of childhood are joyfully stimulated in the scene? Find them and play them.

3. What are the potential evils that the character has escaped? In what way is the character grateful for not being blind, not being crippled, not being old, not being unloved? What does he or she love about her surroundings? Find these and play them.

4. Let your character admire the way he or she talks.

5. Let your character admire the way he or she looks.

6. Let your character admire the way he or she moves.

7. Pick another (but similar) character and go through the previous six exercises. See how many different behaviors are attributable to the different character.

THE SELF-TRANSFORMATION: MAKE-UP

We have covered the mental processes involved in characterization, focusing on the character's thinking, his vision, the outside world as perceived by him, and the particular relish with which he responds to his world and its specific events. Nonetheless, and to be sure, this is not all there is to characterization. Falstaff must still be seen to be fat, Lear to be old, Pantalone to be stilted, and Quasimodo to be grotesque. In these cases the actor must quite deliberately transform himself, to the extent that he does not share his character's physical properties. This means make-up, and make-up has been with the theatre since its inception. "Make-up" is used here not only in the sense of grease-paint, but to include character voices, character movements, and character props.

We should not think of make-up as either purely physical or purely a one-way, actor-to-others statement, however. Make-up is psychological, and it feeds into the feedback which draws forth "characteristic" behavior. Make-up can be part of the whole interaction of a character, and it can induce characterization. Another way of saying this is that make-up can be a self-fulfilling prophecy. Cicely Tyson, who astounded audiences and critics in the teleplay "Autobiography of Jane Pittman" by aging from twelve years old to a hundred and ten with total credibility, reported "after the first make-up session, when I looked at it in the mirror, I really felt that old . . . (I had an) *internal* feeling of old age."

The point is that the actor should not simply apply his make-up, he should *experience* it. He should see its effect on others, and see how others react to it consciously and unconsciously. He should perform improvisations in make-up (and costume, where possible) so that he learns from it.

We should never forget that making up means making *up*. Characters, like the rest of us, invariably want to look their best, not their worst. Quasimodo may be humbled by his hunch, but there are certainly aspects of his appearance of which, at least secretly, he is proud. Make-up must accentuate this positive. Obese by the world's standard, Falstaff can still glory in his girth; it is, at least in part, an intentional obesity, and there was much well-remembered joy in its creation. In general, beginning actors tend to think of make-up as a disfigurement of their already-perfect appearances; this is only another aspect of the "character assassination" approach to characterization mentioned at the beginning of this chapter.

Highly stretched characterizations, like Tyson's 110-year-old Jane Pittman, require the planting of very well-studied obstacles and limitations. One could see the actress-character in that event, struggling to overcome the handicaps of many physical and psychological systems: brittle vocal cords, arthritic fingers, woebegone knee, hip, and neck joints, feeble and disobedient muscles, cloudy memories, waning attention, blocked hearing and seeing; it was Tyson's struggle to overcome these that made them "characterizing" elements of old age—"real," to the audience, and "really" affecting. Dustin Hoffman's masterful Ratzo Rizzo in the film *Midnight Cowboy* is another example of a "stretched" characterization, also played by the actor-character's intense struggle to overcome the limitations of (planted) lameness, pain, ugliness, incontinence, physical helplessness, and fear. Highly stretched characterizations require a great deal of research on behavior as well as on greasepaints, because the extremities of characterization are as much in the mind as on the body. For an affecting and honest portrayal of any characterization highly different from yourself, you must work very deliberately not just at finding how that person, or kind of person looks, but how he *thinks* he looks, and what that does to him.

Characterization by way of make-up has been left to the end of this chapter for a number of reasons, not the least of which is that, to a number of beginning actors, make-up is mistaken for the whole thing. There is a tendency to think of characterization, and particularly highly stretched characterization, as the surest mark of greatness in an actor. Sometimes it is, of course, and the examples of Tyson and Hoffman given above are two of the many thousands in the theatre's history. But the tendency to exaggerate the importance of "stretching" in this direction also has an escapist motive; beginning actors are frequently much more anxious to play a character's vulnerability than their own. This is not stretching, it is shrinking. On the surface level that sometimes passes for character acting, it is easier for many a twenty-year-old actress to play Amanda's aged nostalgic wistfulness than a simple improvisation of love or despair. The character becomes a mask to hide behind rather than a person to assimilate and become. This sort of character acting is safe, chaste, and relentlessly "good enough," but it does not bring characters or audiences to life. The best character acting is like the best slalom race, where the obstacles are planted to inspire a breathtaking performance, and where the performer goes all out in an effort to encircle them and win. That kind of acting is enchanting as well as accurate, involving as well as correct.

SUMMARY

Character acting is not solely, not even primarily, a matter of make-up, character "voices," and character "walks." It is the assumption of a character's thinking from the point of view of a character's own self-centeredness. Characterization is then a subjective process: the actor characterizes the world as his character does, and then interacts reciprocally with that world as characterized. He sees the world in terms of its offered victories (his ideal future, his finish line) and the obstacles in his path—physical, psychological, and physiological. In his homework for the role, the actor "plants" specific obstacles which will lead him through dramatically interesting contours and paths en route to his situational victories. He plants a private audience that influences his behavior unconsciously. He masks himself to the other actor-characters as a tactic to surmount the obstacles and achieve his victories. He enjoys his victories with a special and individual relish. Ultimately, the "character" that he is seen to play will be determined by the audience, who will determine character by what they see of his ideal futures, the obstacles that seem to hinder him, and the masks that he apparently thinks necessary to wear in pursuit of his goals.

CHAPTER 4

PLAYING STYLE

"I used to watch Sir Laurence (Olivier) when he played
Mr. Puff in *The Critic*. To the identical syllable, in
each performance, he would take off his hat, take out
the hatpin and stab the hat with the hatpin. He didn't
vary a hair's breadth from performance to performance,
yet it was always funny and always astonishing.
It occurred to me that it is possible to be a well-trained
instrument, to perform as a craftsman without ever
becoming ordinary, and that if there is such a thing as
perfection in acting it's worthwhile living for and
striving for that perfection."

—*Julie Harris*

As a word in our language, "style" defies attempts
at definition. Everyone agrees that style refers in
some way to the manner in which things are done,
but from that point the word usually disintegrates
into semantic chaos. It is used to denote technical
modes of expression, as in "a flamboyant style."
It is used to denote the shared characteristics of a
historical period, as in "Restoration style." It may
indicate a contextual theatrical format, as in "Ex-
pressionistic style." It may become highly mystical and epigrammatic, as in the classic French
definition "Style is the man himself." Sometimes
it describes an individual, as the "Kennedy style."
Sometimes it describes a group, clan, or race, as

"Divorce Italian Style." Sometimes, even, it can stand by itself without qualifier, as when we say a person "has style." In that case we are saying the person has "style style," and the word becomes its own modifier. It is no wonder that books on the theatre have foundered on the confusion of meanings of the word "style."

For the purposes of making the concept useful, "style" in this book is considered simply as the *behavioral characteristics shared by the play's characters*. It is, in other words, *the play's collective characterization*.

It is like characterization in many ways. It is at the same level of the actor's structure of consciousness; it is planted, like the slalom designer's flags, in such a way as to shape the ensuing dramatic presentation into interesting contours. But it is different from characterization as a mirror twin. *Characterization* is a measure of how the individual character *differs* from the other characters, and *style* is a measure of how much he *resembles* them. If one character in a play is warm and loving, that is a mark of his character; if all the characters are warm and loving, that is a mark of the play's style. If one character speaks in witty epigrams, that is a mark of his character; if all the characters do, it is a mark of the play's—and playwright's—style. If one character speaks in verse, chants intonations, or throws cream pies in other people's faces, that is a mark of a highly aberrant character; if a group of characters behave that way, it is clearly a case of style. Style is a precondition of the whole play—of the social and class values of the people the play is about (whether real or imaginary people)—and the interactions of the play's characters are all governed, to a certain extent, by the preconditions of the play's style.

The basic problem for the actor in a "stylized" play is one of proper alignment. How does the actor enter into style, into social and class values different from his own, without detracting from his situational involvement? How, for example, does he play out of himself, with his own emotions, engaging in genuine relacom with the other actor-characters, and at the same time speak only in blank verse? Or in rhyming couplets? Or in Wildean *bon mots?* Or in the lyrics of Oscar Hammerstein? Conversely, how can actors from today's world step into the "stylized" patterns of the past, or of some director's imagination, without seeming "phony" to the audience, and worst of all, artificial to themselves? How can actors avoid the feeling of affectation when playing in styles that in today's world seem affected, or at least "elevated"? How can style, finally, be integrated with the actor-character's situation? The answer might prove easier than we think at first. If we look through some of life's own experiences, we can see that style is integral not only with life-situations, but often with survival itself. Style is no adornment; at bottom, it is a social necessity.

Let us look, for example, at ourselves as first-time American tourists in Paris. Let us imagine ourselves entering a Parisian cafe and ordering a glass of beer. Being ourselves, we politely order "One Budweiser, bartender, if you please." But the bartender just stares at us, shrugs his shoulders with an incomprehensible mutter, and goes off to wait on somebody else. We realize, to our chagrin, that he doesn't speak our language. Perhaps we can simplify. "One beer!" we cry. The bartender brightens, and soon returns with a "Byrrh." Not the same thing at all. We go get a speaking dictionary, this time, and read the words from the pronunciation key: "uhn dehmee, see voo play." Now, finally, we get our beer. We are not changed people, we have simply changed the way in which we ordered. We have, in short, changed a part of our style, for the language that is spoken in a culture is a part of its style, part of the shared behavioral characteristics of its people. And we have changed our style to get a very real reward. The style is *useful;* whether or not it is elegant, or even "stylized" is not of any real concern to us; at the moment we use it, it is *necessary.*

Now imagine that we go across the Channel to London. Here we are less concerned—after all, they speak English in London. We wander into a dockside pub, and again ask for "One Budweiser, bartender, if you please." Much to our shock, we get the same stare, the same shrug, the same mutter! "Draw one," we say hopefully, "Beer please?" Still, we are obviously not making contact. We find a British phrase book and find the correct expression. Quoting it, we say, "I'd like a half and half, barman, please." But no, still silence. Finally the man at our elbow, a man who had American buddies during the war, looks up at the man behind the bar, "Gi' me mite 'n 'awf 'n 'awf, guv'nuh!" "'Awf 'n 'awf," we blithely echo. The barman breaks into a huge and immediate grin and brings the beer. Again we have changed our style, again we have used a style to get something we wanted.

But the London example makes us feel stranger than the Parisian. In Paris we *expected* to speak a foreign language, and to pronounce words differently; in London we didn't, and we feel somewhat ambivalent about it. We feel a bit foolish, perhaps even affected, asking the bartender for an "'awf 'n 'awf." We feel that he will see through us; we may feel that we are seeing through ourselves. It will take months before we can say, without a great deal of self-consciousness, "bully," or "cheerio." Essentially, and despite all rationality, we retain a deep, unexpressed feeling that our own American pronunciations are the "right" ones, and that the dialect of the barman is a deviation, an "accent." Just as we think of other dialects as accents, and our own dialect as—simply—English. Most Americans can remember a shock upon first discovering that the language they have spoken all their lives is considered an "American accent" by Britishers. Most of us had always believed that it was the British who had the accents; somehow we even assumed that they would have had the grace to understand that as well. This phenomenon, which is not unique to America but is shared by all societies, is called "ethnocentrism," which is the mental reflex that judges all cultures in relation to one's own, which is the "standard." An understanding of this social ethnocentricity is as basic to the actor's playing of style as an understanding of character egocentricity is basic to his playing of characterization.

The fact is, of course, that what we call "beer" is a physical thing, a liquid property, and it is no more "beer" than "'awf 'n 'awf" or "half and half," or "un demi." For that matter, it could be called "Sigaloops" or "Chowchowder"; as long as it slakes thirst and provides nourishment and pleasure, people will call for it by whatever name "works." And that is the first lesson of style. One uses the language, the inflection, the dialect, the mode, the manner, and the format of behavior which *works* within the existing situation. *Style, at bottom, is what works, or can be presumed to work, within a given society or group.*

In the case of the glass of beer, the person who wants it must demand it not in his own language, but (insofar as possible) in the language and dialect of the bartender. Obviously a multilinguist can order a glass of beer in more bars than someone who is restricted to his own tongue, but the multilinguist is not defining himself as a Frenchman because he orders in French, or a Cockney because he speaks in the language of Soho; the multilinguist is merely using his *resources* to get what he needs from the people who can provide it for him. *Style, therefore, is not a definition of self, it is not a limitation of the self; it is a resource for effective action within a group, class, or culture.* Style is essentially tied to action; it is a *tool* toward situational victory and toward survival.

Let us take one further trip out of our own style, and imagine ourselves, like the Connecticut Yankee in Mark Twain's classic novel, transported to King Arthur's court in the tenth century. We would arrive with our present-day clothing, and our wallets stuffed with present-day currency and credit cards. We would be friendless, of course, and without any usable financial resources. Our clothing and our behavior, should they be noticed by appropriate authorities, would certainly serve to denote us as demons; there could be no thought, for the same reason, of trying to explain that we were refugees from another century. Those of us who would survive the transplant would undoubtedly be the ones who most quickly and effectively adopted the manifestations of the place in time. Shedding our dacron and polyester clothing, abandoning our particular dialect and vocabulary, we would as quickly as possible seek to imitate the clothing, language, usage, employment, and even attitudes of our surroundings. It would not be a time to ponder whether or not we were "affected" or "phony" in these adoptions of tenth century behaviors; we would be fighting the battle of survival, and that battle would be fought on the field of style.

In adopting the behavior, manners, and style of King Arthur's Court, we would not at all stop being ourselves; if we were later to return to the twentieth century, we would also be entirely able to return to our customary twentieth-century style. If we could go back and forth, we would simply have picked up a language, like the multilingual tourist. The assumption of tenth-century social behaviors would not be permanent personality changes, only resources for getting food in our mouths and getting our needs taken care of in the tenth century. Style, again, is a resource for effective and necessary action.

There are many styles which operate within our own American culture and within our own century. The courtroom is a stylized environment which is undeniably part of the very real world, giving real punishments and real rewards, but demanding "stylized" behavior. In a courtroom, we are constrained to rise on the bailiff's cue, to address the judge as "your honor," and to speak to the assemblage with a preface like "May it please the court." Attorneys do not speak that way because they are "courtly" people but because they want to win their case; because that is the "style" of language which will most favorably impress the judge. The courtroom has, in addition to its specialized language, a specialized setting, costuming, and decorum. These combine to form a consistent and identifiable style, and anyone who violates that style may well find himself forcibly removed. But the courtroom is only one example of this "stylization" in everyday reality. Political clubs, theatre companies, dormitory groups, coffee klatches, baseball teams, and the informal "worlds" of big business, Madison Avenue, Hollywood, and radical militants all have their styles, their "uniforms," and their collective characterizations which must be followed to a greater or lesser extent in order to gain acceptance and power within the particular unit, and to avoid ostracism and punishment.

Style, therefore, is not something that has been invented by the theatre or by the demands of art. While it is part of the dramatizing of the play, and of the playwright and director, it is also an aspect of human interaction; it is the *special arena in which characters interact, the preconditions of their attempted victories and their struggle for survival.* While the audience may see, or wish to see, certain styles as "affectations," the characters in the play do not. To them, their style is essential, fundamental.

PLAYING THEATRICAL STYLES

The theatre is a vast assemblage of styles. History, geography, culture, and the grand imagination of our dramatic authors have created a myriad of styles—some named, some unnamed, and some misnamed—that are the "special arenas" in which the interactions of most plays take place. How does the actor enter that "special arena," and how does he play style without sacrificing his own, out-of-himself credibility?

Playing theatrical styles is essentially a matter of the actor's understanding the style in terms of *the specific preconditions it places on behavior,* and the actor's subsequent planting of those preconditions between himself and his situational goal. The specific preconditions will then *demand* the style out of him. Like characterization, style is played reciprocally rather than directly.

As in the life-examples above, the American tourist speaks Cockney not because he "feels" Cockney-ish, but because the pubkeeper responds only to Cockney. The Connecticut Yankee wears cotton leggings not because he is intrinsically a legging-wearer, but because the Arthurian courtiers accept them. The attorney for the defense speaks deferentially to the judge not because he feels inferior, or because he is a deferential person, but because the judge rewards deferential language. In every case, style is primarily adopted for the purpose of pleasing, prodding, or persuading the other person in the interaction; it is, in a word, tactical.

Naturally this tactical stylistic adoption is not wholly conscious; most of it, in fact, has developed over the character's lifetime and is habitual—even in many cases beyond the point of its effectiveness. Yet it remains intentional at the unconscious if not the conscious level; style is *intended* by the character, and comes out of the same concentration on winning, intentions, and tactics that derive from the actor-character's situational pursuits. This, ultimately, is the key to how John-Hamlet will play "out of himself," and at the same time play "in blank verse."

Because a character's style has developed in ways suitable to win the character's victories, it is also necessary to realize that style, when mastered by the character, is *enjoyable;* most characters can (and should) be seen to relish their own style. If we feel awkward at first ordering a glass of beer in a foreign language, we ultimately rejoice in ourselves when we have finally mastered that language. The deferential attorney will grumble for years at the "artificial" jargon he must speak, but as his experience teaches him the cybernetic tricks of his trade, he will ultimately revel in his withering "May it please the court" lead-ins. As a master craftsman will grow to love his tools as an extension of himself, and as style is the "tool" by which a character seeks his situational victories, so the character must grow to love his style as he loves himself. Hamlet not only uses blank verse, he loves blank verse, and he loves using it and using it well.

In sum, the actor's essential mechanism for playing a theatrical style is this:

1. He first analyzes the style in terms of its purposes and preconditions; what kinds of behavior are rewarded, and what kinds of behav-

---

"In essence, there is no difference between classical and realistic acting. It's only that they do not take place on the same level."

—*Michel St. Denis*

---

ior are punished; in short, he uncovers and creates the "world of the play" that is the particular framework (the special arena) in which the play's interactions take place, and by which they are regulated.

2. He "plants" that world, with its special rules and mores, as a precondition for all his actions.

3. He "enters" that world, as the Connecticut Yankee would have entered King Arthur's court, and tries to interact successfully within it, according to his intentions, goals, and situations from the play.

4. He grows to relish that world, and his ability to interact within it, insofar as he can.

By this four-stage process, the actor is *seen to be* transformed—he no longer acts as he does offstage—but his pursuit of real goals, really pursued, remains wholly intact. His identity (as we see it) seems to have altered; to himself, however, he is fundamentally unchanged. His vitality·is not only intact, it is enhanced. And that is essential; the problem most young actors have in acquiring style is precisely to seize its vitality, its essence, its exuberance. Just as the American tourist is at first timid in ordering from a Parisian bartender, so the beginning actor is timid in approaching a play by Molière, or Shakespeare, or Congreve. Like the tourist, he is afraid of looking foolish; like the tourist he holds back, rigidifies, shrinks from his task. Trying to look inconspicuous, he only succeeds in what he fears the most: he looks foolish. Only by an understanding of the situational *necessity* of style can the actor liberate himself into its most powerful expression.

Let us look at an example. John, playing Millimant in Congreve's *The Way of the World,* is told by the director to raise his leg, turn his calf inward, and place it on a bench. Granted, there are many pictures of Restoration gallants showing this posture, but it still seems a rather bizarre thing to John, a twentieth-century man, to do, much less to delight in. Therefore John finds himself self-conscious and awkward; this, of course, is the hurdle of approaching an unfamiliar style.

Now let us analyze it. In the Restoration, we find, the calf was considered by young women to be the sexiest part of a man's anatomy. This is the "precondition." Now all John has to do is woo Jane-Mirabelle in an arena governed by such preconditions. He raises his leg in the appropriate fashion, not because he is intrinsically a leg-raising person, or because "that's what they did then," but because, in his own mind, Jane-Mirabelle is going to be sexually excited by the sight of his proffered calf. So John not only does the gesture, he enjoys doing it; he relishes it. And probably that relish will transmit to Jane-Mirabelle as well; if so, the Restoration has come back to life, and the calf is sexy once again!

The point is that to the Restoration gallant, calf-raising is not an affectation, it is a wooing gesture, a tactic for mating play. All the actor has to do to make it "real for himself" is to plant, in the mind of Jane-Mirabelle, a Restoration calf-fetish. He then does the gesture reciprocally—for her, not for himself. It is not posturing, it is *acting*; and he can do it with charm, delight, and enthusiasm. Style, in this example clearly, is something you act *with*. It is useful, not decorative; tactical, not show-offy.

STYLE IS PLANTED IN THE OTHER PEOPLE

In general, therefore, style is not something the actor plays because of his own predilections, he plays it because of the predilections of *other* people. Style, to the actor, is not in himself but in the other characters; they are the ones who are *stylized*, he is simply responding to them as he must. Romeo speaks love poetry to Juliet not because *he* loves it but because *she* does and he happens to be good at it; this any-

"One of the most difficult parts I played was the fool opposite Paul Schofield as Lear. Now what is a fool? The language was practically incomprehensible. The part was wildly difficult to work on until I thought of myself as a little boy of five waiting for my father to come home from work cross and tired. I would try to make him laugh. That's the fool's action in *Lear*—to please, to divert."

—*Alec McCowen*

way, is the precondition that John-Romeo plants in his actor's consciousness. Style, like character, is played reciprocally to these planted assumptions. As the actor-character sees other people as characters (but not himself as one), so he sees other people as stylized (but not himself as such). He does not stylize himself; he responds to the styles of others. He speaks the way they want him to, the way that will gain him the most rewards. At the level of content, of course, he can disagree quite fundamentally with other characters in the play, as can an attorney in the courtroom, but insofar as he stays in the play he must stay in the special arena of the play's style. He must win his victories within the framework of the play's "world," of the preconditions imposed on it, quite unconsciously by the society, quite consciously (in most cases) by the playwright and director. He must win on their terms, in ways they understand and accept. For without their acceptance, there is no victory. The pursuit of an accepted victory, then will define a style without pushing one.

EXERCISE: RECIPROCAL STYLIZATION

A simple exercise will demonstrate reciprocal stylization quite effectively. First a general improvisation is suggested where two persons have conflicting objectives. For example, Person A wants Person B to stand up and make a speech, but Person B has a hole in his pants and doesn't want anybody—including Person A—to know about it. Then the improvisation is "stylized" by planting the following preconditions: Person B has a grave hearing defect, so that he can only hear words spoken in a high falsetto, and cannot read or lip read. Person A, for his part, also has a hearing defect, and can only hear very low tones—the very deepest that Person B can come up with.

The ensuing improvisation has an external style that is quite extreme and extraordinary, resembling certain Punch and Judy or *commedia* stylizations, and can reach high levels of hilarity, and often also of pathos. But the stylization is not imposed contextually; it is *innate to the situation and the described preconditions*. Both actors are improvising only out of situational needs and goals: any eccentricity from their own, ordinary behavior is stimulated by the other person, not from their own wish to stylize themselves. The exercise, then, is entirely "real" in the sense that it can be played as a pure interaction, and utterly "stylized" by its preconditions; in this case the actors' dramatizings and their situational involvements are perfectly and completely aligned.

EXERCISE VARIATIONS: RECIPROCAL BEHAVIOR

These exercises ask you to adapt your behavioral patterns reciprocally to a group.

1. Person B is schizophrenic, and can comprehend only rhymed speech. Perform an improvisation with this person. Both A and B are similarly schizophrenic; perform an improvisation together.

2. Person B grew up as a "wild child," has no verbal language, and is frightened of human sounds. Perform an improvisation with this person, trying to make him understand that the building is on fire.

3. You enter a room full of chained, foreign prisoners of war, whose language you do not speak, and who have been blinded. They are terrified of you; calm them and win their trust, and free them.

4. You find yourself in a political meeting filled with increasingly violent partisans of a candidate you despise. Join with them in singing "For He's a Jolly Good Fellow" without betraying your true feelings and endangering your safety.

5. Talk to an imaginary group of kindergarteners. Talk to a group of your peers, and imagine them as kindergarteners. Have the entire group imagine that *everybody else* (themselves excepted) is a kindergartener. Perform an improvisation under these circumstances.

THE WORLD OF THE PLAY

The world of the play is not a simple matter, and rarely can it (or should it) be reduced to a single word. Contributing to the world of a play, and its style, are several factors: the historical period (including the present) in which the play is set, the particular cultures or classes to which the characters belong, the particular cultures or classes to which the characters aspire, the style of theatrical expression common to the author's period, the personal style of the author himself, and the specific style the author may have implanted on this play and its collection of characters. Sometimes these worlds are multiple: Jean Paul Sartre's *The Flies,* for example, portrays a historical world of archaic Greece through the language of 1940s existentialist dialecticalism; T. S. Eliot's *Murder In The Cathedral* portrays the historical world of medieval England in the language of modern verse; Shakespeare's *Titus Andronicus* portrays Imperial Rome in tones of Elizabethan melodrama; Shaw's *Caesar and Cleopatra* portrays romance in Rome and Egypt in the spirit of rhetorical Edwardian debate; *All In The Family* portrays contemporary Brooklyn domesticity in the format of television situation comedy. The combinations of these stylistic components are perhaps infinite; what draws them together in the actor's mind is that they are all determinants of his character's tactics for achieving situational victory. They are defined operationally, and not necessarily verbally or intellectually.

Example: Man and Superman   Let us examine, by way of illustration, the world of George Bernard Shaw's *Man and Superman.* It is a play whose characters differ from most of us by nation, dialect, historical period, and social class; it is also a play whose world is somewhat imaginary, and not quite like any world that has ever existed outside of Mr. Shaw's own fertile brain. Here is a sample passage from that play:

RAMSDEN (very deliberately): Mr. Tanner: you are the most impudent person I have ever met.

TANNER (seriously): I know it, Ramsden. Yet even I cannot wholly conquer shame. We live in an atmosphere of shame. We are ashamed of everything that is real about us; ashamed of ourselves, of our relatives, of our incomes, of our accents, of our opinions, of our experience, just as we are ashamed of our naked skins. Good Lord, my dear Ramsden, we are ashamed to walk, ashamed to ride in an omnibus, ashamed to hire a hansom instead of a coachman and footman. The more things a man is ashamed of, the more respectable he is. Why you're ashamed to buy my book, ashamed to read it: the only thing you're not ashamed of is to judge me for it without having read it; and even that only means that you're ashamed to have heterodox opinions. Look at the effect I produce because my fairy godmother withheld from me this gift of shame. I have every possible virtue that a man can have except—

RAMSDEN: I am glad you think so well of yourself.

TANNER: All you mean by that is that you think I ought to be ashamed of talking about my virtues. You don't mean that I haven't got them: you know perfectly well that I am as sober and honest a citizen as yourself, as truthful personally, and much more truthful politically and morally.

RAMSDEN (touched on his most sensitive point): I deny that. I will not allow you or any man to treat me as if I were a mere member of the British public. I detest its prejudices; I scorn its narrowness; I demand the right to think for myself. You pose as an advanced man. Let me tell you that I was an advanced man before you were born.

TANNER: I knew it was a long time ago.

RAMSDEN: I am as advanced as ever I was. I defy you to prove that I have ever hauled down the flag. I am more advanced than ever I was. I grow more advanced every day.

TANNER: More advanced in years, Polonius.

RAMSDEN: Polonius! So you are Hamlet, I suppose.

TANNER: No: I am only the most impudent person you've ever met. That's your notion of a thoroughly bad character. When you want to give me a piece of your mind, you ask yourself, as a just and upright man, what is the worst you can fairly say of me. Thief, liar, forger, adulterer, perjurer, glutton, drunkard? Not one of these names fits me. You have to fall back on my deficiency in shame. Well, I admit it. I even congratulate myself; for if I were ashamed of my real self, I should cut as stupid a figure as any of the rest of you. Cultivate a little impudence, Ramsden; and you will become quite a remarkable man.

RAMSDEN: I have no—

TANNER: You have no desire for that sort of notoriety. Bless you, I knew that answer would come as well as I know that a box of matches will come out of an automatic machine when I put a penny in the slot: you would be ashamed to say anything else.
(The crushing retort for which Ramsden has been visibly collecting his forces is lost forever; . . .)

We can certainly see, in this passage, all the earmarks of what can be called "Shavian style." There is the very deliberate phrasing: no stammers, no sloppy reasoning, no grammatical sins. No one could mistake this for everyday speech, even everyday Edwardian speech; speech is rarely if ever transcribed with semicolons. Rather this is

Shavian-styled debate rhetoric. There is the building of assertion upon assertion, the use of rhetorical climaxes and extended outpourings of crescendoing epithets: "Thief, liar, forger, adulterer, perjurer, glutton, drunkard." There are multiple listings, such as Tanner's "ashamed's," and parallel phrasings, such as Ramsden's "I detest its prejudices, I scorn its narrowness, I demand the right to think for myself." There is literary allusion (to *Hamlet*), wit ("I knew it was a long time ago"), sophisticated irony ("Cultivate a little impudence"), simile ("as a box of matches will come out of an automatic machine when I put a penny in the slot"), and the "crushing retort" which is prepared but never delivered. The "Shavian style," however, does not apply to any one character as much as to both of them; it is respected by both of them, it *works* on both of them—that is why they use it. The world of *Man and Superman*, we see right away, is one where brilliant verbal rhetoric is going to be rewarded, and inarticulate bullying will prove hopeless. If Stanley Kowalski could walk out of *A Streetcar Named Desire* and into *Man and Superman*, he would be utterly ineffective in any pursuit. The process of evolution and natural selection has gathered onto Shaw's setting only those characters who can survive in the glittering intellectual climate of Shavian discourse.

So the actor assuming the role of Tanner must play toward a dual objective. At the content level, he must win his control of Ann's guardianship. At the relationship level, he must make clear to all concerned (and particularly to Ramsden) that he is cleverer, smarter, better read, more quick-witted, more pursuasive in debate, and in short, more Shavian than Ramsden. Ramsden pursues the identical objectives, so that the battle between them goes on at both content and relationship levels; that is, as they argue over who shall control Ann's future (the content debate) they are simultaneously trying to achieve the superiority of style which would entitle them to dominate the relationship, and therefore win the final victory at the content level. They are trying, in other words, to gain control of Ann (content) by "out-Shawing" each other (style): their *situational* victory, therefore, is entirely dependent on their *stylistic* excellence, and their levels of behavior are exactly aligned.

That alignment is what makes "stylized" acting possible without any sacrifice of power or credibility, but, indeed, with the enhancement of them instead. Style is not "something added," it is instrumental to the situation. The actor engaged in Tanner's situation is engaged in his stylistic attack. Like Tanner, the actor playing him must

appear cleverer, smarter, better read, more quick-witted, more persuasive in debate, and more "Shavian" than his fellow actors. As the characters compete with each other for Ann's attention, so should the
actors compete with each other in this "out-Shawing" battle for su-
premacy. They should learn Shavian debate tactics, they should master them, perform them, improvise them, and absolutely delight in
them. Above all, they must make the Shavian tactics situationally
useful; they should make them tools in their character's behalf. As
Shaw himself says in the Preface to this same play, style is nothing
but "effectiveness of assertion."* It is that which asserts effectively,
in other words: that which has impact and focus, that which *works.*

STYLE AS A WEAPON

Style is a situational tool even in totally non-naturalistic styles. It is
hard to imagine a less naturalistic style than opera singing, for example,
but the great soprano Maria Callas has said that "the voice is a weapon,
the voice should serve the person [character] you are on stage." What
could be sillier, from a naturalistic point of view, than a Japanese lady
named Butterfly singing a Puccini aria (in Italian, yet) as her American
sailor-lover called Pinkerton goes off to sea? And yet Callas sings her
way into our hearts because Butterfly sings her way into Pinkerton's.

Given Callas' rationale that "the voice is a weapon," we may presume her mechanism as a planted precondition: that Pinkerton is an
opera fan—even a Puccini fan! This plant lets her sing her heart out to
him; it lets her try to be *successful with her singing as well as with her
song;* with her form as well as with her content. Callas-Butterfly not
only sings the aria, she sings singing; she is "saying" not only the words
of the song, but conveying the implicit message: "I am a great singer—
if you leave me you will never hear an aria like this again!" So *Callas'*

---

*"Effectiveness of assertion is the Alpha and Omega of style. He who has nothing to
assert has no style and can have none: he who has something to assert will go so far in
power of style as its momentousness and his conviction will carry him. Disprove his
assertion after it is made, yet its style remains." Probably no one understood better
than Shaw the "power of style."

"The performer is obliged to make the concern of the character he is portraying so unconditionally and consistently his own that to him and to the audience all basic musical functions—rhythm, meter, harmony, tempo, dynamics—do not appear to be prescribed by the score or the conductor but seem to be determined by his, the character's, intentions and sensations."

—*Walter Felsenstein*

---

magnificent voice becomes Butterfly's weapon; we, the audience, are merely the observers and vicarious co-participants in this intense musical-dramatic experience.

RELISHING THE WORLD OF THE PLAY

But style is not *only* a weapon, not *only* a tactic. These are only the foundations of style, the reasons why styles develop. In the final analysis, the style of a play becomes a magnificent world to experience. And this leads the actor toward one of his deepest and most profound glories—the joy of inhabiting a new and magnificent world. Like the old cliché about travel, acting style is broadening.

As the American tourist finally makes himself at home in the Cockney pub, he finds out not only that he can order himself a glass of beer with relative ease, but also that he can share in the values, language, humor, feelings, culture, and spirit of a world previously foreign and inaccessible to him. For most people—and all actors—this should be an exquisite experience. The style of a culture, whether the "real" culture of an ethnic bar, or the imaginary cultures of Shaw's or Puccini's worlds, is a shared set of understandings among people and environments, understandings that have profound if unspoken connections. Style, ultimately, is a union, a brotherhood, a transcendent social relationship. It is a cultural and spiritual unity of values, history, modes, and philosophy. As Michel St. Denis suggests, "Style . . . is the expression of real understanding, of deep communication with the world and its secrets, of the constant effort of men to surpass themselves." Style is an escape from the confines of our own environment, and from the narrowness of our own understandings.

Therefore it is the task of the actor to consider an assignment in style as a voyage into a strange, wonderful, and vast new world, one in which he can discover new things about his capabilities, and devise new tactics to work through new preconditions. He must meet with relish the challenge of dealing with new people, new ideas, new values, and new modes of expression. The worlds of *Man and Superman* or *Madame Butterfly* are not necessarily better ones than our own, but they are wildly different, they are whole in themselves, and to their inhabitants the life within those worlds is thrilling indeed. The thrill of living in those worlds, the thrill and relish with which style is played and experienced, will radiate through any cast and any audience.

THE WORLDS OF THE PLAY: SHAKESPEARE'S SPEAKING STYLES

So far we have been speaking of overall styles—Shavian and operatic, for example—which form the arena of manners for their particular plays and pieces. This is not to say that every play—or even any play— can be reduced to a single style. Shakespeare is a playwright who, perhaps more than any other, provided a broad palette of styles in every play, a variety of dramatic languages in which content and relationship, form and function, are inextricably entwined. The overall stylistic format of Shakespeare is a combination of earthy prose, blank verse, Elizabethan song, witty stichomythic repartée, Senecan melodrama, Marlovian bombast, and Lylyan balance. These are not "real world" formats in any way, but dramatic constructs created by an author of unprecedented linguistic skills. Shakespeare uses the speaking styles of his characters to enormous situational effect; his characters are defined as much by how they speak as by what they say.

Hamlet provides us a very good example of this, and shows us a great many speaking styles that relate directly to situation, or to plot points. In the world of *Hamlet,* blank verse is the accepted mode of speaking among educated and royally connected Danes; Hamlet speaks it because it is spoken to him, and he has learned to speak it from the time he learned to speak. The first time Hamlet speaks extended prose is when he tries to persuade Polonius that he (Hamlet) is mad (the "fishmonger" scene, II, ii); that is, he changes his style of speaking in order to re-mask himself and create a new image at court. This stylistic change is as shocking as the content of Hamlet's remarks. Both his blank verse and his prose are then chosen behaviors from his repertoire. They are chosen for pragmatic situational ends, not because they happen to be "Shakespearean." Hamlet switches from verse to prose as suits his purpose, prose being convenient for friendly exchanges with non-royal friends—the players, Horatio, and the two gravediggers. He also uses it to confuse and taunt his quasi-royal adversaries (who otherwise speak in verse, and clearly prefer to); these include Polonius, Osric, Rosencrantz, Guildenstern, and even Ophelia, whom he suspects of spying on him. In the remarkable Act IV, scene iv, Hamlet speaks prose to the King, while the King, speaking verse, dispatches him to England. Not only are Hamlet's lines in that scene a matter of insubordination (calling Claudius his "Mother," for example), so is his lack of metrical regularity in speech, since blank verse is utterly established, by this time in the play, as the language of the court: Claudius and Gertrude, as well as Laertes, Fortinbras, and the ghost of King Hamlet, speak nothing else. Hamlet's use of prose here is more insulting to the King than what he actually has to say. Hamlet's ability to speak verse at court and prose in the graveyard testifies to his stylistic versatility and his ability to don various masks as occasions require. It makes him less of a limited "character," and more of a flexible "anybody" who can move cybernetically toward situation goals, adopting stylizations as necessary to his progress.

This is not at all to define "Shakespearean style" as a matter of prose versus blank verse. We must speak, first, of Shakespearean *styles* in the plural, and identify the several varieties of behavior which seem to be drawn out of each play's world. *Hamlet* demonstrates numerous speaking styles, for example, which are tactical in their very syntactical construction. For example,

HORATIO: Stay illusion!
If thou hast any sound, or use of voice,

Speak to me.
If there be any good thing to be done
That may to thee do ease and grace to me,
Speak to me.
If thou art privy to thy country's fate,
Which, happily, foreknowing may avoid,
Oh, speak! (I.ii.126–35.)

Comment: Rhetorical interrogation. The ghost of a late King would hardly listen to adolescent whining or verbal threats. Horatio's repeated phrases form a singsong incantation designed to pierce the silence of the apparition. When the incantation fails, he cries to Marcellus to stop it, and Marcellus strikes at it with his "partisan" (spear). The best style is whatever works; in this case rhetorical interrogation fails, and so does the "show of violence," but they were used as attempts to win situational advantages.

HORATIO: But look, the morn, in russet mantle clad,
Walks o'er the dew of yon high eastward hill.
Break we our watch up, and by my advice
Let us impart what we have seen tonight
Unto young Hamlet, for upon my life,
This spirit, dumb to us, will speak to him.
Do you consent we shall acquaint him with it,
As needful in our loves, fitting our duty?

Comment: Poetic elaboration. The first two lines, justly famous, have frequently been cited as examples of Shakespeare "painting the scenery with words." But there is a situational point here, too. Horatio is trying to force agreement from Marcellus and Bernardo, both to break up the watch and to go to the palace and talk to Hamlet. The introductory phrase serves as a turn-taking device for Horatio to focus attention on himself, on the new business at hand, and on his own eloquence which will be needed to carry this matter to the prince. Horatio does not "throw off" this line as though it were not eloquent; rather he uses it to enhance his own position with his cohorts, and to establish his right to a position of authority. Obviously Marcellus and Bernardo respect poetic eloquence more than contemporary military men might be expected to, and that is why Horatio uses it.

CLAUDIUS: Though yet of Hamlet our dear brother's death
The memory be green, and that it us befitted

To bear our hearts in grief and our whole kingdom
To be contracted in one brow of woe,
Yet so far hath discretion fought with nature
That we with wisest sorrow think on him,
Together with remembrance of ourselves.
Therefore our sometime sister, now our Queen
The imperial jointress to this warlike state,
Have we, as 'twere with a defeated joy—
With an auspicious and a dropping eye,
With mirth in funeral and with dirge in marriage,
In equal scale weighing delight and dole
Taken to wife.

Comment: Regal address. The tortuous syntax of this opening of Claudius' first speech—two sentences with multiple dependent and independent clauses spread over fourteen lines—indicates a man who can say what he wishes without fear of being interrupted, and who is assured that his listeners will take it upon themselves to unravel his meaning. If, as Hamlet, says, "the time is out of joint," here we have Claudius explaining how, with his new "jointress" wife, he is rejoining the society together; and he is saying it in his very construction, as well as his literal message. His blanched phrases, his oxymorons and antinomies, his alliterations ("sometime sister," "delight and dole"), all seek to create the appearance of a completed syntactical and genealogical complex which proves to the hearers that the throne of Denmark is rock solid. The tactic apparently works—on everybody but Hamlet.

> CLAUDIUS: Give me the cups,
> And let the kettle to the trumpet speak,
> The trumpet to the cannoneer without
> The cannon to the Heavens, the Heaven to earth,
> "Now the King drinks to Hamlet." Come, begin.
> (V,ii, 285–90.)

Comment: Incendiary oratory. The King, having poisoned the drinks as well as Laertes' sword, now tries to intoxicate the duelists (as well as the spectators) so that his murder of Hamlet can be speedily accomplished in a welter of drunken confusion. The crescendoing phrases are calls to action—drinking and duelling. Again, this tactic does not completely succeed, but it is clear what his goal with it is.

FORTINBRAS: Let four captains
Bear Hamlet, like a soldier, to the stage.
For he was likely, had he been put on,
To have proved most royally. And for his passage
The soldier's music and the rights of war
Speak loudly for him.
Take up the bodies. Such a sight as this
Becomes the field, but here shows much amiss.
Go, bid the soldiers shoot. (End of play.)

Comment: A show of grief. Regardless of whether or not Fortinbras feels true grief at Hamlet's death (he never knew Hamlet, and of course Hamlet's father had killed Fortinbras' father), he recognizes that it is politic to show some: he is about to take over the Danish crown as a foreigner, and he could lose any advantage he might have if, at this moment, he seemed overly gleeful or overly "rehearsed" for what he is about to do. Therefore his verse is strikingly broken, in the overlong (six-foot) fourth line, and the abruptly curtailed sixth and ninth lines. The rhyming couplet, proper but somewhat clumsy, is Fortinbras' manner of concluding the event, assuring himself of having the final word about it. Rhyming couplets are common in Shakespeare at the end of scenes. They should be played as such—as attempts to conclude conversations in one's own favor—of having the last word and shutting out the other characters.

There are many more possibilities of relating the syntax of speeches in *Hamlet,* or in any play, to the situational involvements

---

"God, give me language. The No. 1 thing with (Pinter and) Paddy Chayefsky, too, is that you don't piss it away. You learn it. When it's really going, it's like a souffle. Even the rhythms are written in."

—*Faye Dunaway*

---

of the characters who speak them, and to demonstrate the tactical use of these syntaxes, which form the basis for the verbal style of each characterization, and in sum, of each play. This discussion only creates the beginning of an analysis of *Hamlet*'s stylization, and does not even touch upon the visual stylizations of dress, manners, postures, and expressions which might find their way into the stylization of a production. But the analysis of these five speeches should suggest the deep integration of speaking styles with plot situations—particularly in the work of a master playwright.

PHYSICAL STYLES

To this point we have concentrated on speaking styles, specifically in Shaw and Shakespeare. There are, of course, physical styles as well, having to do with costume, carriage, movement, bearing, posturing, gesture, and comportment. In fact these are the stylistic attributes we learn in infancy, before speaking; it is to physical stylization that children's mothers refer when they instruct their charges to "mind their manners."

Physical styles, like speaking styles, are behaviors that are directed toward situational victories. We have already seen that the Restoration rake's elevation and turning in of his calf was an attempt, on his part, to display what his lady would consider the most suggestively erotic portion of his anatomy; it is a gesture identical in function to Stanley Kowalski's stripping off his shirt in the first act of *A Streetcar Named Desire*, an act differing in outward form but not in purpose or intent. The actor playing the rake "plants" in his mind the precondition of fair ladies being excited by the calf, instead of the chest, and plays his situation accordingly.

Gesture, in most cultures, is frequently as specifically communicative as spoken language. It is therefore *intentional* rather than simply expressive. The Italian who purses his fingers and shakes them is not merely releasing his feelings, nor is he trying to "look Italian"; he is, instead, communicating a very specific message in the physical language he has been brought up with. Even non-specific gestures—shrugs, grunts, waves of the hand—are usually socially derived and represent attempts, if unconscious ones, to *do* something rather than to *be* something. In studying and adopting the gestures of a culture (historical stylizing) or of an imaginary theatrical format (theatrical stylizing), the actor must search for the *intention and purpose of the style; whom it is directed to, and what it is intended for.* Only then can the actor transform his gestures into the stylized ones with the requisite authority and power.

Costume is, of course, one of the great hurdles for many inexperienced actors; and this is easy to understand. Most of us feel uncomfortable even in formal dress; it is only natural that we will at first tend to be uncomfortable in doublet and hose, or in hoop skirts and petticoats. Almost nothing marks the amateur production of Shakespeare as much as young actors fiddling with their costumes, and obviously wishing they were able to wear their rehearsal jeans and T-shirts. It is the actor's old enemy, egocentrism, that creates this hurdle; the actor's innate belief that his everyday clothes are "real," and that tuxedos, doublets, periwigs, togas, and zebra skins are "stylized"—unreal, affected, peculiar. Jeans and T-shirts, however, would be just as stylized and unreal to the Elizabethan, the Greek, or the Zulu.

Costumes must be worn as clothes, and enjoyed as clothes. That does not mean they should be worn as we wear *our* clothes, but rather that they should be worn for the purposes for which they were intended. For the style of dress we adopt, like everything else in style, is intended and intentional. At least in the case of those characters who can be presumed to have chosen their own clothes (excepting, by this rule, prisoners, babies, and hospital patients—although even these have some control over the deployment of their garb), characters like what they wear; they *want* to wear what they wear. Some dress for specific effect, some for fashion, some to stand out, some to fit in; the fact is that no dress is wholly purposeless; no costume is wholly without a tactical consideration.

To wear a costume of a style different from our own requires that we analyze the style for its purposes. The actor, instead of seeing his costume as an awkward embarrassment, must see it as a source of strength, an emblem of his power. He must inwardly love his costume; after all, he chose it. Costumes can be the character's weapons. Playwrights often capitalize on this: Tennessee Williams gives Stanley Kowalski a pair of bright red silk pajamas so that he can dazzle Blanche; Shakespeare gives Hamlet a "suit of inky black" so he can shame the court; Molière gives Monsieur Jordain a grotesque turban so he can (try to) awe and impress his family. In the consciousness of the actor, his costume is aligned with his struggle and allied with his efforts. The actor must learn to understand the uses of his character's costume, he must grow to use it, gain power from it, and love it.

Carriage, movement, and deportment are similarly physical styles that present problems when the actor is required to move out of his own time and place, or his own (usually limited) vision of the world of the play. One of the great curiosities of the modern theatre was the insistence of the American "method" actors on performing a Shakespearean script, for example, with the shrugs, grimaces, stammers, and halting, sluggish movements common to their own time. This could perhaps have succeeded if the plays involved had been reset into the contemporary period, but they were not; the actors had simply been instructed—or had decided themselves—to use "real" movements instead of "stylized" ones. But of course this is ridiculous—egocentricity again—for no style of movement is intrinsically more "real" than any other, except as viewed from the relative and narrow perspective of one's own habits and the habits of one's surrounding society. A shuffling, muttering, foot-dragging Henry V could hardly inspire the English army through the gates of Harfleur; and a sloppy, bedraggled Hamlet could hardly enlist Horatio's aid, Ophelia's love, or Laertes' respect. Elegance, in King Henry and in Hamlet, is simply a prerequisite for effective action within the royal arena. Conversely, regal-like elegance would be ineffective around Stanley Kowalski's poker table, where another style of movement and bearing is required, and where even Mitch's clumsy efforts at eloquence are futile.

LEARNING TO PLAY STYLES

Learning to play a particular style demands, at the outset, a thorough understanding of the world of the play, including its period and locale, the political and social environment portrayed, and the special preconditions which the author has imposed upon his characters. This ordinarily involves a good deal of research, some of which might be suggested by the director; research involving the study of those pertinent and related works of art, music, philosophy, science, religion, and literature that help reveal the texture of life in the author's world. And, of course, the actor must understand the mental mechanisms

"What is it that makes the so-called 'star'? Energy, an
athletic voice, a well-graced manner, certainty of
execution, some unusually fascinating originality of
temperament? Vitality, certainly, and the ability to
convey an impression of beauty or ugliness as the part
demands, as well as authority and a sense of style."

—*John Gielgud*

for translating his knowledge of a play's style into the "plants" that will
make it play. But to understand all this, unfortunately, is only a first
step in playing style. Even if we fully "understand" from Mme. Callas
that the voice is a weapon in behalf of the character, we cannot simply
go from there to be able to sing like Maria Callas. Nor does our understanding of Jack Tanner's rhetoric, Hamlet's versifying, or King Henry's
regal bearing lead us directly to the capacity to perform in these styles.
Understanding provides us with the base, the mental alignment, and
the liberation from egocentrism which makes learning possible; but
of course, these are only foundations.

Essentially, the actor learns style in a way similar to the process
by which the character learned it, or the person represented by the
character learned it. Style, after all, is *learned* behavior; it is not innate
or genetic. Environment, not genes, determines whether a child will
speak Cockney or Scots or Brooklynese. Tanner, insofar as we consider
him a real person (or even as an author's idea of a real person), was not
born rhetorical, he learned to be rhetorical, and King Henry learned to
be regal, and the Restoration rake learned how to attract ladies. The
learning processes involved at least three things: instruction, imitation, and real-life trial and error. And while they must be telescoped
down in time for the actor, the same learning processes will apply.

The learning of style by instruction is, of course, the most obvious
way, if also the hardest to find. Jack Tanner went to school; the actor
playing Tanner, most desirably, would simply go to an accelerated

program in the same school. Of course schools like Tanner's don't exist any more, so the actor is forced to find what kind of comparable instruction he can. Most classical acting styles are taught at the major acting conservatories, where student actors work under the tutelage, and sometimes the apprenticeship, of professional classical actors. There is certainly no effective substitute, in the development of a classical actor, for personal instruction by an experienced master. Written analyses of particular styles, such as those above with regard to *Man and Superman* and *Hamlet*, are also instructive in isolating the purposes and uses of a certain style, which when coupled with the actor's imagination and self-application, can produce marvelous results. A combination of academic study and conservatory training, as would be offered by the Royal Academy of Dramatic Art, the Comédie Française, or the Julliard Conservatory in New York, is a proven producer of fine performers, flexible and capable in a variety of physical and vocal styles.

Imitation must not be ignored in the development of style, because imitation is the process by which we learn much of our day-to-day behavior; naturally, it is also the way in which characters in plays may be assumed to have learned their behavior. Tanner not only went to school, in other words, he spent a great deal of his childhood observing people like Ramsden, and fashioning his behavior after them. We all, in life, find and imitate role models. The child, after all, learns to speak by imitating others; he learns and retains his dialect by imitating others, and the actor who wants to play that dialect will invariably learn it at least in part by the same process. Likewise the young debu-

"I sometimes think that if professional actors reflected a little more on how we all learn acceptable social manners, it would be a valuable guide to many of the techniques of their craft."

—Tyrone Guthrie

tante learns deportment from fashion models, the Prince learns regality from the King, and the athlete follows the behavior pattern of his childhood hero. Imitation is the means by which we pick up the countless attitudes and behaviors that are not important enough to talk about formally, but which comprise the bulk of our daily actions; imitation is, therefore, one of the ways in which an actor develops stylized performances.

Imitation, though, of what? Obviously the actor cannot directly imitate the performance of another actor without a mammoth sacrifice in his own creativity, spontaneity, and even credibility; the actor who tries to play Hamlet by copying Olivier's inflections from a record album will certainly fail in all respects.

Where possible, of course, the actor learns style from living exemplifiers. Stanislavski, when he directed a play set in a brothel, took his cast to live several weeks in a brothel. Film actors, shooting on location more than in the past, also use this technique.

Imitating recordings of living exemplifiers is a once-removed technique, particularly useful for learning a dialect. Bearing and deportment, physical styles, can be learned similarly by imitating paintings and photographs: candid ones, which show the subjects as if unobserved, and portraits, which are perhaps even more useful because they show how the person wanted to be seen; the intention of appearance, as well as its manifestation.

The imitating of other actors, whether through recordings, pictures, film, or live contact, is a second-removed technique, and, as mentioned, it is stultifying if attempted directly. But there can be a very effective indirect use of this second-removed technique, particularly for classical and theatrical styles, and where no living exemplifiers can be found. In exercise eight, below, you are urged to "Play opposite Olivier," by taping his speeches in a given two-person scene, and blanking out the speeches of the other character. Then, memorizing those blanked out speeches yourself, you play *opposite* Olivier—not with his lines but *to* them. Olivier's performance is your starting point: you must impress this man, you must appeal to him, dominate him, debate with him. You must, in short, become a member of his world just as Jack Tanner became a member of Ramsden's world. Imitation, therefore, is indirect and reciprocal in this exercise; it is the same kind of imitation which we do ordinarily in life, both in growing up and in adapting to new situations and new people. The actor grows into character, of course, in a much shorter time; his goal must be to synchronize himself with the style of Olivier (or whatever style is attempted), to master it for his tactical purposes, to relish it, and then to be able to break out of that synchronization when he is ready to grasp the particular victory that his own character needs and desires.

Trial-and-error, of course, is the cybernetics of behavioral development; the way in which our behavior is shaped from day to day until it reaches the patterns of the present. Trial-and-error informs and redirects both instruction and imitation. The actor uses trial-and-error as a technique for getting into a stylized world in concert with the other actor-characters; he must, in addition to using his style as a weapon, continually evaluate and improve the weapon's effectiveness. Style is not rigid and not fixed; it is a fluid, ever-adjusting attempt to find the best vehicle, the best tactic, toward victory. In the examples given above, most of the character's attempts at style are somewhat unsuccessful; most are at least partial failures: Tanner does not really close out Ramsden's arguments, Stanley Kowalski does not really dazzle Blanche, Hamlet's inky black suit does not really shame the court, Monsieur Jordain's turban does not really awe his family, the Restoration rake does not always excite his damsel, and Butterfly does not keep Pinkerton from leaving. Style is weapon, but it is not all-powerful; it is *attempted* rather than displayed, and it can never be proffered glibly.

Trial-and-error, therefore, is important in the actor's development of style because it is important to the character as well. If actors find that style is a struggle, they may be comforted to realize that it is a struggle for their characters as well. It is not that Claudius would, like us, rather be speaking prose. Claudius, as a regal pretender, would have been speaking blank verse for years and years. The point is that *Claudius is struggling for his regality;* it does not come all that easy to him. That his political situation demands him to speak regally, and this theatrical situation demands him to speak in verse, does not mean that he is so terribly facile. He must concentrate and he must *work* to get his proper style—his "effectiveness of assertion," in Shaw's phrase. It is all too easy for us to ignore the struggle for expression experienced by characters who speak and act differently than we do; often we simply assume that they are "Shakespearean people," for example, and that this sort of language rolls effortlessly off their lips. Perhaps it comes easier to them than it does to us, but it is not effortless. Characters strain against the limitations of style, they struggle to perfect it and to make the best use of it. The struggle toward victory takes place not only at the plot and situation level, but at the level of style. Style is part of relacom, and the actor who struggles to achieve victory in his situation also struggles to achieve victory in his style.

EXERCISES: PLAYING STYLE

These exercises do not teach styles; as should be clear from the foregoing discussion, styles are acquired only by an effective combination of personal instruction, apprenticeship, imitation, and trial-and-error. The exercises do tend to liberate stylizing mechanisms, however, and to demand an understanding of the tactical *use* of style.

1. Group domination   In an improvisation, or in an imaginary self-exercise, try to dominate a group by being its very best member—in the eyes of the group. Avoiding parody, try to become:

a. The belle of the ball
b. The king of the mountain
c. The star of the show
d. The chief of the ratpack
e. The chairman of the investigation
f. The bishop of the archdiocese
g. The Speaker of the House
h. The sweetheart of Sigma Chi
i. The team spokeswoman
j. Miss America
k. Mr. America
l. Big Man On Campus, 1920s style
m. Ditto, 1950s style
n. Ditto, late 1960s style
o. Ditto, present style
p. The best poker player in Stanley Kowalski's gang (*Streetcar*)
q. Your father's best friend
r. Your mother's best friend

2. Analyzing group styles   Take any of the groups mentioned above and analyze them by answering the following questions:

a. What draws the attention of these people? What holds it? What makes them look up?
b. What makes these people respect me?
c. What kind of words do these people respond to? What kind of syntax? What is their span of verbal attention? Do they fear eloquence? Do they admire it? Do they respond to it? Does it annoy them?

d. How do they respond to casualness? in dress? in
   speech?
e. How do they respond to the expression of feelings?
   Of passion?
f. What puts these people down? How does it make
   them feel?
g. What shuts these people up? What happens to them
   when they shut up?
h. Who are their allies?
i. How frightened are they of physical force?
j. How repressed are they? How open to seduction? What
   are their professed morals? What are their real morals?
   What do they desire from me?
k. What turns them on?
l. What turns them off?
m. What frightens them most? How do they react when
   frightened?
n. Do they have a sense of humor?
o. Do they like to have fun? To be seen having fun?
p. What do they like in people?
q. What makes them trust people?
r. Do they treat their friends well?
s. Who are these people?

3. *Analyzing historical styles*   Ask the same questions, above,
about the following historical groups. Research the answers, and
where research fails, speculate:

   a. Hamlet's Wittenburg schoolfellows
   b. Courtiers to Charles II (English Restoration)
   c. Courtiers to James I (Jacobean England)
   d. Courtiers to Oedipus (archaic Greece)
   e. Courtiers to King Lear (archaic England)
   f. Judges of the Spanish Inquisition
   g. Moscow aristocrats before the 1917 Revolution
   h. Courtiers to Caligula (Imperial Rome, Decadent era)
   i. German weavers during the Industrial Revolution
   j. French followers of Robespierre, during the Revolution
   k. Puritans in Salem, Massachusetts, during the witch
      trials
   l. Slaves in Alabama, 1860

Now, in an improvisation, integrate with the group as you have analyzed and defined it.

4. Creating imaginary styles   Ask the same questions about a wholly imaginary group, and by your imaginative answers, define a wholly imaginary style evolving from the group. For example:

  a. The fairies in *A Midsummer Night's Dream*
  b. The ondines in *Ondine*
  c. The trolls in *Peer Gynt*
  d. The frogs in *The Frogs*
  e. The Furies in *The Eumenides*
  f. The gods of *The Goodwoman of Setzuan*
  g. The Seven Dwarfs in *Snow White*
  h. The Characters in *Six Characters in Search of an Author*
  i. The Madwoman in *The Madwoman of Chaillot*
  j. Martians
  k. Witches
  l. Talking trees

In an improvisation, integrate with the group as you have analyzed and defined it.

5. Opera   Go back to the contentless scene or the *Woyzeck* scene from Chapter Three, or any simple two-person scene that you and a partner have memorized. Improvise, without parodying, an operatic version of the scene. Improvise it as a Mozartian, Puccinian, and Wagnerian opera by turns. Listen to recordings of various operas with your partner, and try to make your opera improvisation fit into the operative structure that you hear. Do your opera improvisation with the recording playing in the background. *Use* your singing to win situational victories.

6. Blank verse   Memorize any of the *Hamlet* speeches in this chapter. Perform them according to the tactics described in the accompanying commentaries. Make the style of the speech useful to the character and the fulfillment of the character's intentions. Master the style, revel in it, take delight in its usefulness. Concentrate not on yourself, but on the character you are speaking to—and what is happening to him. Do not judge yourself, and do not judge whether or not you are doing the exercise well. Just do it.

7. Shaw   Memorize any of the speeches of Ramsden or Tanner in this chapter, or, with a partner, memorize the scene. Perform the speech or the scene in accordance with the accompanying commentary. Try to destroy the position of the other character, try to make him squirm, try to hit him where it hurts the most, in his self-opinion. Humiliate your real or imaginary partner.

8. Play opposite Olivier   Find a recording of Laurence Olivier (or any other great actor) performing a two-character confrontation scene from a play by Shakespeare, Shaw, Wilde, or Congreve. Learn, *from the text,* the other part. Then record Olivier's lines on a tape recorder, leaving blank spaces for the other character's lines (which are to be yours). Now, playing the tape, act opposite Olivier! Without consciously trying to imitate him, try to better him in the confrontation. If it is a Shakespearean play, try to "out-Shakespeare" him. Try to top him according to the "rules" of debate that he seems to be playing. Repeat the exercise many times, and over a period of many days and weeks. Concentrate on winning in the situation, and let the style grow in you cybernetically; don't push it, it will come, evolving out of the feedback you receive. Expand your repertoire: play opposite Glenda Jackson, Nicol Williamson, Hume Cronyn, Uta Hagen.

9. Learn a dialect   The process of learning a dialect is identical to the process of learning a style: dialect *is* a style, and is invariably part of every style. Learning a dialect is not only a useful exercise in style, it is a useful tool for an actor in the employment market; once you learn a dialect, you will have it for the rest of your career. Learning a dialect is best accomplished by *both* phonetic study and imitation of live or recorded examples; many phonetic books include records of spoken examples, and record and book are meant to be used together. But you can learn and use dialects that are not written about in phonetic books just by going into the appropriate area, or purchasing dialect recordings. Certain bars and taverns in major cities, if you can find them, are favored by certain ethnic groups possessing interesting and assimilable dialects. When you learn the dialect, try to "pass" with it. If you know of a recording of a play in the dialect, re-record it on tape as in the previous exercise with one part—the one you will take—blanked out. Then integrate yourself with the Abbey Players, or whatever the recording group is.

10. Face down a portrait   Get a book of the paintings of various periods, preferably with a large number of portraits. Find a full-page portrait with the eyes looking straight out, and put the portrait at about eye level with yourself. Stare down the portrait. Try to dominate the person you see there. Try to seduce the person that you see. Try to figure out what frightens him, what excites him, what appeals to him. Get to know him, and in so doing, adjust yourself to get to know him better. Develop an intense relationship; repeat the exercise a day later. If you can, go to a portrait gallery (there are splendid ones in Washington, D.C., and in London) and stare down the portraits of famous people. You will find yourself adopting the style of the person you try to dominate. Find full length portraits when possible. In staring down the person in the portrait, imagine yourself wearing comparable clothing.

11. Wear a costume   Get a costume from an obliging wardrobe department, or make your own. Do a mirror exercise with yourself in front of a full-length mirror. Speak to your image in the mirror. Let yourself "grow into" your own costume. If the costume has pockets, put your own possessions in the pockets. Write a letter to someone while wearing the costume. Watch TV; make yourself breakfast. Return to the mirror and do another mirror exercise with yourself. Spend a day by yourself in the costume.

BUILDING A STYLE: THE DIRECTORIAL FUNCTION

We have concentrated in this discussion on the mechanisms for finding, analyzing, and "entering" styles, rather than on the strict definition of the conventional stylized manifestations of, for example, the Greek and Elizabethan era. We have tried, in other words, to look at style from the inside, and from the perspective of the actor.

However, style cannot, and should not, simply be built into a production by the actor. Style is a collective characterization, and it demands a composite view. It requires a *general* understanding among all actor-characters as to what the preconditions for survival and success might be within the social fabric of the play's situation. This general understanding comes from the era, from the playwright, from the particular play, and from the director's concept. It is the latter of these, and through the person of the director, that the others are synthesized and brought together. For good or for ill, the style of a play is essentially shaped by the director, unless someone takes that function out of his hands (invariably an unpleasant circumstance). So it might be useful at this point to outline some of the director's responsibilities in determining styles, and indicate the collaborative actor-director function in stylistic creation.

One cannot get dogmatic about styles, even about those that seem most conventional and "established." To say that a play will be formed in "the conventional classic Greek style," for example, is to say almost nothing at all. Does that mean the heroic style of Aeschylus or the cynical-realistic style of Euripides? Does it mean the Apollonian or Dionysian elements of Greek culture? Does it mean chanting or choral speaking; masks, half-masks, or no masks; colored or white himations; scenery or no scenery; a raised stage or no raised stage; indoors or outdoors; mass spectacle or intimate; fifth century B.C. or tenth century B.C.; "Rex" or "Tyrannus"; chorus in unison or chorus broken into semi-choruses and soloists; three actors or eight; men and women, or an all-male cast? All of those possibilities could be—and have been—justified as "conventional classic Greek style." Obviously a guiding hand must make some decisions upon which everyone's performance will be able to rest comfortably.

So it would be futile and misleading to try to list the standardized rudiments of any fixed conventional style; they simply are not that fixed nor that conventional. What we can show, instead, is a possible directorial approach to the building of a coordinated and comprehensive style; a directorial approach that will coalesce with the actor's need and desire to enter a stylized world of the play.

Essentially this directorial approach is to find by research, or to create by imaginative reconstruction and speculation, the common denominators of ideal futures, tactics, and private audiences that would have been shared by people of the play's "world." So far we have talked of ideal futures, tactics, and private audiences as personal to each character, some of them, however, while pursued by each character personally, are also pursued by a given society collectively; style, again, is collective *characterization*. Common ideal futures, common favored tactics, and common private audiences characterize each society, each real or imaginary "world," and each dramatic style.

The directorial approach might take the form, then, of a worksheet of assumptions and preconditions that apply to each of the play's characters (or when a play has two "classes" of characters, courtiers and rustics for example, the preconditions applying to each of the two classes). The worksheet (which may or may not be written down) is developed, discussed, and disseminated at the first rehearsal or rehearsals; it becomes the underlying set of "plants" that shape the production style.

Following is a sample worksheet illustrating a directorial approach to a certain style.

WORKSHEET: SHAVIAN PHILOSOPHICAL DRAMA (*Man and Superman*)

1. *Ideal futures* Each character pursues these specific goals:
Respect
Impenetrability
Comprehensive understanding
Rhetorical domination

2. *Tactics.* Each character uses the following tactics, wearing the appropriate masks:

Lucidity: I can express a point of view with such absolute perfection that I will be able to structure the conversation, making you able only to defend yourself rather than attack me. I understand your position better than you do yourself.

Penetration: I see into you and through you.

Conclusiveness: I am not arguing with you, I am simply explaining what should be obvious if you were intelligent enough to shut up and listen. There is simply nothing more to be said.

Logic: My argument is a perfect construct, a geodesic structure of inextricably connected truths. My syntax is strength itself.

Wit: You amuse me.

Pride: I delight myself.

Contempt: Nobody else can quite do it, can they?

Privacy: You will never know who I really am.

3. *Characterizing Others:* Each character characterizes the other characters as fools.

4. *Private Audience:* Each character plants a private audience consisting of the following persons, and plays for their approval: George Bernard Shaw, Bertrand Russell, Henry Higgins, Friederich Nietzsche, Nietzsche's Superman, and Karl Marx.

5. *God:* Myself.

6. *Dialect:* Standard English (Received pronunciation).

SUMMARY OF STYLE

Style is the collective characterization of the play. It is those behavioral characteristics that are common to the characters in a play, or a group of those characters; sometimes it is historically derived, and sometimes it is wholly an imaginary creation of the playwright or the director. The actor asked to play something in style makes a transformation from his everyday behavior, but there is nothing unreal about behavior that is thus transformed, it is only different. The actor plays style by understanding its purpose in the situation: why the appropriate style is an attempt to be situationally effective, effective in the *plot* of the play. He then plays that style reciprocally; it is drawn from him by the goals his character seeks, and the preconditions (which he plants) that regulate interactions within the group in which he seeks them. Playing style, the actor begins to relish it. He begins to enjoy and appreciate the world which he has entered. His style becomes his weapon and his love; he can play powerfully and without embarrassment or tentativeness toward situational victory with and within the framework of style.

Style is a struggle, not an accomplishment—for the character as well as for the actor. Neither the actor nor the character will ever be the total master of any style; they are always trying to top themselves, they are always reaching for style; they never completely arrive, they never completely rest. Specific styles are learned by research, by instruction, by imitation, and by real-life trial and error; we are always adjusting and perfecting the styles which, like languages and dialects, are part of our behavioral equipment, part of our acting versatility.

Style is built into a play first of all by a director, who sets up the collective "common denominators" of ideal figures, tactics, character-izings of others, private audiences, and dialects which serve as the universal preconditions that determine, to a greater or lesser extent, each character's thinking. Whether the director does this formally or informally, it is the responsibility of the actor to adapt, by reciprocal mechanisms, his actions and behaviors to the demands of a world thus "stylized" in its appearance and in its intrinsic and extrinsic rules.

CHAPTER 5

PLAYING
THE PERFORMANCE

"The whole business of marshaling one's energies
becomes more and more important as one grows older.
Where to use it, where not to waste it, how to cover
the fact that it may be forced, how always to leave an
audience feeling that there's more there. How to lead
an audience to a point where the smallest nudge can
push them over a precipice of feeling instead of
trundling them downhill."

—Hume Cronyn

It is a great temptation to think that when the
actor successfully plays the dialogue, the situation, the character, and the style, he has then done
everything he needs to do. This is erroneous. The
actor must also *perform*. He must play the performance. He must create an effect on the audience.

What, exactly, does this mean? What does it
entail? Among other things, it means that the
actor must be heard in every seat in the house.
And this is a bare minimum, a passive responsibility. He must also make the audience know what
his character is all about. More than that, he must
make the audience *care* what his character is
about. He must make them guess what his character *could be* about. He must create, in addition to the external behavior of the character, the

177

potential of the character. And he must create this with impact. These are active responsibilities.

When we look at it freshly, we realize that acting is not simply a job that must be done competently; it is an art form that must be executed brilliantly, ravishingly. It must not only satisfy an audience's expectations, it must exceed their expectations; it must raise their expectations. It must excite them; must electrify, entertain, and transport them. It must, in good measure, be hilarious enough to make them laugh, engaging enough to make them think, empathic enough to make them weep, and intense enough to make them gasp. Acting that fails to do any of these things fails to retain the theatre which houses it. There is, after all, no requirement that people attend the theatre, no requirement that the theatre even exist. Theatre exists only because it is overwhelming, because its acting is astonishing. Where a theatre and its acting are merely "good," merely "correct," merely "in the proper style," theatre dies a slow death.

The actor, then, is faced with an obvious problem. He must perform his role at the same time that he acts it. He must "sell" his character at the same time he "becomes" it. This problem touches the very paradox we have thus far avoided; for how does the actor "perform" without sacrificing credibility? How does he electrify, ravish, and excite his audience without mugging, indicating, hiding, flag-waving, and all the amateurish, contextual gimmickry we have seen as anathema to his situational involvement? How can he be "theatrical" without disgracing himself, his characterization, or his style? How can he perform, in the words of two Broadway commentators, "internally and without shame?" The answers to these questions can be approached only by examining a final level of acting behavior, the performance level, the level of *theatricality*.

"Etonne-moi!" ("Astonish me!")

—*Sergei Diaghilev*

THEATRICALITY: THE FINAL LEVEL OF ACTING BEHAVIOR

Theatricality is not a bad word at all. It is essentially the short form of "the theatrical process," or "the theatrical arrangement." It is the specific way in which actors and audience are linked in the theatre.

Theatricality is not a mere vehicle. It is not simply an outward gloss that the director or the actor grafts onto situation in order to make it palatable to an observing audience. It is not the sugar coating of the play's medicinal theme. It is intrinsic to the play, and it is played *with* the play, not on top of it. It cannot be dismissed from the actor's mind; the question is: how does it fit into the structure of his consciousness? How does the actor play the performance as well as the part?

Before addressing these questions directly, it might prove illuminating to examine further our analogy of the skier. This analogy has been advanced earlier at two levels:

1. The downhill skier, who pursues his intention (the finish line) in any way he can, with a total commitment to victory (getting there first), is analogous to an actor playing a situation, who pursues intentions in the quest for a victory—an ideal future. This is the first level— the "life level" of acting behavior.

2. The slalom skier, who pursues the same intention and commitment to victory, but does so in a way shaped by the flags of the slalom designer and governed by the rules of the slalom, is analogous to an actor whose situation has been "dramatized" by the considerations of characterization and style. The slalom skier's path, while just as goal-oriented and just as intensely pursued, is made more elaborate and sophisticated by the flags planted by the slalom designer. The actor in a dramatized role pursues a path similarly contoured by the specific obstacles and rules placed there by the playwright, the director, and the actor himself during his homework. This is the second level—the dramatized level—of acting behavior.

We can now take this analogy to its third and final level: the theatrical level. To do so we need add but one element: *a crowd of rooting spectators.*

Imagine the slalom skier in an Olympic race. He sees the finish line far down the hill, the flags scattered down the course, and a line of cheering, yelling, rooting partisans lining the route. As he races by them, their cheers increase. His pulse, raised to its seeming extremity by the race itself, surges even faster. There is an edge of new recklessness that creeps into his racing style, a previously unseen daring that the crowd seems to bring out of him. There is a burst of—for want of a better word—"spirit" that tempts him to challenge the limits of human endurance. Persons unacquainted with "performance," whether in sports or on stage, may doubt the effectiveness of the crowd's cheers upon an athlete, particularly upon a skilled and disciplined athlete, but that effectiveness is quite real, quite measurable. Hard-nosed and skeptical bookmakers, who set their odds on facts, not theories, figure in the "hometown advantage" in all their wagers, knowing that the athlete— or team of athletes—who has intensely loyal rooters will invariably get a solid boost from them. "Boosters," in fact, is the name of some of the "rooting clubs" that follow their chosen athlete-heroes from competition to competition.

The psychological reasons for the "boost" the fans provide include, at the least, three features:

In the first place, they raise the athlete's expectations, and allow him to share in the crowd's highly idealized expectations for him. These become tugging, cybernetic forces urging him on, compelling him to victory. Much of this is purely physiological. The cheers stimulate the secretion of adrenalin: the heartbeat increases, the spleen contracts releasing its red blood cells, the liver releases its sugar, the viscera release blood to the muscles, and the bronchi dilate to deepen respiration. All these add up to greater physical energy, greater muscular power, greater stamina and control.

In the second place, the crowd encourages recklessness. By declaring itself at one with the athlete, the crowd also declares itself a supporter for the athlete should he overextend himself. The cheers and screams encourage fearlessness in the athlete, and induce a greater willingness to take chances in the pursuit of superhuman physical attainments.

Finally, the crowd threatens punishment for a failure of effort. Having, by their cheers, raised the athlete to a position of eminence, the crowd implicitly suggest to the athlete that they now *count* on him—he is carrying their honor, their hopes, and he must not let them down. The effect of this implicit punishment for failure, coupled with the reward for recklessness in the pursuit of victory, is a tremendous spur to the athlete; it can compel him beyond the merely "good" to the truly "great."

What is the athlete's position with regard to all this? Naturally he does not "play to" the supporters, the fans, the boosters who surround him. During the race he never gives them so much as a glance—were he to do so, that rooting would cease, he would be seen not as a hero but as a grandstander. His conscious concentration on victory, and on the best possible route around the flags, seems virtually total. Nonetheless, *a feedback loop between the skier and his fans exists,* though it is not acknowledged. The skier cannot *not* be aware of his rooters. He cannot *not* be affected by their cheers. He cannot *not* know that they bring out his best efforts. Unconsciously, inevitably, *cybernetically,* he will realize that they can help him win his victory. He will learn, perhaps unconsciously and perhaps not, to *cultivate* his audience.

Eventually, what the athlete finally realizes is this: the more he stimulates the crowd by his efforts, the more they will stimulate him to *increase* those efforts; the more they stimulate him, the more he can stimulate them, and on and on in a self-feeding, self-fulfilling, cycle of increasing energy. It is a symmetrical feedback loop; the athlete and his fans will win together or they will lose together; each uses the other to bring out the best performance. And the sole criterion of "best performance" is the athlete's victory.

Crowd and athlete, then, seek the same thing: victory at the finish line. The crowd can only get its victory through the skier; the skier cannot get his through the crowd. The skier is not looking for an award from his fans; he is looking for an award *for* them. If he fails to achieve his victory, they are useless to him; all the "nice tries" and pats on the back are the dimmest, saddest of consolations. He does not stimulate them, then, for any reason but for assisting his victory; for adding fuel

---

"Actors should be handled not as employees (even though they are) but in much the same way a prize fighter is handled, or a bullfighter. They are the creatures (finally) who must appear before the crowd and hold the attention of the crowd. They are the gladiators of the arts."

—*William Redfield*

---

to his feedback fire that will draw out of him that last burst of spirit, that last full measure of dedicated devotion to the goal.

But what if there is no crowd of spectators? What if this is not the Olympics but merely a practice run? What if the observers are in fact rooting for someone else?

Anyone who has ever performed in an athletic contest knows the answer to this: *the athlete imagines his rooters,* and he can be "boosted" by these imaginary rooters almost as much, sometimes, as by real ones. These imaginary rooters can take many forms. They can be the grand *imaginary* crowds of a major sporting event, cheering the athlete because he is ahead, or because he is catching up, or because they like his style. They can be members of the athlete's own, personal, "private audience"—his parents, for example, or the person he hopes to impress. They can be the press box, or the announcer who breathlessly reports his every action to a nationwide television audience. Children at play are quite uninhibited at imagining such witnesses to their athletic competitions, and they frequently "act out" the presence of their rooters simultaneously with performing the actions which are thus "rooted." "Johnny takes the sign, nods his head; now he's going into his windup," says Johnny, to himself, as he takes the sign, nods his head, and winds up. The athlete stimulates himself by imagining himself observed, encouraged, egged on. This, too, can be a powerful weapon for the competitor.

THE ACTOR THEATRICAL

The actor in the theatre—the actor theatrical—is in several ways analogous to his athletic counterpart. Like the athlete, the actor can stimulate a crowd of observers; also like the athlete he can in turn be stimulated by them. No one can expect an actor to be oblivious to this; it is the fundamental dynamic of the theatre, as it is of spectator sports.

The actor can, therefore, "use" the audience in much the same way that the athlete can, but there is one absolutely crucial understanding that must precede this "use." It is this: the audience will only support and stimulate the *character;* they will not directly support the actor. The audience, in other words, does not root for the actor to be a good actor, but for the character to win his victory. The actor, insofar

"Occasionally, an actor can completely dominate any
house, and so, like a master matador, he can work
the audience the way he pleases."

—*Peter Brook*

as he "plays to the audience" in any way, does so on behalf of his character and his character's struggle; *he uses the audience to help his
character win.*

As with the skier, the actor-character seeks a single victory, and
that is in the situation, not in the context. To create a theatrical experience, the actor must make the audience "overhear," observe, and
finally root for his character. The actor's concentration is entirely on
the winning of his character's victory, and in that effort he must try to
draw the audience—real and imaginary—into a fierce partisanship with
his character.

What is being suggested, therefore, is the precise opposite of our
"objective" dramaturgy which holds that the theatrical event is a dramatized situation, a situation "brought into a theatrical context." On the
contrary, *from the actor's viewpoint, a subjective perspective, it is the
theatrical context which is brought into the situation.* It is the audience which is brought into the world of the play, not the play which is
brought into the world of the audience.

In the actor's viewpoint, the audience must be made to *work,* to
work for the benefit of the character. The audience must become the
character's boosters. As with style, the theatrical context, in the actor's
order of thinking, becomes a *weapon* of his character.

How does the actor do this *specifically?* By making a mental
"plant" of an audience potentially favorable to him and his efforts,
and by making that audience important to his victory. The actor says,
"I, character X, am attempting to threaten (seduce, defeat, convince)
character Z. There is an audience observing this attempt: I want them

on my side. I want them to root for me. I want Z to *know* that they're rooting for me. I want them to inspire me. I want to be their hero."

Let us fill this out with the example of Hamlet in his first court scene: "Seems, Mother, I know not seems." Let us say that with this speech Hamlet wishes to shame Claudius. Certainly his manner of speaking, posturing, gesturing, and staring will all serve tactical purposes in this effort. But so will his "playing" to the audience of the surrounding Court. Insofar as he can sense their support, he will become emboldened; his tactics will become firmer, braver, more dynamic. Insofar as he can detect that he is winning them "from" Claudius, his sense of incipient victory will egg him on even further and finer. His cutting edge will sharpen; his wit will penetrate deeper; he will glisten with ironic brilliance.

It is clear that the court setting, with its onstage audience of potential supporters, brings the best out of Hamlet; moreover, it brings the best *Hamlet* out of Hamlet. Now let us simply expand that court to include the offstage (in-house) audience as well. Let the actor playing Hamlet seek *their* support as well—their support of Hamlet and Hamlet's quest, their agreement that Claudius is shamed. This "plant" only redoubles Hamlet's force and energy; it makes him not merely reach Claudius and the audience at the same time, it makes him reach Claudius *through* the audience. It "tells" Claudius: "Look, the people are against you, the people find you shameful." Theatricality has a situational, not merely a contextual function.

What about Claudius? He, of course, is trying the same thing. His tactics in the scene are a demonstration of political force and pragmatic rationality. He, too, is trying to convince the Court that he is the appropriate man for the throne, the most deserving of their support. He should try to convince the larger audience as well. Both characters, in their battle with each other, are playing all out for victory, and are bringing in both the onstage and offstage audiences as weapons in that struggle. And this is the mechanism that is at the very heart of a vigorous, credible, and aesthetically consistent theatricality.

This mechanism does not depend on the presence of an actual onstage audience, such as the Court. The "plant" of an audience of rooters can be made even in a one-character play. It is a mechanism, and it becomes the basic precondition for theatricality, for performance. The actor does not, certainly in the case of realistic plays, play directly to the audience at all. But he knows that they are watching, and he takes advantage of that fact on behalf of his character, and on behalf of his character's quest for victory. Insofar as the audience seems to be rooting for his character, he exploits this and attempts to increase it. Insofar as they are neutral, he tries to stimulate them to action. He identifies them with members of his character's own private audience, and tries to stimulate and please them. Insofar as they are hostile, he tries to change them into being supportive and loyal. He need do none of this consciously; the feedback loop exists, and it cannot *not* operate. He must only allow the loop to operate in its only effective way: on behalf of his character's intentions.

This turns out to be easier than it might at first appear, since the transformation is a simple extension of a well-known psychological phenomenon—human egocentrism, the feeling that we are all the heros of our own plays.

THE CHARACTER AS HERO

The slalom skier considers himself the hero of the fans, and if the fans do not in fact appear on the slopes, he imagines them there. He is, in any event, a hero to his private audience; and he is quite able and willing to imagine his private audience as part of his public one.

The actor, in the same way, imagines his character not only as the hero of the play, but as "heroic" and worthy of the audience's support, encouragement, and cheers. Osric, for example, feels that *"Hamlet* is a play about Osric"; but more than that he also feels that

---

"Directing George (C. Scott) is a wonderful experience. He follows direction so easily, knowing that wherever he sits it will be the head of the table."

—Jose Quintero

---

any fair-minded audience will identify with Osric. He is, in his own mind, not only the hero of the play but the hero of the play's audience. This is a subjective opinion, of course, utterly unconfirmed by objective analysis, but it remains a dominant theme in Osric's mind. All characters, like all people, assume the inevitability of final validation.

This is an aspect of the universal egocentrism of man. Fundamentally, all persons innately think of themselves as "right"; "right," in our minds, is essentially defined as "what *we* do." While we may be consciously aware of our faults, our flaws, our regrettable habits, foibles, and affectations, we nonetheless feel that if there were an all-seeing, all-knowing, all-just observer of our thoughts and actions, we would find ultimate vindication. Insofar as we find ourselves ridiculed, unappreciated, or despised, we feel ourselves to a like degree misperceived. This egocentrism is a holdover from earliest infancy. Piaget, the child psychologist, has shown that the infant "feels that others share his pain or his pleasure, that his mumblings will inevitably be understood, that his perspective is shared by all persons, that even animals and plants partake of his consciousness." The infant, in other words, feels he is at the center of the world, with all eyes upon him, and all values are his own. Maturity gives rude shocks to these infantile delusions, but it does not eradicate them. Rational development diminishes, but does not destroy, our egocentricity; it remains a precondition for all our thinking.

Characters in plays share that egocentric precondition. No matter how vile, despicable, or malicious they might be in our eyes, they *themselves* feel confident that we will, given the whole story, take their side. Iago, in Shakespeare's *Othello*, is a fine example of this; Iago, who is clearly the most loathsome character in Shakespeare, addresses himself to the audience in a number of soliloquies. It is clear in those soliloquies not only that Iago delights in himself, but that he fully expects us to delight in his delight. In his many confidences shared with us, his audience, he charms us with wit, with frankness, and with his unabashed contempt for the witlessness of the other characters. He appeals to our sense of justice, to our appreciation of his intellectual superiority, and to our prejudices. He acts as though we like him and admire his style. With every speech he gives us a message that says, "I know you can't admit it out loud, or to the person you're sitting next to, but you know I'm right, don't you? You share my sense of irony, you admire my cleverness and resourcefulness—in fact you *like* me,

"To survive, an actor needs extraordinary quotients of the active and the passive in his make-up. Passive in that you have to wait for the phone to ring; passive in that you have to please a great many people— agent, producer, director, playwright, even the secretary who may get you to that producer or director. You have to take so much nonsense from so many people for so many years. And in spite of the bad breaks, the disappointments, you must hold on to your innocence, you must remain open and receptive no matter how much you get hurt. And then comes that moment, if you're lucky, when you step out in front of an audience—and suddenly you can't be passive any more. You have to be aggressive. You have to deliver, take the stage, be the boss."

—*Alec McCowen*

don't you?" And, if the performance is sufficiently powerful, we *do* like him; grudgingly perhaps, but genuinely.*

Egocentricity is the subjective state of us all; no matter how feeble, how reviled, or how downtrodden, we all share the essential feeling of innate nobility. Even suicide, to its practitioner, is seen as a heroic act, expressing not the suicide's unworthiness in the face of society,

*A rather extraordinary example of this phenomenon was occasioned by Albert Finney's portrayal of Tamburlaine the Great in the Peter Hall production that opened the National Theatre (Great Britain) in 1976. There has probably been no greater monster in history or literature than this Scythian murderer, rapist, betrayer, and genocidal maniac, and Hall's production was spare, cold, and brutal. Yet Finney's sheer power in confronting the audience, his seeming confidence that they would approve of him, led to an enormous subjective sympathy for his character, utterly in conflict with "objective" opinion. The confrontation of these two feelings in the audience, favorable versus unfavorable, created much of the production's theatrical charge.

but society's unworthiness in the face of him. If we read the letters and the diaries of the world's great villains, castoffs, and unappreciated souls (Hitler, Arthur Bremer, John Wilkes Booth, Vincent Van Gogh), we will find a feeling of ingrained, heroic self-approval that is quite equal to that of the announced heros of our time, such as Kennedy, Namath, Salk, and King.

Egocentricity is the phenomenon that keys the character's relationship with the audience. It allows the character's relationship with the audience. It allows the character to make the basic assumption that the audience is *potentially* on his side, eager to overhear, and ready to approve the logic of his position and the superiority of his manner. No matter what his part, the actor may presume that the audience is prepared to "root" for his character. He can encourage it, stimulate it, and he can imagine it. The audience is, to begin with, fair. It is objective. It is everything the character could want in a final "judge." The character need not be defensive with the audience. He can "lean into them"; insofar as they may be predisposed, they will be predisposed for him, not against him. They will want him to win. They will identify with his victory; his victory will be theirs. He will be their hero. For this reason his attitude toward them is one of confidence and positive expectation. He has their initial support, he needs only to preserve and develop it. They already want him to win. He wants to win for them. They want to share his victory. He wants to share their cheers. He will be their hero, vindicated from all his faults and celebrated for all his skills, for all his nobility.

"I know the excitement an audience experiences in coming to hear a performer do something extraordinary. That audience out there can tell it's going to happen by the first inning. There's a kind of electricity crackling in the theatre."

—*Beverly Sills*

This is the basic mental precondition for an immensely powerful and theatrical performance. And, since the precondition is based absolutely on the solid foundation of the character's situational victory, it elicits a theatricality that is entirely real to the play, honest to the character, and credible to the audience. It is a theatricality totally aligned with situation, style, and character; it is utterly different from mugging, showing-off, and amateurish contextual self-indulgence.

EXERCISES: PUTTING BACK THE AUDIENCE

Earlier, we discussed exercises that would "remove the audience." That removal is necessary when the actor feels an obligation, or a desire, to demonstrate himself to the audience. But the audience cannot be removed forever; the audience, after all, exists. The following exercises seek to "put back" the audience, in a way that is properly aligned with the actor's concentration on his character's situational intentions.

In these exercises, the actor must not consciously play to the audience. Rather he should try to have them work for him and for his intended situational victory. He should use their support, in other words, as a weapon to get what he wants. He need not pretend to be oblivious to them, but he should not court them directly in any way.

Avoid, in these exercises, any tendency to reduce them to parodies.

1. Sex rooting Choose a scene of fierce conflict between a man and a woman, and have two people perform the scene before an audience of men and women. Then bring the audience into the scene by having its male members become partisan "rooters" for the male performer's position; its females partisans for the female's. Repeat the scene, and let the rooters join in by vocally expressing support, cheering their spokesperson on, and trying to aid their spokesperson to achieve a victory in the scene.

Repeat the exercise, this time allowing it to go into improvised additional dialogue.

Repeat the exercise a final time, and this time let the "rooting" be internal.

2. Team rooting   Choose a two-person scene of ideological conflict, in which both sides have a viable position. Have the acting group declare sympathies with one side or the other, and divide into two teams on the basis of their declaration. Then have the groups separate to discuss why the ideology they support is the "right" one, and to elect one of their members to be their spokesperson. The opposing spokespersons then read the scene aloud, as a debate, with the other team members rooting behind them and joining in.

Repeat the exercise, exchanging spokespersons.

If there is time to memorize the scene, do so—or begin the exercise with an already memorized scene, or repeat the scene on a later date after it has been memorized.

3. Bilingual improvisation   If the acting group is fortunate enough to include two or more people who are fluent in the same two languages, have them improvise a quarrel with one speaking in, say, Spanish, and the other in English. The audience, surrounding the performers, is "instructed" to understand only one of the languages. Midway through the exercise, they are instructed to understand only the other one.

4. Leaning on the audience   Choose a scene of emotional, personal conflict between two people, and perform it once before an audience. Then have the audience "support" one character by physically standing and kneeling beside him or her. Have some of these supporters go down on all fours, and provide a human chair, or chaise longue, for the supported actor. Have others act as armrests and headrests, making the supported character feel regal. Have still others act as bodyguards, standing fiercely behind the supported character, staring suspiciously at anyone who would do him or her harm. Then repeat the scene.

Repeat the scene again, with the audience giving their physical support to the other character.

5. Political speech   Memorize a political speech, such as Marat's address to the Assembly for *Marat/Sade,* or John Kennedy's Inaugural Address, or Henry V's speech before Agincourt. Deliver the speech *to* an audience of cheering supporters.

Repeat the exercise, this time delivering the speech to an

imaginary audience, but with real cheering supporters *behind* you—you being their spokesperson.

Repeat the exercise once more, with both audience and cheering supporters being imaginary.

6. *Lead a delegation*   Improvise a situation in which a student delegation comes to the president of the University to demand a specific change in academic procedures. Perform the improvisation, casting one person as the president, one as the head of the delegation, and the rest of the group as the members of the delegation.

THE AUDIENCE AS CHORUS

The great Greek tragedians endowed the theatre with a device of great theatrical utility—the chorus, which serves a dual function as both party and witness to the play's major lines of action. While the chorus may ally, during the course of the play, with one character—or group of characters—it does not deny its ear to any claimant of rightness, and it serves as a sounding board and judge for all the play's characters and all the play's claims. Therefore, all the characters in Greek tragedies look to the chorus as a source of potential support for the struggles in which they find themselves engaged.

We can see this very clearly in the great arguments between Oedipus and Tiresias, Oedipus and Creon, Creon and Tiresias, Creon and Haemon, in the familiar Theban plays of Sophocles. These arguments take on added urgency and piquancy when we realized that they are not private debates but public ones, and that they are waged, ultimately, for the final opinion of the chorus. Haemon, particularly, exploits this in his debate with his father, Creon, in the *Antigone:*

HAEMON: I wouldn't urge respect for wickedness.
CREON: You don't think she is sick with that disease?
HAEMON: Your fellow-citizens maintain she's not.
CREON: Is the town to tell me how I ought to rule?
HAEMON: Now there you speak just like a boy yourself.

Haemon has succeeded in goading Creon into making a very arrogant remark in front of the wrong audience, for when Creon denounces the right of the "town" to tell him how to rule, he has momentarily forgotten that he is speaking in the midst of a chorus representing that same "town." This is a low point for Creon, and eventually the town will turn against him.

In a larger sense, however, the chorus is simply a representative of the Greek audience itself. In its function as a character, the chorus of *Antigone* is composed of Theban elders in the archaic time of Oedipus; in its function as an audience, however, the same chorus represents contemporary Athenians in the time of Sophocles. The judgments the chorus makes in the play, by and large, are the same judgments the audience will make in watching the play. The chorus, then, is both part of the play and part of the audience. And while the evidence is sometimes contradictory, it seems likely that this relationship was echoed by the physical arrangement of the Greek theatre, with the chorus in a circular "orchestra," located between the audience in the theatron, and the actors on a somewhat elevated stage behind them.* If this physical relationship is the true one, therefore, *from the actor's viewpoint the chorus comprised, essentially, the first row of the audience.* In that case, the actor's relationship with the audience, whether by direct address or by indirect behavior, was simply an extension of his character's interactions with the chorus.

The Greek device of the chorus is immensely useful to the actors in Greek plays. It establishes a theatricality that is perfectly aligned to the play's situation: the character's interaction with the chorus and the actor's interaction with the audience are identical, they are shared. Whatever is addressed to the chorus is simultaneously addressed to the audience; the arguments that move and impress the chorus will move and impress the audience, and the more persuasive the character, the more theatrical the actor. With this sort of alignment, performances of great power and eloquence can come through with an unfiltered impact. It is unfortunate, perhaps, that we have lost this device through the break-up of the classical conventions; modern choruses, like Anouilh's in his modern *Antigone,* are interesting for what they tell us, but they don't listen very well.

---

*"Contradictory" is something of an understatement, for this is one of the most hotly contested debates among historians of theatrical architecture. Nonetheless, it is certain that there was a raised stage in the Hellenistic period of Greek tragedy, and evidence seems to be building up for a temporary trestle-type raised stage even in classical fifth-century times. See Peter Arnott, *Scenic Conventions in Greek Tragedy* (1962).

"There is always a chorus. There is always a play-
within-the-play. . . . A dramatic hero is always
surrounded by a social group, actual or implied, who
press upon him with extraordinary attention,
extraordinary threat, just as the audience in the theatre
does. Even in one-character plays . . . the character
must direct his remarks to a real or imagined audience
whom he makes take on a choral role."

—*Michael Goldman*

The concept of the Greek chorus can be useful to the actor in the
non-Greek play as well, however. *It can become a metaphor for his
own performance context.* Suppose the actor, on his own, were to in-
vent an imaginary chorus? This is identical to the skier, on a practice
run, inventing imaginary rooters. We have explored the theoretical
principle that the actor, in becoming "theatrical," in leaping to the
final level of acting behavior, is in his own mind the hero of the play.
If he is a hero, he needs a heroic chorus. The creation, in the actor's
imagination, of a silent chorus in the first rows of the audience is a
potent mental device for liberating a theatricality that is totally aligned
with situation—just as it is for Creon and Oedipus. The presence of an
imaginary chorus "brings the audience on stage" in exactly the right
place: as the character's confidante, supporter, and appeal judge.

EXERCISES: AUDIENCE AS CHORUS

1. Memorize and perform any of the classic debates of Greek
tragedy, in the midst of a "chorus" that surrounds the action.
For example:

> a. Prometheus and Oceanus in Aeschylus' *Prometheus
> Bound*

   b. Haemon and Creon in Sophocles' *Antigone*
   c. Oedipus and Tiresias in Sophocles' *Oedipus Tyrannus*
   d. Electra and Clytemnestra in Sophocles' *Electra*
   e. Electra and Clytemnestra in Euripides' *Electra*
   f. Theseus and Hippolytus in Euripides' *Hippolytus*

Let the chorus be characterized (for example, as Theban elders, or Palace women) but not rehearsed or directed; let them make up their minds as they wish at the time.

2. Repeat the exercise above, but have four people from the "chorus" become an "audience," and have them take seats a few steps behind the remaining chorus members. Perform the scene.

Now reverse this, and have the "chorus" stand behind, and the "audience" around the performer. If the exercise is done in a theatre, have the "chorus" in the back row of the house, the actors and "audience" on stage.

The point of this exercise is to show that, for the actor-characters, *it makes no difference whether the faces around them are labeled "chorus" or "audience."* The same should apply despite changes in magnitude occasioned by real performance, in which there might be a chorus of fifteen and an audience of one thousand; from the actor's perspective the two groups, structurally, are indistinguishable.

3. Repeat the first exercise with a wholly imaginary chorus and no audience.

4. Repeat the first exercise with a wholly imaginary chorus and a real audience.

5. Memorize and perform one of the following scenes in the same manner as the previous two exercises: with each character imagining his character's own "tragic chorus" surrounding him, and both with and without a real audience observing the scene:

   a. Tom and Amanda in *The Glass Menagerie*
   b. Willy and Charlie in *Death of a Salesman*
   c. Blanche and Stanley in *A Streetcar Named Desire*
   d. George and Martha, opening scene, in *Who's Afraid of Virginia Woolf?*
   e. Ramsden and Tanner in *Man and Superman*
   f. Woyzeck and The Jew in *Woyzeck*

    g. Any scene of strong conflicting values and interests

    h. Any of the contentless scenes in Chapter Two.

6. Repeat the previous exercise, imagining the chorus in the back of the house.

THE SHAKESPEAREAN SOLILOQUY

Shakespeare never used a listening chorus (in some plays, notably *Henry V*, he employed a speaking chorus), but he did use a convention common to his time which served a similar function. This was the direct address, or the soliloquy. There are, of course, many interpretations of the soliloquy's intended function, and many analyses as to how the soliloquy was originally delivered. Some soliloquies appear to be overheard ruminations—"thinkings out loud," as it were. Others seen to be quite specifically directed to the audience, such as Puck's curtain line in *A Midsummer Night's Dream*, and the comical addresses of Grumio, Tranio, and Petruchio in *The Taming of the Shrew*. Others are more internal, as self-rehearsals and self-encouragements. Petruchio, in *Shrew*, concluding his soliloquy on how he shall win Katharine, says to himself at his soliloquy's end (and at Katharine's simultaneous arrival), "Now, Petruchio, speak." It is as if Petruchio is trying to tell us that what he has been doing for the past few minutes—soliloquizing—is not actually "speaking," but some other process altogether. The soliloquy, then, is a somewhat mixed communication, and, like the Greek chorus, occupies a half-way stage between the situation and the audience.

    For the actor, the soliloquy is best seen not as thinking out loud, and not as a presentation to the audience, but as an *interaction between his character and the audience.* As an interaction, the soliloquy has all those aspects discussed in Chapters One and Two, including invocation, tactics, feedback, relacom, and the pursuit of victory.

    When played as interactions, soliloquies develop their deepest theatrical meaning and most vivid intensity. Interaction, we remember, is a two-way communication. It is not simply the laying on of ideas, eloquence, brilliance, or wit. Interaction is action and response. The soliloquy which is an interaction is, essentially, a speech demanding a response. It is the fishing line with the sharpened hook, the wriggling bait, and the eager, expectant, demanding fisherman. Interactive soliloquies *demand* response; and the actor performing an interactive soliloquy hunts for clues in the audience with whom he is interacting.

This does not at all mean that the actor, in delivering a soliloquy, stares at the audience until they become embarrassed; dialogue is not a response which the audience is capable of giving. What it does mean is that the character soliloquizing to the audience is invoking their respect, their warmth, and their approval. What he is trying to sense from them are *bodily* clues; changes in their breathing, the glaze of their eyes, the attention of their consciousness, the favor of their expression. In the physical Shakespearean theatre, with the jutting platform stage surrounded by standing patrons and three tiers of very nearby spectators, all as equally illuminated by the afternoon sun as was the actor, this was a literal reality. Hamlet, Iago, Grumio, and Puck were all within about forty feet of perhaps 2500 spectators.*

This gives the soliloquizing actor-character a very real chorus, and a chorus which is not simply in the first rows of the audience, but which is the audience itself. Once addressed directly, this "audience-chorus" remains chorus to the character in his imagination—a potentially friendly group to whom he can return time and time again for support, encouragement, and validation.

What does the character want from the audience, if not dialogued answers? He may simply want their quiet, while they listen patiently to his explanations. He may want their laughter, when he pokes fun at his enemies. He may want their smiles, when he demonstrates his wit or his intellectual superiority. He may want to test himself on them before going against the harder opponents he faces on stage. He may want their concentration, their sympathetic figuring out, along with him, of the perplexities that surround his situation. And he may even want their applause, the rush of blood to their cheeks, their gasps of excitement, their ovations. He wants anything at all that shows they are in his camp, and that they are "his" chorus. He may, of course, not get what he wants: what he must do is *try*. Naturally, the Shakespearean soliloquy is an unabashed incidence of theatricality totally aligned

---

*The Fortune Theatre, for which we have dimensions, was a square eighty feet per side, with the downstage center roughly in its middle. There were three tiers of seats, at 11, 21, and 30 feet above ground, and standing room around the stage. The entire building would have fit within the orchestra of the Greek Theatre. Audience capacity has been estimated at close to 3,000.

with situation, and as such it is one of the glorious contrivances of all dramaturgy.

EXERCISE: THE SHAKESPEAREAN SOLILOQUY

1. Memorize and perform a Shakespearean soliloquy to a real audience, considering the soliloquy as an interaction between yourself and an audience-chorus. Try, with the soliloquy, to convince the audience-chorus of your character's rightness, your character's superior intelligence, your character's superior wit, your character's winsomeness. Try to develop a bandwagon effect on the audience/chorus, and convince them that you are going to win, and that it is to their advantage to join with you now. Try any of the following soliloquies, drawn from comedies as well as tragedies:

  a) Richard III, in *Richard III.* His opening soliloquy. This is a particularly difficult soliloquy, since it is usually played with the actor obviously intending to show us how loathsome Richard is. Play it, instead, *as* Richard instead of *about* him, and show us how *marvelous* you are. If you must tell us that you are "rudely stamp'd," then do so either for our sympathy or for our amusement (which you share). When you tell us that "dogs bark at me as I halt by them," either make that a sarcastic joke (meaning "the world says all kinds of slanderous things about me—that dogs bark at me when I pass, that sort of stuff—but you and I know different, don't we?") or as a testament to your unflagging self-knowledge and superior honesty ("look, I know who I am, which is a heck of a lot better than the other characters in this play"). Emphasize that you, as Richard, "delight" to "descant on mine own deformity"; that is, that you like one thing above all, which is to make lovely music out of your physical handicap; that plots and murders you are now planning are a glorious fugue which the audience will be privileged to admire. Play Richard's soliloquy, then, as a positive, goal-oriented interaction with the audience, and get them on your side.

b) Petruchio's "Thus have I politicly begun my reign,"
   The Taming of the Shrew, end of Act IV, scene 1. Here
   the goal is to convince the audience—which you may
   suppose, by an imaginary "plant," to be male and male
   chauvinist—that you are the cleverest marital expert of
   all times, and that your plan is the best, most humane,
   most inspired ever invented. When, at the end of the
   soliloquy, you demand of the audience "He that knows
   better how to tame a shrew; now let him speak," make
   that a real challenge; make the audience want—and
   fail—to answer.

c) Romeo's "He jests at scars that never felt a wound,"
   Romeo and Juliet, beginning of Act II, scene 2. This
   speech is not ordinarily played to the audience; but, as
   an exercise, play it to the audience trying to get their
   moral support for the pursuit of your loved Juliet.
   Convince the audience—your personal chorus—that
   your love is great enough to transcend the obstacles you
   will face wooing a Capulet. Make the tentative self-
   commands a test; when you say "Her eye discourses, I
   will answer it. I am too bold, 'tis not to me she speaks,"
   try to sense which course of action (to answer or not
   to answer) your audience-chorus will support. Try, with
   the soliloquy, to ferret out your audience-chorus's
   position on all this.

   There is an interesting quirk to this scene. Juliet, of
   course, appears above at line one. It is not unrealistic
   to assume that Romeo might be having this interaction
   with the audience-chorus in order that it be overheard,
   as it were, by Juliet. In that case, the ordinary theatrical
   relationship is completely reversed: the audience has
   become a character in the play, and Juliet, a character
   in the play, has become the ulterior audience. Play the
   scene as an interaction with the audience-chorus and
   as a meta-action with the observer-Juliet.

d) Viola's "I left no ring with her," from *Twelfth Night,*
   the conclusion of Act II, scene 2. Try to get the
   audience-chorus's assistance to "untangle this . . . knot"
   that leaves you in such great distress. Make the ques-

tion "what will become of this?" a *real* question to the audience-chorus, try to make them give some sort of answer, with their eyes, their expression, their interest. Try out various hypotheses on them, try to get their help.

e) Hamlet's "To be or not to be" (III, i), "Now I am alone" (II, ii), "Now might I do it pat" (III, iii), "How all occasions do inform against me" (IV, iv); Ophelia's "O, what a noble mind is here o'erthrown" (III, i); or Claudius' "O, my offence is rank, it smells to heaven" (III, iii), all from *Hamlet*. These are perhaps the most famous soliloquies in dramatic literature, but they are not, for that reason, mere poems played upon a stage. There is a political nature to this play, which concerns not just fathers and sons, kings and princes, but general public opinion. Claudius explains to Laertes that he cannot act directly against Hamlet because of, among other things, "the great love the general gender bear him; who, dipping all his faults in their affection, would . . . convert his gyves to graces" (IV, vii, 18ff). Claudius also worries about "the people muddied," and Laertes comes in leading a "rabble" of them. Clearly there is a general public to be persuaded in this play, and the soliloquies can and should be played, at least in part, as the efforts of each soliloquizing character to win their support, to gain the love of the "general gender."

f) Iago's "Thus do I ever make my fool my purse," in *Othello*, end of Act III, scene 3. Try, with the speech, to make the audience share your disdain for Cassio and Othello. Make them laugh with you. Make them enjoy you. Enjoy them!

Alternate: Edmund's first soliloquy in *King Lear* (I, ii).

g) Othello's "It is the cause, it is the cause," *Othello*, beginning of Act V, scene 2. Try to make the audience validate your intended action, and the moral rightness of your cause. Try to go to heaven with this speech.

h) Lady Macbeth's "The raven himself is hoarse," in

Macbeth, Act I, scene 5. The soliloquy is ostensibly addressed to the "spirits that tend on mortal thoughts." Place those spirits in the audience-chorus. When you ask them to "unsex me here," try and make them do exactly that. Do not play these statements as mere rhetoric, make them invocations for real action. Demand results, Madame Macbeth, with your invocations!

THE IMAGINARY AUDIENCE-CHORUS

The Greek chorus is decidedly real, since it consists of costumed actors who actually speak lines and express specific opinions about matters. In the Shakespearean soliloquy examples and exercises, the chorus is imaginary; it is an audience-chorus in the mind of the character who addresses them in private remarks.

The audience-chorus does not disappear, however, when the soliloquy ends. Iago, who addresses the audience directly on many occasions, does not suddenly become oblivious to their presence when Cassio enters. He continues to "play to" the audience-chorus in the ensuing scene, he continues to solicit their support. The analogy might be made with a trial attorney in a criminal case. The attorney will sometimes address the jury directly, as in his summation speech. In that case, he interacts with the jury, and he is clearly and directly "playing to" them. Then there are the occasions when the attorney will be cross-examining a witness. He does not, on those occasions, suddenly stop "playing to" the jury. During his cross-examination he is interacting with the witness, but he is also performing for the jury. He is still, finally, attempting to win their support. And so is the dramatic character. If the character has created, in his mind, an audience-chorus, which we might now designate an "audience-chorus-jury," he "plays to" them all the time, albeit at different levels. He is always striving for their approval.

We can now take this one step further. There is no reason at all why this need apply solely to characters who soliloquize. The fact that Iago turns to Cassio when he comes in does not mean that Iago stops playing for the audience's approval, and the fact that Cassio never soliloquizes to the audience does not mean that he—Cassio—does not also play for their approval.

The imaginary audience-chorus is a fabrication of the character, soliloquizer and non-soliloquizer alike. It is imaginary, and at the same time it is as real as anything mental is real; it is as real as hope, fear, and headaches. It stems from psychological realities, particularly the universal egocentricity by which each character feels the presence of a favoring audience-chorus, feels that the world revolves around him and his actions, and feels that the people in the world are eager observers to his behaviors, and are, potentially, the "general gender" which will, in the final analysis, rally to his support. And this runs true regardless of whether the character ever addresses the audience directly. It is as true for Osric and Lodovico—and for Biff and Charley—as it is for Hamlet, Iago, and *The Glass Menagerie*'s Tom.

The actor's job, then, in "theatricalizing" his character, is basically to develop the character's audience-chorus, to characterize them, to plant them, and to play to them. Two marvelous mechanisms tie this all together in one final, perfect, alignment: (1) The audience-chorus can be the character's "private audience," (see pp. 110–13); and (2) the audience can be planted in the back rows of the real audience. These mechanisms pull theatricality out of the actor *together with* characterization and style. They provide the preconditions which make theatricality a necessity of the character's situation rather than an exigency of the actor's context, and which make theatricality real and dramatic reality theatrical.

THE PRIVATE AUDIENCE IN THE PUBLIC

The private audience are those people the character carries about in his head; both those individuals who draw from him the unique inclinations and incentives that determine his character and those who induce from him the collective social behaviors that define and describe his— and his play's—style. Having created and embodied that private audience (pp. 113–15), the actor's next—and final—mental task is *to "plant" his character's private audience in the public one.* He plants them as the audience-chorus to his character's behavior, not in the first rows of the public audience, as a Greek chorus, but throughout the real audience, in the back rows as well. From that point on, he never has to look at them directly, talk to them directly, or acknowledge their existence in any way. His relationship to them is like the skier's relationship to his partisans lining the route. But he will know they are there. He will *project* to them. He will stimulate them. He will play for their highly specialized, highly special support, and toward their highly characterized and highly styled demands.

Example: Shaw   In the *Man and Superman* example, for instance, the actor playing John Tanner should create Tanner's private audience, should imagine them in full embodiment, and then should "plant" them in the real audience watching the *Man and Superman* production. In arguing with Ramsden, then, he will also be arguing on behalf of his private audience "out in the house." He will use them to help him get the most out of himself. And by so doing he will be working simultaneously toward a specific characterization and a specific style, both calculated to win him a great victory over Ramsden, conveyed to the real audience with a tremendous and infectious theatricality. The real audience then becomes a real weapon in Tanner's quest for the Ramsden defeat. Every laugh he gets from the real audience is another blow to Ramsden. Every shudder he gets from them for his brilliant rhetorical twists digs the knife deeper into his foe. Every gasp at his stunning linguistic reversals makes Ramsden all the more outnumbered and abashed. Theatricality serves Tanner's purpose as well as the actor's; it is his way of reaching his private audience and strengthening their support.

The actor using the imaginary audience-chorus as his stimulus for theatricality, therefore, does not play to the "real" style of the "real" audience, but to an imaginary audience sitting in the real seats. The transformation the actor makes, then, is not in himself but in the audi-

---

"I so respect Pinter. I always had an image of him sitting out in front. I knew how he wanted it played."

—*Robert Shaw, on his performance*
in Pinter's The Caretaker

ence. He characterizes them. He stylizes them. It is not that he makes the audience see him as a Shavian character, but that *he sees them as a Shavian audience.* Theatricality, like character and style, are played reciprocally, not directly. Theatricality comes from assumptions and preconditions planted in and about the real audience—essentially, the precondition that the real audience is the character's own private audience, and that it can be addressed as a heroic chorus to the character's heroic actions. In making these plants, these preconditions, the actor becomes the ultimate creator of his own performance. He becomes an artist.

Example: Restoration comedy   The comedy of the Restoration affords us a grand example of the potential for this transformation. The nature of the English audience at the time of the Restoration is well known from a variety of contemporary accounts. It was composed of a highly elite crowd of sycophants to the court: a group characterized by great amorousness, wit, bitchiness, competitiveness, pseudo-regality, anti-intellectuality, and a widespread contempt for all classes beneath the aristocracy. Peasants were accounted positively vile. Physical beauty was in great demand, particularly if it was developed with great artifice and contrivance. The city was the epitome of the life force; the country was one vast and unendurable wasteland, and the only other civilization that existed (and then but dimly) was in Paris.

The actors of the Restoration catered blithely to this audience, both onstage and off. The comedies were as much about the audience as for them, and the plays were filled with local and immediate allusions, references to members of the audience, places the audience would be gathering after the performance, affairs between the actors and their patrons.

In creating the special Restoration theatricality of the seventeenth century, then, it is necessary to create not merely the Restoration "style," but the Restoration audience. The actors must address the audience not as a collection of twentieth-century theatregoers, but as a court of sycophants to Charles II.

What this does is quite astonishing: *it makes the audience act!* If the actor-characters address the audience as though the audience were a group of Restoration fops, the audience will consider itself a group of Restoration fops! Then the actor can "fop" at them with all the confidence, enthusiasm, and foppishness at his command. He will be inspired with his foppishness and so will they. A truly theatrical experience has the effect of changing the audience's collective pre-

"The unity of music and theatre is equivalent to the
unity of expression and technique in a singing actor's
performance. This unity is achieved when the dramatic
action alone determines all vocal statements. Only then
can the singer recreate a dramatically valid musical
score according to the intentions of the composer;
only then will he appear sufficiently free and relaxed
to turn everything in him and around him into music;
and only then will he make singing actually his most
convincing expressive device. In that case the human
truth of the event being portrayed and sung will attain
such power of conviction that the spectator will be
drawn into the metamorphosis as a co-actor, and will
experience a more intense feeling of reality and
community than he has known before—one which
perhaps it is not even possible to experience outside
of the theatre."

—*Walter Felsenstein*

conception of itself, of "transporting" the audience to another world.
The audience members at a *successful* Restoration comedy, for example, should not feel so much as though they were twentieth-century
"peekers-in" at a Restoration happening; they should feel that *they
themselves are in the Restoration*. That, of course, is why people come
to the theatre in the first place: not to watch something, but to have an
experience—which is *to act*. This is the final—and most laudable—goal
of theatricality: to liberate the audience, to "move" them into a different world, to give them not a moving picture of reality but a real experience in living.

   Example: Realism—The Zoo Story   This is not to say that theatricality is involved only in highly stylized productions, of Shaw or the Restoration. It is equally essential in realism or naturalism, for in both of

these styles the actors must make their principal points clear and engaging to the real audience.* In both styles the actors must project meaning, characterization, and intensity.

We may look at *The Zoo Story* by Edward Albee as a fairly well-known, realistic play that can exemplify this. In the play a gutty, neurotic social outcast (Jerry) meets a timid, middle-rank publishing executive (Peter) on a bench in Central Park. Jerry badgers Peter into talking with him, and after a long, rambling, seemingly discontinuous conversation he prods Peter into fighting with him, and eventually killing him. Most of the dialogue is conversational, and while the play may have philosophical, social, and religious themes, it can certainly stand as a credible, if unusual, interaction between two individuals.

Jerry's private audience is obviously a strong factor in his behavior, since his long rambling speeches are clearly not addressed, in the main, to his present hearer. Jerry's private audience must include, primarily, his parents, who in his mind abandoned him at an early age. His private audience is exemplified by the two empty picture frames which, he explains, adorn the wall of his rooming-house garret. There are also faithless and deserting lovers, rooming-house neighbors, a sister, and a dog. And there is God, "who turned his back on the whole thing some time ago." Clearly much of Jerry's extended conversation, while aimed at Peter, is more profoundly intended for Jerry's private and imaginary audience. Peter, for his part, has a private audience which we can only guess at: his wife, who presumably resembles his mother, and is something of a feared and dominating figure; his executive supervisor; the authors whose work his publishing job makes him read, depend on, and at the same time resent; and his parents, to whom we may feel Peter finds himself a disappointment. And finally there are common members of their private audiences: potential Central Park policemen and passersby, to whom much of their mutual behavior is directed. When Peter says, at one point, "I feel ridiculous," and Jerry replies "You look ridiculous," it is in the eyes of the imaginary Central Park passerby that his "ridiculousness" takes shape.

The actors in *The Zoo Story* can bring out the theatricality of their situation (which, like the situation of any good play, is theatrical) by

*Naturalism is usually described as extreme realism. Neither form is absolute, of course; both are metacommunicational styles of conveying interactions to an audience. Occasionally persons consider "style" as something that is distinguished from naturalism or realism; naturalism and realism, however, are themselves styles and cannot really be considered otherwise.

"The eye of the camera and the eye of God are very similar, I think."

—Gene Wilder

---

planting those "private audience" members in the back row of the house, and by playing the Jerry–Peter interaction as though it were being overheard and overseen by those particular individuals. Jerry, that is, is still trying to please his (dead) father; Peter is still trying to impress his long-given-up wife. If the actors imagine Jerry's father and Peter's wife, plus the whole private audience cast, seated in the back row of the theatre in which *The Zoo Story* takes place, there need be no further question of the play "getting across the footlights." It will get across, and with its credibility not diminished but positively enhanced.

Example: Brecht   The theatre of twentieth-century playwright and director Bertolt Brecht illustrates another type of theatricality, one somewhat more complex than either the Restoration or realistic type. Brecht's theatre is one of self-declared "distancing" (the *Verfremdungseffekt*), or, in some translations, "alienation." The Brechtian actor remains a solid step apart from his role; he does not, directly, try to *become* his character, but tries to *indicate* and *represent* his character instead. According to Brecht, the actor "never forgets, nor does he allow anyone to forget that he is not the one whose action is being demonstrated, but the one who demonstrates it."

The "alienation" or "distancing" in Brechtian theatre is dual: there is a sense of removal between the actor and his role, and a similar sense between the audience and their feelings. An "alienated" audience, Brecht reasoned, would not be so swept up by the story and its attendant feelings that they would neglect the more important social issues that comprised the play's theme. Social themes, not personalities or "stories," are the ultimate focus of Brecht's plays, at least in the playwright's intention.

The theatre of distancing permits, through various Brechtian mechanisms—songs, signs, direct address, and other plot interruptions—an open acknowledgment of the audience's presence much like in the Shakespearean soliloquy convention. But what distinguishes the theatre of alienation above all is that the real audience and the private audience become one and the same; and that the characters—Mother Courage, Grusha, MacHeath—perform for the twentieth-century audience that comes to see them and learn from them. This divests the characters of their everyday psychology and fixations, and makes them exemplifications of principles, theses, and themes; demonstrators rather than completely filled and fleshed human beings.

The audience in a Brecht play is not expressly characterized: it is seen as an audience of contemporaries, somewhat predisposed to Brecht's socialist humanism (else why would they be coming to a Brechtian play?). The Brechtian audience is seen, by the Brechtian actor, as part of his own extended family; interested as he is in the progressive development of a humanized, socialized civilization. The Brechtian actor-character will look at the audience, speak to them, and share his feelings, gestures, ideas, and dialogue with them. More importantly, he will listen to them. He will study and observe them, and openly receive feedback from them. He will make them as important, in the play's development, as he is himself. The alienation in Brechtian theatre is not at all between the actors and the audience, as a few misguided American directors seem to think.* Quite the contrary, between Brecht's actors and Brecht's audience there flows great mutual trust, great love, and a great spirit that says "together we will build a better world."

Since Brechtian theatre is socially oriented, and the playwright's focus is on overall themes rather than individual character plights or random idiosyncrasies, there is a collectivity in the approach to the acting that includes actors and audience—the entire theatrical context—as a group. The actor's portrayal is not so much the portrayal of a character as of a company member playing a character. Thus instead

---

*One of the ironies of Brechtian production in America is the seeming reversal of this idea, where alienation is actively introduced between the actors and the audience, by the actors treating the audience as if they were a bunch of dolts, fascists, racists, or worse. Brecht's plays are not exactly "pleasant," but he certainly did not expect to find his enemies in his audience; rather he enlisted his audience's support to hunt out and destroy enemies common to him and his audience alike. His plays were never intended to be diatribes against the people who came to see them.

of saying, as we usually would, that Helene Weigel "played Mother Courage," we could more accurately say that she "played a member of the Berliner Ensemble (Brecht's company) playing Mother Courage." This is the "distancing" of the Verfremdungseffekt, the filter between the actor and his role. The use of the word "alienation" to describe this process leads, therefore, to a certain confusion, for what Brecht tried to do was to dissolve the difference between interaction and performance, and make actors and audience alike communicate at the single, interactive level. Unfortunately, this seems to have worked out better on paper than it did in Brecht's otherwise splendid productions.

Does the Brechtian actor also "become" the character he demonstrates? Brecht insisted that he does not, but this we must dismiss as rhetoric, needed to distinguish his theory in a striking manner. "Becoming a character" is not a physical transubstantiation; a "character," unlike a "person," is not a fixed, unique, physical presence but an idea, a compilation of attributes, an abstraction, a person in quotes. We cannot become King Henry V, but we can become "King Henry V"— or, more specifically, a "King Henry V." Becoming a character simply involves engaging in the character's interactions, and that the Brechtian actor clearly does. In fact, Brecht's own plays succeeded almost in direct relation to the degree to which the audience accepted the actor *as the character* he played, much to Brecht's chagrin. The separation between "actor" and "character," after all, is a pure abstraction; there is but one body, one face, one voice. Impersonation, no matter in what spirit it is undertaken, carries an undifferentiated impact.

The effect of the Brechtian theatre can be absolutely staggering, and its great influence on contemporary staging and acting theories is a fact of modern theatre history. The Brechtian theatre, when artfully produced, transports the audience into a state of dignified social criticism and awareness. Brecht, in treating his audiences with enormous respect, makes them respect themselves, and respect themselves particularly for sharing his views. Brecht's theatre is called "didactic," but it does not lecture as much as Ibsen's theatre, nor harangue as much as Shaw's. Rather it induces, by the process of direct interaction, the development of its audience's social consciousness. It is this audience that must be the actor's private audience in Brecht, and this audience that he must see in the auditorium seats before him. Then his performance takes on the "alienated theatricality" that Brecht intended; alienated not from the audience and not from the play's ideas, but from anything extraneous to their coming together.

"There's nothing like comedy to me, because it's a
therapy for both sides. You look out there and see the
audience laughing, and it does something to your
adrenalin. It pumps me up. When you turn the audience
on, it's sheer joy. It's like being on the winning team.
When you're floating free, when the laughs are coming
in large, you regulate your timing in a great
free-wheeling style."

—*Bob Hope*

PRESENTATION

Presentation of a role, whether in realism, in Shaw, in the Restoration, or in Brecht—or, for that matter, in opera, ballet, Shakespeare, TV sitcom, TV "soap," or cinema vérité—is a matter of creating an audience, planting the audience, and using that (partly imagined, partly real) audience as a weapon in your character's behalf. Presentation is a two-way street; the actor presents himself to the audience as the hero and partisan of their interests, and he demands that the audience present themselves to him as his supporters. This is a common line in characterization, style, and theatricality. If you play Madame Butterfly, you must imagine the audience as partisan to your predicament, and also particularly disposed to an elegant soprano. Then you can align the soprano to the character, the style to the situation, without hesitancy and without internal conflict.

"Performance" and "theatricality" are the demands of the theatre; they simply cannot be avoided, for they are the origin of the theatre and the only product of the theatre. We are suspicious of performance and theatricality only insofar as they are dishonest, and they are dishonest only when they directly serve the actor's needs to the exclusion of the character's. This happens because actors see too clearly the possible results of performance, and the rewards of theatricality. Having the capacity for theatrical performance, they want to show it off rather than use it; they wish, as it were, to act the role of the great actor rather than to act the *role* of Hamlet or Amanda Wingfield. There is nothing dishonest about theatricality, nothing unreal about performance, so long as they are clearly part of the experience of a character. If they are so, then they become part of the experience of the audience. And that is the function of the theatre; to provide, and to share, experience. "Theatricality," and "performance" are the conveyance modes for that provision and that sharing. They are the cables that knit audience to actor to playwright to character in the grand circuit of induction and communication that defines and distinguishes the theatrical art.

EXERCISES IN THEATRICALITY

1. Costume the audience   Choose and memorize a scene from *The Way of the World*, a Restoration comedy by William Congreve. Study the historical resources that can acquaint you with the details of the original audience to that play—paintings, illustrations, samples from Pepys' Diary, and so forth. Create, in your imagination, a Restoration audience for your scene. Imagine the real audience in Restoration costume. If you can, get some ribbons and feathered hats and literally costume the audience. Put some audience members on stools on the stage with you. Rely heavily on your imagination to make up the missing details; chandeliers, rococo decor, and so forth. Now perform the scene, playing for that (largely imagined) audience's support of your character and his plight.

Do this exercise with a variety of scenes from different periods.

2. The private audience in the public   Take any realistic scene and imagine specific people in the real audience as being specific people of your character's private audience. Play the scene for the private audience's support of your character.

CHAPTER 6

ACTING POWER:
A SYNTHESIS

"What you do as an actor is what we are all trying to do as people. And what the artist tries to do is to get back, is to stop all that terrible self-conscious clothing we put on ourselves. Not that one doesn't get older and one doesn't learn more things or one doesn't grow in certain ways, but we leave that most valuable purity behind, that great courage, that great open stuff."

—Dustin Hoffman

Power comes from alignment.

You can easily hold twenty plates in your hands, but you cannot hold twenty ping-pong balls, even though the ping-pong balls are smaller and lighter than the plates. That is because the plates can be aligned, and the ping-pong balls cannot.

If you want to hold twenty plates in your hands, all you have to do is stack them. Then you simply pick up the bottom plate correctly, and the rest will follow. You need only concentrate on the bottom plate—provided you have stacked the plates correctly to begin with.

AN ACTING ALIGNMENT

It is the same with acting. You cannot at any moment concentrate on situation, style, characterization, theatricality as though they were so many loosely arranged ping-pong balls. You must stack them so that one rests upon another, so that by handling one of them correctly, you will take care of all of them at the same time.

The bottom plate, the foundation of acting, is the character's intended victory in his situation. It demands the actor's total concentration, and all of his conscious, controlled energy.

Characterization, style, and theatricality must all be "stacked" on that bottom plate with the best possible alignment. Then they are carried along with the situation; they are supported by the situation, they are part of the situation. In playing the situation directly, the ac-

---

"You're really driving four horses, as it were, first going through in great detail the exact movements which have been decided upon. You're also listening to the audience, as I say, keeping if you can very great control over them. You're also slightly creating the part, insofar as you're consciously refining the movements and perhaps inventing tiny other experiments with new ones. At the same time you are really living, in one part of your mind, what is happening. Acting is to some extent a controlled dream. In one part of your consciousness it really and truly is happening. . . . To make it true to the audience . . . the actor must, at any rate some of the time, believe himself that it really is true. . . . Therefore three or four layers of consciousness are at work during the time an actor is giving a performance."

—*Sir Ralph Richardson*

---

tor plays character, style, and theatricality reciprocally, automatically. He stacks them atop the situation to which, in performance, he gives his total and undivided attention. It is by this means, by a structuring of the actor's consciousness, that the actor drives Ralph Richardson's "four horses" without falling off or falling apart.

A STRUCTURING OF CONSCIOUSNESS

Situation, character, style, and performance—the four modes—must be aligned at the moment of performance. The actor cannot be expected to think in a rotating alternation of each one, and he cannot give a quarter of his consciousness to each. He must, on the contrary, develop mental mechanisms by which these four playing consciousnesses can derive from a single concentration. If the four playing consciousnesses can be made to *feed into* each other, they will redouble rather than fragment the actor's concentration, and allow him to perform with four times rather than one-fourth his strength and power. Obviously the attempt to find a structural alignment for the actor's thinking must have a high priority.

To this end, a three-leveled model of acting consciousness has been pursued throughout this book.

Playing the situation is the first level. It is the foundation of acting. At this level the behavior of the actor is "pulled" entirely by the ideal futures the actor-character seeks, and the relacom victories he pursues in his interactions with the other actor-characters. This is the *life level* of acting, whereby the actor creates a human being with human intensities.

Playing the character and playing the style are both at the second level. Here the behavior is drawn from scripted and directed sources; from the play, from the director's blocking and coaching, and from the actor's homework. This is the *dramatic level* of acting, whereby the actor creates a dramatized human being whose intensities are dramatically interesting.

Playing the performance is the third level. Here the behavior is drawn from the real or anticipated audience. This is the *theatrical level* of acting, whereby the actor creates *and projects* a dramatized human being.

"Once you set the things you do and make them mean
certain things, you then respond to the stimuli you
yourself have set up. Then you *feel*. You might set
it up as a combination of mind and feeling, but the
feeling usually takes over."

—*Maureen Stapleton*

If the situation is properly constructed—if it is dramatically and theatrically constructed before the actual "acting" begins—then that situation will simply *demand* the most unique, appropriate, and theatrical forms of characterization, style, and performance. By finding the mechanisms for aligning the dramatic and theatrical levels with the human one, acting becomes organically integrated; and character, style, and performance become mutually aligned spines of the action, not add-ons or detractions.

The alignment is a mental one; it is a way of looking at things, a structuring of the actor's consciousness. Whether the actor makes his alignment consciously or spontaneously, of course, depends on the actor, and it may depend on the play as well. Most actors who talk about it at all insist that they do it spontaneously. John Wayne, as we have seen, describes his acting theory as "I read what's in the script and then I go out there and deliver my lines." But he does create an alignment and act reciprocally with it. "I don't call myself an actor," continues Wayne, "I'm a re-actor." Diana Ross, describing (in a television interview) her acting in the film *Lady Sings the Blues,* says "I don't act. I let the others do the acting. I just talk to them." Both of these actors have obviously created their alignments and are capable of playing powerfully toward them. Actors tackling more subtle roles, however, or attempting to attain more difficult styles or characterizations, might wish to pursue their acting alignments more consciously and purposefully.

ACTING POWER:
A SYNTHESIS

When the alignment is perfect, the results can be staggering. We have turned, from time to time in this study, to sports for examples of this alignment. Sporting events provide a valuable metaphor for the theatre; they are "games" in which there is situation and context, and they are public events that attract great followings. Sports and the theatre, in fact, have had an intertwined history since the beginnings of recorded time. The Greeks had two great festivals, a Dionysian one for theatre and an Olympian one for games. The Romans presented plays and games simultaneously in their circuses; the Elizabethans presented them alternately in theatres designed to hold bear-baiting contests on days when no plays were performed. Today it is sporting events and dramatized teleplays that, together, occupy the vast majority of television time in the major Western nations. And yet rarely do we find a theatre that competes successfully with the excitement, the open-ended passion, even the "drama" of a great sporting event; rarely do we find an actor who is as thrilling as a great sporting competitor. This is because the alignment of the athlete is easier to come by; it is less abstract.

The example of Dr. Roger Bannister is illuminating in this context. Bannister, in 1954, became the first man to run a mile in less than four minutes. This was not just an ordinary athletic record; for years people had said that the four-minute mile was a physical impossibility, that its demands exceeded human capability. Yet after Bannister ran his sensational mile, his feat was almost immediately bettered. Within a few months, four-minute miles were common; people ran four-minute miles and came in third. The breaking of the four-minute mile was not, obviously, merely a physical feat. It seems to have re-

"I like to watch a prizefighter or a basketball player, not another actor, whose clichés I might automatically pick up."

—*Walter Matthau*

quired not only the speed and stamina of the athlete, but the daringness, the sense of *creative discovery,* that we expect from the artist. Bannister described the final moments of his run thusly:

> My mind took over. It raced well ahead of my body and drew my body compellingly forward. . . . There was no pain, only a great unity of movement and aim. The only reality was the next two hundred years of track under my feet. . . . I drove on, impelled by a combination of fear and pride. . . . The noise in my ears was that of the faithful Oxford crowds. Their hope and encouragement gave me greater strength. . . . There was fifty yards more. My body had long exhausted all its energy, but it went on running just the same. . . . The faint line of the finishing tape stood ahead as a haven of peace, after the struggle. The arms of the world were waiting to receive me . . . I leapt at the tape like a man taking his last spring to save himself from the chasm that threatens to engulf him.

This description is quite obviously the one we have been pursuing in this book with the analogy of the skier and the actor. Bannister's mental state is entirely cybernetic. He is looking only ahead; his mind is already there, drawing his body "compellingly forward." Nothing exists except the future, the next two hundred yards, the finish line. The crowd is "faithful." It is his private audience and also the public one; it is the "Oxford crowds" and it is also the "arms of the world." It is real and it is imaginary, provoking in him both pride that he is their champion and fear that he may let them down. His spirit transcends his body, his energy seems to come from an external source, from the cheers of the crowd and the arms of the world. In the final leap to the tape everything comes together; there is no second thought, no holding back, no hesitancy; rather, an alignment, "a great unity of movement and aim." He is aligned for superhuman power.

It can be the same with acting. Great acting, like great athletic performance, comes from a transcendent effort, in which everything—audience, character, style, dialogue, costume, staging, self—comes together in complete accord. Alignment can create the accord. The actor must make the transcendent effort.

Effort is sometimes underrated as an actor's tool. There is an inclination, perhaps a defense, to consider an actor's talent hereditary or God-given; a "gift" that one has or one hasn't and there is nothing to be done about it. Nothing could be more deceptive. Heredity, training, psychological background, and cultural experience might all be vitally important in the growth of the actor, as they may be in the devel-

"When I go out there on stage I'm battling the world,
I have to be the best."

—*Richard Burton*

"Acting is a sport. On stage you must be ready to move
like a tennis player on his toes. Your concentration
must be keen, your reflexes sharp; your body and mind
are in top gear, the chase is on. Acting is energy.
In the theatre people pay to see energy."

—*Clive Swift*

opment of a track star, but none of them outweighs effort; all they can do is make the effort easier and more spontaneous. Effort, powerfully and effectively aligned with the character's situation, is the directive of acting energy. It is the dynamic of stage presence.

PRESENCE

Great acting is often said to involve "presence." It is easy to say this, but hard to say exactly what it means.

Audiences, who are more willing than actors or aestheticians to discuss the concept, consider that a performer has presence if and when he is "convincing," "commanding," "captivating," or "charming." In each of these cases, however, the audience is describing not the actor but themselves: they are saying, in effect, "I was convinced," "I was commanded," "I was captivated," "I was charmed." They are saying that the actor made them have an experience. This, of course, is the entire goal of theatricality in the first place.

The American drama critic John Lahr gave one of the most acute analyses of a captivated audience—himself—when he described his reaction to the singer Tina Turner:

> "Hi, Tina!" we say, forgetting where we are. . . . She is toying with us; but that's why we came—to be played with. . . . She lifts grown men out of her seats; they wave at the stage; they talk to it. . . . She comes up against the audience with a street-fighter's lust for battle. And she wins. (We want her to conquer us.) And wins completely. . . . People are coaxed out of isolation and into a community. . . . She has enough life for a whole auditorium. People move toward this luminous presence like moths to a light. Her energy is superhuman. The audience is *feeling* something.

This, obviously, is presence.

Presence derives from the word "present," and can be considered to mean something like "now-ness," or "present-ness." An actor trying to win a victory in a situation is experiencing his action at that moment,

---

"Performance is *in the present*—it's one of the few times when you're living totally in the moment. . . . Your reflexes are totally automatic, and the reflexes have to do with the tasks—with the movement and how you speak. Your mind stops working except for that little part that functions practically, that knows what to do, tells you where to move, senses how you should place dynamics and how to rhythmically work that evening. It's a level where judgments are made instantly, like a basketball game when a guy is moving in on someone else, and he uses peripheral vision to see him coming over his left shoulder. You use your mind practically and instantly. It's more like sports, I think, and not like any other kind of activity."

—*JoAnne Akalaitis of Mabou Mines*

---

in the absolute present. Jean Louis Barrault, the great French actor and director, says that "The actor lives uniquely in the present; he is continually jumping from one present to the next. . . . Characters . . . are continually in action and reaction. They reason, they plead, they argue, they fight with or against others, even with or against themselves. They dispute, answer back, dissimulate, deceive others or themselves with greater or less bad faith; but they never stop." Being in the present—having "now-ness" or "present-ness"—being engaged in the experience of the situation and the feedback of the situation at the moment you are performing the situation—this is the precondition for presence. It is what allows the audience to be transported, to be moved, to experience and feel.

Being in the present, of course, means concentrating on the future, on the road immediately ahead. Paul Claudel, the French playwright, reminds us that "Often we are moved not so much by what the actor says as by what we feel he is *about* to say." Expectations are no less real than actions. Expectations, after all, are what makes the world go around, what makes people *act*. Expectation is the soul of the human potential.

POTENTIAL

The existentialists say that "we are our acts and nothing else." This may have philosophical validity, as seen by an outside, objective observer. It has no validity from the subjective perspective: we "know"

"There is always about a moment of fine acting a kind of fringe of wonder."

—*Stark Young*

---

we are more than our acts, and that knowledge is no less "real" because it is subjective. Helene Deutsch, the great Viennese psychiatrist, looked back over her immensely long and rich lifetime and wrote: "Everyone lives two lives simultaneously. One of them is devoted to adapting to the outside world and improving one's external circumstances. The other consists of fantasies, longings, distortions of reality, undertakings unfinished, achievements not won." The objective, existential analyst looks only at the first life. The person in life, the character representing him, the actor playing him, and the audience empathizing with him, see and "know" both. That knowledge, the knowledge of human *potential*, the knowledge of things that have *not* been done, is the *subjective* reality of life. In many ways it is the most interesting aspect of any individual. It is certainly the most theatrical. In order to create a character with presence, it is necessary to create that character's potential, to create potential itself.

Where does the actor find that potential? Ultimately, he finds it in himself. Finally, the source of an actor's power is himself; this is the key that links him to his character and to the here-and-now of the present. Acting, at bottom, is the most personal of arts. Peter Brook, the English director, suggests this quite clearly in his famous essay on "The Immediate Theatre," a theatre directed to "present-ness." As Brook says, "The actor is giving of himself all the time. It is his possible growth, his possible understanding that he is exploiting, using this material to weave these personalities which drop away when the play is done." In other words, Brook suggests that the actor exploits his own, personal possibilities, his own potential. This is the wellspring of a profound creativity.

For what is the actor's personal potential? Obviously it includes the actor's instincts for fulfillment, engaged as the actor participates in feedback with the other actors, his continual *trying to win* in situational involvements, relationship communications, and dramatic tactical endeavors. The hopes, wishes, lusts, longings, expectations and commitments of the actor—shared with the character—are all a vital part of the actor's and character's potential, of the actor's and character's life and vitality. But that is not all.

So far throughout this book we have concentrated on the actor's positive efforts; his win-directed behavior. That is because these are the character's concentrations. Now we must turn to a grayer and less conscious preoccupation: fear and the threat of destruction. For these, too, lie within the realm of human potential; though peripheral rather than central to our vision, they are nonetheless galvanizing in their effectiveness. Runner Bannister's whole conscious focus may have been on the finish line ahead of him, but his report is also of a "chasm" that threatened to engulf him from behind. The human potential is as much for disaster as it is for glory.

Great actors always manage to give the audience a sense of that potential, impending disaster. Of Marlon Brando, certainly one of America's finest actors, the critic Ronald Hayman has written: "Brando's acting is exciting because it seems so dangerous. There may be a framework of conscious preparation, but he keeps it well hidden and he looks likely to burst at any minute through the walls of any situation that contains him. Like Olivier, he has a volcanic quality and he makes us feel that if he erupts, there is no knowing where the flood of lava will stop." The comparison with Olivier is particularly apt, for the "volcanic quality," the "dangerousness," is the main link between the century's most celebrated "method" actor and its greatest "technical" performer. Nothing so distinguishes great acting—in any style, in any historical period—than the feeling that the actor has the poten-

---

"I think your breed of actors like McQueen are very exciting to act with and bring a marvellous immediacy. They are 'stars,' and I know it's sort of a dirty word in a way, but stars are actors or creatures that look as if they are going to blow up any minute. They have an in-built violence within them."

—*Richard Attenborough*

"Whoever has seen a great actor knows that he is not an animal to be stalked in its lair but a tiger leaping out on the spectator from the bush of mediocrity."

—*James Agate*

"Watching Brando was like watching a dog or a cat walk across the stage. You had no idea what he was going to do next. He also had a kind of contempt, which Olivier has too, a violent self-dissatisfaction which I found riveting."

—*Alec McCowen, referring to the stage production of* A Streetcar Named Desire

---

tial to "go off" at any moment, and to unleash an explosion—a flood of lava, that will be totally out of the frame, totally uncontrolled and uncontrollable. Great acting always dances with danger.

DANGER

Danger, then, is a virtual precondition for presence. If there is no danger at all, the performance cannot electrify an audience, cannot move them, cannot thrill or transport them. Sporting events are notoriously dangerous, and their records of broken bones, blows to the head, "spills and chills" are as frequently reported as are the heroics needed to win victory over those threatening catastrophes. The skier's ride would be of no interest to us, no matter how fast or elegant, were it to be entirely safe—were he to be tracked, for example, down a mechanical rail. Similarly, the actor's performance has no great interest for us if the character we see is never threatened, never endangered. Something must be on the line, something must be risked. The fine actress Lee Grant, in accepting an Academy Award for her performance in the film *Shampoo*, thanked her director "who encouraged me to fly without a net." That is the difference between "safe" and "dangerous" performing.

Yet how do we liberate that sense of danger into performance?

Where do we find it? Again, we find it within ourselves. Danger is hardly unknown to our consciousness; no one is totally without an inner volcano of his own, without the boiling lava of primordial imagination. Theatre, as Antonin Artaud reported with insights sharpened but not defeated by psychosis, serves to remind us that the sky can always fall on our heads, and that the plague can always land with the next ship. As the search and struggle for victory must be played by the actor, with single-minded absorption, so must the ever-present potential for catastrophe be latent in his mind.

And we do not have to go very far afield to find that ever-present chasm, that catastrophe, always threatening to catch up to us, as the bear threatens to catch up and destroy the man running in the forest. We know the catastrophe by personal experience; it is vivid in our imaginations. It is, of course, mortality; the inevitability of death. Universal mortality is the final link between actors, characters, and audiences; it is the most fundamental sharing we experience—the basis of our deepest alignment, and perhaps the basis of theatre itself. The inevitable awareness of our mortality, far from draining our enthusiasm for life, can serve as an inspiring source of power and shared energy, a springboard for heroism.

It is wise, in this context, to examine the remarkable suggestion of N. S. Shaler that "heroism is first and foremost a reflex of the terror of death," a suggestion that lies at the heart of Ernest Becker's justly celebrated study, *The Denial of Death*. In this latter work, Becker draws upon the entire range of twentieth-century psychological and philosophical literature to explore the "terror of death" which lies far more deeply and pervasively behind human actions than most of us dare to admit, even to ourselves. Death, Becker says, is not at all a conscious preoccupation; rather it is a lingering unconscious dread which promotes our greatest energies in our attempts to deny it. The urge to action, suggests Becker, is an urge toward the denial of death, toward heroism.

Death, obviously, stalks us all. When the man in the forest runs for the safe haven of a cabin door, death is the bear that chases behind him. The man does not need to look back at the bear, or study the bear, in order to run from it. The bear may not even be there, as a matter of fact; the bear's presence in the man's imagination is quite sufficient to induce his speedy charge, his "drivenness." The man is not particularly "afraid" of the bear; or at least he does not, at the time, conceptualize his feelings as "fear." Fear is a feeling we entertain at leisure; yet it

---

"It's very important to realize that we're up against an
evil, insidious, hostile universe, a hostile force. It'll
make you ill and age you and kill you. And there's
somebody—or something—out there who for some
irrational, unexplainable reason is killing us. I'm only
interested in dealing with the top man. I'm not interested
in dealing with the other stuff because that's not
important. The only questions of real interest are the
ultimate questions, otherwise who cares about anything
else?"

—*Woody Allen*

---

affects us whether we entertain it or not. In Becker's view most of what
we call "character" and most of what we call "behavior" is stimulated,
at the deepest level, by the bear of death behind us, the bear to which we
pretend, by all these mechanisms, to be oblivious.

If this is true—if this model is sufficiently in agreement with our
own beliefs so that it can be used—it provides the actor with two deeply
telling points of collaboration with his character, with *any* character.
These are the unconscious terror of death, and the more conscious affirmation of life. The character, if he is real, is mortal. He represses his
fear of death—by living, by *acting*. So does the actor. Through his behavior, his character, and his style, the actor affirms life and affirms
the present. Like the character he plays, the actor will, in the words
of William James, "plunge ahead in the strange power of living in the
moment." In this case, the actor is not only aligned, in a profound
way, with the fundamental situation, character, and style of the person
he represents; he is aligned with his own life and the life of his audience.
He is aligned with *immediacy*, with the present, and with the forces
that converge on actor, character, and audience alike at every moment.
By giving his character the potential to die, in other words, he creates
the opportunity, even the necessity, to make his character *live*.

"The actor is able to approach in himself a cosmic
dread as large as his life. He is able to go from this
dread to a joy so sweet that it is without limit. Only
then will the actor have direct access to the life that
moves in him, which is as free as his breathing. And
like his breathing, he doesn't cause it to happen. He
doesn't contain it, and it doesn't contain him."

"I look at the audience and I think, 'I'm playing the
finiteness of this character' and I have these peculiar
thoughts like 'How could I have gotten through this
performance? It's so arduous.' And some nights I don't
think I can do it at all and I feel I might not come back
the next night. And then I say that I have been close to
death myself and that maybe this experience, this play
is also about my familiarity with being near death.
I sometimes feel like I'm going to die onstage and
then I think, 'That's very melodramatic—that's a very
romantic actor's fiction,' and then I think, 'But in fact
this moment is passing, and it's the end of this
moment.'"

—Joseph Chaikin

ACTING IS AN AFFIRMATION

One of the greatest direct treatments of this affirmation of life is the
theatrical masterpiece of Thornton Wilder, *Our Town*. At the end of
the play, the young heroine, Emily, dies. The townspeople gather
around her grave and sing the hymn "Blessed be the tie that binds."
And as they sing, Emily's spirit rises from the grave to take its place

---

"No one lives more lives than the actor. When I played
Lord Nelson, I worked the poop deck in his uniform.
I got extraordinary shivers. Sometimes I felt like I was
staring at my own coffin. I touched that character.
There lies the madness. You can't fake it."

—*Peter Finch*

---

in the town graveyard. It is, even in the most inelegant production, a
terribly sad scene, deeply affecting to the audience. And yet what gives
the scene its poignancy is not a preoccupation with death, but rather
the converse. It is the muffled *affirmations* of the townspeople's singing. With every verse, the townspeople declare to each other, to their
private audiences, and to their God, "I am still alive!" The scene is moving because the characters *fight* the sadness and they fight against
death; not only Emily's death, but also their own—and ours, too, by
the extension of our feelings. And rather than having the choruses
fading out into despair, Wilder has them increase to a crescendo. Mere
living is, itself, a positive affirmation of life. Acting only intensifies the
affirmation. Acting, or behavior, in other words, is the moment-to-
moment conquest of death. It is "playing against" the biggest and pro-
foundest of obstacles. Playing it as such can tie the actor to his deepest
source of power.

Acting, therefore, is an affirmation of *living.* It is a positive act.
Everything we do in life is an act intended to extend and improve our
lives; it is this aspect of behavior, the positive aspect, with which audiences will identify. It is this aspect they will understand.

Jack Nicholson, the superb film actor, says "I'm at least 75 percent
of every character I play. For the rest, I try to find a character's *positive*
philosophy about himself. You have to search out and adopt the character's own justifications and rationalizations." This positiveness is
the key to Nicholson's brilliant "good bad boy" performances, and
what character is not a "good bad" character when all is said and done?

"(Robert) De Niro's instinctive insight into perverse
behavior is one of his credentials as the most
expressive actor of this moment. All great acting has an
ethical dimension, and De Niro always suggests
positive energy that has been perverted. Even his poor,
crazy, shaven-skulled Travis Bickle, aiming his vigilante
guns at pimps and politicos in 'Taxi Driver,' expresses
a diseased gallantry that's a tragic part of an era in
which you can't always tell the saints from the swine. . . .
As with all the best actors, his acting is a riveting,
unexplainable blend of pure abstraction and absolute
reality."

—Jack Kroll

The "justifications" and "rationalizations" which Nicholson finds
are not objective ones; objectively, justifications and rationalizations
are considered distortions, blindnesses, shallowness, even neurotic
symptoms. Nicholson's findings are subjective. He finds how the character's behavior to *himself* is positive; how, to him, his behavior is
both "just" and "rational." Nicholson plays his characters as heroes,
he plays them heroically, and as he does so, he affirms their life and
the life within them.

PERFORMING IS AN AFFIRMATION

And performing, too, is an affirmation of life. Performing is itself a form
of action, a positive act. The townspeople at Emily's graveside are
affirming life by their singing, but no less than the actors who play
those townspeople. *The actors are affirming that they are alive by*

being in the play. They celebrate life as they represent it. Even in the darkest tragedy, that affirmation can be joyous. Essentially, the actor says with every act: "I survive. I live!" Theatre exists on that vitality.

Robert Frost, the great American poet, wrote several witty and revealing essays on the nature of artistic performance. Certainly poetry is the most private of the public arts. And yet Frost wrote, with evident sincerity as well as wit:

> What do I want to communicate [with a poem] but what a *hell* of a good time I had in writing it? The whole thing is performance and prowess and feats . . . why don't critics talk about those things? . . . I look at a poem as a performance. I look on the poet as a man of prowess, just like an athlete. He's a performer. . . . You excel at tennis, vaulting, tumbling, racing, or any kind of ball game because you have the art to put all you've got into it. You're completely alert. You're hotly competitive and yet a good sport. Putting up the bar in the high jump, for instance. You deliberately limit yourself by traditional, artificial rules. What you try for is effective and appropriate form. And success is measured by surpassing performance, including the surpassing of your former self.

Frost, quite obviously, found in his art the alignment of the great athlete, or the great actor. He found the ability to make goals, obstacles, artificial rules, feats, prowess, and competition with—among others— his former self aligned with his creation of splendid artistic monuments. His writing, as a result, has not only insight and eloquence, it has power. It has undifferentiated impact. It speaks with its totality as well as with its parts. For Frost, the job of "performance" was both part of his artistic process, and of his artistic product. It is the same with the great actor.

As the actor affirms life through his character's actions, so he affirms life by the mere act of his own performance, and by the discipline of his training and his rehearsal. When the actor's alignments and concentrations are true, and his consciousness is not fragmented and inhibited, performance of even the darkest, saddest plays brings with it a wry feeling of glee, of satisfaction, of joy. The actors, like their characters, have danced on their own tombs. As the poet William Butler Yeats observed:

> All perform their tragic play
> There struts Hamlet, there is Lear
> That's Ophelia, that's Cordelia;
> Yet they, should the last scene be there,

The great stage curtain about to drop,
If worthy their prominent part in the play,
Do not break up their lines to weep.
They know that Hamlet and Lear are gay:
Gaiety transfiguring all that dread.

And the same goes for the performers who play Hamlet and Lear. They, too, are "gay," affirming, filled with the power and spirit of life.

DEFENSES

Great acting is not easy; anyone who says it is is either shallow or a charlatan. And one of the hardest things about acting is admitting that it is, in fact, hard.

Peter Brook says, "Time after time I have worked with actors who after the usual preamble that they 'put themselves in my hands' are tragically incapable however hard they try of laying down for one brief instant even in rehearsal the image of themselves that has hardened round an inner emptiness." Conditioned as we are to hide our vulnerabilities, to demonstrate "control" in interpersonal relations, to obliterate the fear of death and the fear of failure, and any showing of these, it becomes difficult or impossible to develop the sense of presentness, of volcanic potential, that characterizes the truly talented actor. And the less-than-great actor (one hesitates to call him "bad," more likely he is simply, and stultifyingly, "good") has many rationalizations for his less-than-greatness. These are his actor defenses, and he can always, if he wishes, polish them to a high degree of sophistication.

"Anti-intellectualism" is one of the commonest of actor defenses, and it has a long history. It can be seen in the John Wayne remark with which this book begins, and in similar remarks by highly elegant performers like Jason Robards, who has said, "I always felt I had to get up on a stage and perform before people; studying didn't matter." Many directors echo this attitude with the explicit command: "Just *do* it!" It is easy to take these comments at face value, and to consider more complex attitudes about acting as simply "mental games."

There is a profound error in this, because *theatre itself is a mental game.* It is a mental game from start to finish; a giant mental game, perhaps the greatest of mental games. It is a game in which actors and audience alike agree to consider as reality a whole host of arbitrary pretenses. On its face, theatre is absolutely preposterous. It exists only because of a massive collective will that these pretenses are worth assuming, are worth building into the consensus of pretenses which form a play. Theatre exists only insofar as actors and audience agree to play out mental games with themselves and with each other; that this is a natural, if not spontaneous, process seems to be implied in the 2500 years of success with the consensus so established. The actor, therefore, will be playing a "mental game" whether he wishes to or not; the only question, then, is whether he plays it well or badly. No amount of avoidance can obliterate this issue.

A great deal of the anti-intellectualism professed by the successful actor is, perhaps, as much a pose as a reality. Jason Robards, of course, studied acting at a fine acting academy. Most actors are quite conscious, and quite articulate, about the intellectual problems of acting—that is, about what the actor is thinking while he's acting. Every actor knows how harmful certain kinds of thinking are to acting; thinking about how your voice sounds, for instance, or how your make-up looks, or whether you've got your lines right. One cannot avoid these sorts of problems by abolishing thinking altogether. The mind cannot be told to stop. It rebels; it thinks in any event. But it can be *aimed*. The goal of

---

"One mustn't allow acting to be like stockbroking—you must not take it just as a means of earning a living, to go down every day to do a job of work. The big thing is to combine punctuality, efficiency, good nature, obedience, intelligence, and concentration with an unawareness of what is going to happen next, thus keeping yourself available for excitement."

—*John Gielgud*

"It's an odd paradox of the stage that as soon as you
start pretending to do something and enlarge it to the
scale that is necessary to carry it to the back of the
theatre, you not only portray what you're pretending
to do, but you portray yourself, your innermost self,
in capital letters, red ink and underscored three times.
Homosexuality peeps out from the most butch men—
gentlemen who carry on, you know, like they're great
lechers and things, suddenly they have to do some
kind of a revealing scene, and you see suddenly that
inside all this facade of tweed and manliness is a
terribly frightened little spinster lady. And not only in
the sexual department: sweet-faced spinster women,
pillars of the Presbyterian Church, have to get up and
show something and suddenly you see that inside all
this, there is a raging, voluptuous tigress. Well, that's
not awfully funny; it can be very shaming for those who
have to undergo it."

—*Tyrone Guthrie*

an acting theory—of thinking about acting—is to find a way to aim,
not to still, the actor's mind.

"Using yourself" or "acting out of yourself" is another acting task
that is often resisted, unconsciously if not consciously. Many actors
find themselves hamstrung by any act of self-revelation, needful as
they are of protecting what Brook calls that "image of themselves that
has hardened round an inner emptiness." It has been said that the actor
feels himself a hypocrite for pretending to be somebody he is not. It is
more likely that he feels himself "caught" if he shows the world what
he really *is*. Both "hypocrisies" are dissonances—differences—between
the actor's image and his character's. The merely "good" actor will
make the audience think they have seen a character different from what

"What you use in acting is everything you are as a human being."

—*Kim Hunter*

they know about him, the actor. The great actor will make the audience think they have seen things they never before knew about the actor himself. The dissonance will be resolved in the great performance, in other words, by the audience's greater understanding of the actor, rather than by their narrower understanding of the character. One of the most telling comments about a performance is when the audience member tells the actor "I didn't know you had it in you." Great acting is a revelation of that which is "in you," rather than an elaborate depiction of what is in somebody else.

Reliance on a simple, single theory or "method" is another actor defense, one that is crippling both in the long and the short run. An actor refuses to study, because he claims that acting must be instinctual and nothing else. An actor refuses to learn scansion because verse must be spoken "naturally." An actor refuses to study the character's psychology, because acting is simply a matter of "technique." The actor refuses to act out of himself, because the character is "someone else." The actor refuses to audition, because he must be discovered. The actor need not examine himself, because his favorite movie star does not (or says he does not). The actor does not think about acting, because thinking sullies art.

The folly of these approaches need not be discussed at length. The author has pointed out in another book that professional acting careers demand comprehensive and versatile greatness, not mere sufficiency. Earlier in these pages we have discussed alignments which can take into account, which can synthesize, the great complexities of acting. The defensiveness of the blinded adherent of simplistic "methods" and clichés is simply and clearly that: defensiveness. The simplistic actor knows it—he knows that there are things about acting that confuse him, things he must somehow keep out of his mind, things about himself that he must consciously suppress (including the fact that there are things that confuse him that he is suppressing). He knows the trap he's in, but avoids the work on himself needed to get out, because it would amount to an admission of defeat. His acting becomes scared, shallow, a cover-up for his hollowness. He is, finally, powerless; straddled in impotence and hopeful only of not being found out.

ACTING POWER

Power comes from alignment, and power builds upon power. The exercises in this book are calculated to build, one atop the other like plates in a stack, the alignments an actor needs to enter a situation with the confidence that his characterization, his style, and his need for theatricality are his allies, not his enemies. As allies, they give the actor strength. That strength leads to confidence. That confidence leads to more strength. It is the ultimate power spiral.

Jason Robards, who said that "studying didn't matter," also said (in the same article), "Acting is strange. You are split in many ways. You have about six things going on in your head. You have to be completely in it, yet aware of . . . the audience. It's all there if you trust yourself." Confidence, finally, is its own reward. It is that which allows the actor full play of his tactics, full pursuit of his intended victory. It allows him to *use* the audience in the same way the skier, or the mata-

---

"It is by no means naive to state that at a certain point
in the development of a character, confidence is all.
It is by confidence that the actor finally triumphs."

—*Jean Vilar*

---

dor, uses his appreciative fans. Confidence—the faith in ourselves—implies that we are split personalities, and that both parts of us, "we" and "ourselves" have faith in each other. We *are* split personalities. That is why actors can be actors, and at the same time, characters; and why audiences can remain themselves and at the same time empathize with the people on stage. If acting is complex, it is because we are complex, because life and any conceptualization we may make of life are complex. It is the goal of acting to learn to manage that complexity, to learn to *use* it, and to create a powerful and subtle art out of it.

Theatre, after all, is the art we make out of ourselves. It requires, in the end, neither scenery, nor costumes, nor lighting fixtures, nor apparatus of any kind. It does not even require a text. It requires behavior within a context; people acting and people watching them, or in the French term Peter Brook likes to use, *assisting* them. Theatre is as vital as life, as cruel as death, and as unfathomable as unconscious experience. And acting that does not "re-present" these—that does not "put them again into the present," as the word "represent" essentially means—is not the acting that brings art or life to the stage, or to ourselves.

APPENDIX
DETERMINISM, CYBERNETICS, AND COGNITIVE DISSONANCE

This book introduces to the study of acting several theoretical and experimental terms that are not customarily encountered by actors or students of acting. For the interested reader, some of these terms are here explored in somewhat fuller detail.

DETERMINISM AND CYBERNETICS

Determinism and Cybernetics are two different epistemologies or "ways of thinking." Neither is definitively "right" or "wrong"; both are simply perspectives, viewpoints. In the subject we are examining here, determinism and cybernetics are different perspectives from which we may view behavioral systems, different ways of describing the relations we observe between people and events.

What we want to know about behavioral systems is how they work—how they get into operation, how they get their results. The weight of scientific literature on behavior until fairly recent times has been based on deterministic reasoning which, more or less, likes to see things "happening" because somewhere in the past they were "caused." Thus the knee jerks because the physician hit a certain tendon with a hammer. To the deterministic scientist, any happening, event, or effect can be precisely predicted or understood only when and if the prior determinants have been isolated and identified. Determinism was the basic epistemology, or method of reasoning, of the nineteenth century. It served well for the industrial revolution, and led to great sophistication in engineering, where, for instance, a gunsight could be quite accurately fashioned given awareness of the force of gravity, the exit velocity of the bullet, the friction coefficients of the barrel, and the various calculated trajectories over various distances. Determinism combined well with Victorian morality (divorce causes damnation) and preventive medicine (mosquitoes cause yellow fever). In neurology, deterministic scientists developed the concept of the body as a reactive machine, with neural mechanisms on a reflex arc, and bodily systems were explained as a series of cause-and-effect reactions: finger touches fire, sending impulses to the brain, sending impulses to the muscles, pulling finger from the fire. In psychology, the deterministic epistemology led to the stimulus-response findings of Pavlov in his famous experiments with canine salivation, and also to the more ethereal causalities of Freud, involving repressed trauma causing subsequent tics, slips, dreams, and other "symptoms" of their cause.

The findings reached under determinism were magnificent in their time, like the deterministic physical systems reached by Newton; however, also like Newton's work, they can only be first approximations. Determinism depends on several prior assumptions, namely: *simultaneity*, whereby various phenomena can be examined irrespective of the time of their examination; *isolation*, by which phenomena are seen separated from their normal context, as on a microscope slide; *immobility*, whereby phenomena are examined in a fixed position in space; and *atomism*, whereby it is accepted that the whole is always no more than the sum of its component parts. These prior assumptions, sometimes (now quite eccentrically) considered "scientific method," were certainly necessary for the development of the industrial revolution, and were largely satisfactory up through the advanced technology of the Second World War. They disintegrate, however, under the volatile speeds and behaviors investigated through relativity physics and cybernetic psychology. Basic to the principle of Einsteinean relativity, the general acceptance of which need no longer be demonstrated, is the discarding of simultaneity, isolation, and immobility as valuable concepts in understanding the physical universe. The Principle of Uncertainty (or Indeterminancy), developed by Werner Heisenberg in 1927, not only confirms the basic epistemology of relativity in those aspects, but makes atomism meaningless as well. According to this principle, we understand that insofar as the position of a subatomic particle is known, its velocity cannot be determined; yet insofar as its velocity is known, its position cannot be determined. In plain terms, if we stop something in order to see it, it is no longer the "it" we wanted to see; instead have seen "stopped-it" which is something altogether different. The Principle of Uncertainty is an unavoidable reality and creates a new "scientific method" whereby the scientist admits that his "knowledge" is ultimately restricted to the adding up of a number of uncertainties and indeterminates, which at best will lead to probabilities and statistics, not absolute causes or effects.

The breakdown of determinism is not, of course, merely a subject of philosophical disquisition. While deterministic engineers could build a proper gunsight, they could not design a rocket-guidance system. Determinism could be used to build adding machines, but not computers. It could never be used even to approximate the enormously complex systems being uncovered in high energy physics, molecular biology, or genetics and neurology. And without question it has left us lacking effective models for the behavior of the one phenomenon least able to be considered atomistically: man.

CYBERNETICS

For some of these reasons, perhaps, the growth of cybernetics has been widespread in all these areas of inquiry and action. Cybernetics has been described by a physiologist as "a new branch of science, engendered in our times under the pressure of necessity, whose study is associated with the general problems of control theory, information theory, and communications theory."* Cybernetics was developed in the 1940s primarily by Norbert Weiner, a mathematician at the Massachusetts Institute of Technology, and was first used in the development of high-speed digital and analogic computers. The word was coined by Weiner after the Greek word for "helmsman," and it generally refers to systems which, by acquiring information about their own behavior and that of the outside environment, "steer" themselves toward designated targets or goals. At first glance, cybernetics

*N. A. Bernshtein, "Methods for Developing Physiology as Related to the Problems of Cybernetics," in Michael Cole and Irving Maltzman, eds., *Handbook of Contemporary Soviet Psychology* (1969), p. 422.

seems to resemble the earlier Greek teleology, which held that even physical behavior was ultimately purposeful, and that rocks "want" to fall, water "seeks" its own level, and stars shine because that is their "purpose." Cybernetics differs from this set of epistemological conclusions because a cybernetic system continually acquires and processes information, and regulates itself according to the information it receives.

One of the most common examples of a cybernetic system is the thermostatically controlled furnace, which is set to maintain a given temperature. While the furnace provides the actual heat, it does not do so in carefully premeasured units, but simply by turning itself off when the temperature is sufficient, and on when the temperature falls. *Information* is vital to the system: it is acquired by the thermostat, and translated into an electrical command to the furnace via an information-processing device made for the purpose. One noteworthy feature of the thermostat-furnace system is the fact that it is continuously self-correcting rather than continuously correct. That is, if the thermostat is set at 70 degrees, the furnace will, in practice, turn on when the temperature falls to 69, and turn off when it reaches 71; thus the temperature, if graphed, would show an oscillating pattern between 69 and 71, and be absolutely 70 only during the (theoretical) split-seconds of passage on its way up and on its way down. This is going to be true of any cybernetic system, even if the parameters are made terribly precise, and the calibrated off-on temperatures are narrowed to the gamut between, say 69.999999999 and 70.000000001 degrees.

A more sophisticated cybernetic system is that used in missile and rocket guidance. If we remember Jules Verne's *Rocket to the Moon*, a piece of deterministic nineteenth-century science fiction, it was suggested there that lunar travel could be accomplished by precisely aiming a rocket on a moonward trajectory, then shooting it out of a huge cannon. The original aiming would have to be absolutely perfect, of course, or else the rocket would sail blithely into outer space. (Disregarding the moon's gravitational field, which is not involved in this particular consideration.) Modern rocketry does not depend on aiming. Indeed, the moon-bound spaceships are simply aimed "up," and only after launching do they begin to develop their precise direction. They do this by continuously monitoring their position with respect to their destination, and calibrating that received information into course corrections that eventually land them on target. While manned moon missions do this via humanly aided calculations and corrective firings, the so-called "smart bombs" are ingeniously devised lethal missiles that self-correct their course continuously and automatically until they make their final strike. Neither the spaceship nor the guided missile is ever on its *exact* trajectory at any given point; it is always a little off to the left, or a little to the right, or a little high, or a little low. But it is always subject to correction; in fact, we could say, subject to overcorrection, since the correction must then be corrected, and so on. Instead of thinking of the rocketship as "pushed," by the configuration of the cannon barrel and the explosion of gunpowder, we can cybernetically consider it "pulled" by the information it receives from its target and its configuration designed to get it there.

FEEDBACK

The information solicited and received by a cybernetic system is called *feedback. Positive feedback* is information generated by the system to indicate that it is off course or malfunctioning, just as a radio amplifier announces positive feedback by an ear-piercing scream. *Negative feedback,* by contrast, indicates that the system is operating well, is on course, and within tolerances. Unfortunately, popular usage of these words have frequently ascribed the opposite connotation: we may incorrectly refer to "negative feedback" as though it were roughly synonymous with "negative criticism." It isn't, and in fact could better be stated as "no criticism." To remember the strict sense of feedback, we may think of it as roughly synonymous with "self-criticism."*

The use of cybernetics and feedback in the study of mankind has been enormous, and has directed itself toward the elimination of "determinants" as explanations of human and animal behavior, at both the physiological and the psychological levels. Cybernetic models

---

*It is fairly easy to see how this reversal of connotations came about. Determinism is based on the general concept of inertia, which states in general that it is in the nature of things to keep going in the same direction until countered by an outside force. Cybernetics is based on the Principle of Uncertainty, which in general says it is in the nature of things to disintegrate into chaos. Thus the determinist tends to think of "the universe at large" as basically supportive of human pursuits, while the cyberneticist sees the universe at large as tending to confound man's efforts at creating any kind of order. Thus to the determinist, feedback from the universe would be expected to be "good." To the cyberneticist, without question, no news is good news. The connotations of what is "positive" feedback then has become confused. To the cyberneticist, positive feedback means essentially "the damn universe is doing its thing again, and we have to fight it and get back on course."

focus on the animal's ability to generate feedback even in its autonomic processes, and even possibly in its *cellular* processes. The leading Soviet physiologist N. A. Bernshtein wrote shortly before his death in 1966:

> It is now recognized that a feedback principle governs the regulation and control of all of an organism's functions. This fact compels us to admit the urgent need to replace the concept of the reflex arc by that of the *reflex loop*, which includes as an essential component a continuous stream of afferent signals that are vital for control and action. . . . The idea of an atomized chain of elementary reflexes connected only in a sequential order has been replaced in modern physiological thinking with the theory of a *continuous* cyclical process of interaction between the changing conditions of the external and internal environments which develops and proceeds as a whole action. . . . A loop process, which includes continuous participation of effectors and receptors, can . . . begin with equal ease at any link of its block diagram.*

Bernshtein's model of the reflex loop makes clear that living matter does not behave in accordance with a "chain of elementary reflexes," but a "*continuous* cyclical process of interaction," a process that for the student of human behavior weakens the concepts of simultaneity, isolation, immobility, and atomism which are vital to the deterministic viewpoint. Cybernetics, among other things, has led to a major revolution in psychology and psychiatry, turning them in the direction of psychosociology and social psychiatry. It has led away from the concepts holding human behavior as an outgrowth of intra-psychic forces, and toward the viewing of behavior as a function of feedback-loop interactions. In psychiatric practice this is made explicit in the movement away from classical Freudian on-the-couch psychotherapy, and toward conjoint family or group therapy systems, where the patient, now renamed the "identified patient" (to contrast him with the "unidentified patients," or his family) is seen in his social and familial context, and "his problem" is seen as an overall problem only partly his, and partly an aspect of the feedback he exchanges with others. Feedback, then, is essentially a process of continuously emitted and received information; it is a form of communication in which we are involved at the cellular autonomic and tactical levels, and it elicits our observable behavior.

*Bernshtein, in Cole and Maltzman, eds., *Handbook of Contemporary Soviet Psychology*, p. 444.

COGNITIVE DISSONANCE

The theory of cognitive dissonance was developed by Leon Festinger in 1957, and has been put to many applications over the years. In his landmark experiment, Festinger induced subjects to assert beliefs that Festinger secretly knew the subjects did not, in fact, believe. What Festinger did was to administer a very tedious examination to a group of volunteers, and then request the volunteers to "help" him by telling the new volunteers that the test was "fun to take." Festinger paid some of these "helpers" $20 to lie in this way to the newcomers; others he paid only $1 to do the same. Then, at a subsequent date, he asked his helpers if they had, in fact, enjoyed the original examination. The result was, at first, quite surprising. The helpers who had been paid $20 agreed, at the subsequent date, that the original test had been quite tedious. The helpers who had been paid only $1 to lie, however, reported that they had, in fact, *enjoyed* taking that test. What had happened, as subsequent investigation has shown, was this: the $1 helpers felt guilty for lying to prospective volunteers for so paltry a reward. Looking back over the act—perhaps unconsciously—they could not accept *even to themselves* that they had been so immoral as to lie for a mere dollar. They suffered, as Festinger reported, a *cognitive dissonance:* a discrepancy between what they found themselves doing, and what kind of person they thought they were. Not being able to change the kind of people they thought they were, they resolved the discrepancy— the dissonance—by changing the nature of what they found themselves doing. That is, they came to believe in their own lies (or to believe that they believed in their own lies) in order to quell their guilt about lying. The higher paid subjects had no such guilt: they simply remembered telling a little white lie for a very reasonable reward; thus they suffered no cognitive dissonance, and they retained their original beliefs—that the original experiment had been tedious—without alteration.

The implication of the Festinger experiment, and of subsequent ones which have confirmed it, is that we have a tendency to come to believe in what we find ourselves doing, particularly when we can find no other reason acceptable to ourselves for having done it. Debaters thus often find themselves coming to believe in the positions which they—quite arbitrarily—have been asked to defend. Attorneys come to identify with the interests of their clients, although the clients may have been randomly assigned by the court. People engaged in certain sexual activities with others tend to develop the feeling that they must be "in love" with those persons—or why would they have had sex with them? Persons who shout political slogans tend to come to believe in the principles behind the slogans, even though they began their partisanships to impress a similarly engaged friend or would-be lover.

Cognitive dissonance makes clear that the actor's tendency to identify with his role is quite normal, even inevitable. It is a psychological mechanism that works well on behalf of the actor, and he is lucky if he is mentally free enough to take advantage of it.

The literature on cognitive dissonance, together with the original report of Festinger's experiment, is collected in Alan C. Elms, *Role Playing, Reward, and Attitude Change* (New York: 1969).

SOURCE NOTES

INTRODUCTION

12/15–17   Quoted in William Fadiman, *Hollywood Now* (1972), pp. 88–89.

CHAPTER 1

18/8–23   Edward E. Jones and Richard E. Nisbett, *The Actor and the Observer: Divergent Perceptions of the Causes of Behavior* (1971), p. 2.

22/25–28   Anton Chekhov, *Letters*, ed. Michael Heim and Simon Karlinsky (1973), p. 122.

36/10–13   Paul Watslawick and others, *The Pragmatics of Human Communication* (1967), pp. 44–45.

43/2–5   Quoted in Judith Cook, *Director's Theatre* (1972), p. 64.

CHAPTER 2

54/29–32   Eric Berne, in *Transactional Analysis in Psychotherapy* (1961).

54/32–34   Virginia Satir, *Conjoint Family Therapy* (1967), p. 81.

76/27–31   Constantin Stanislavski, *Building a Character* (1949), p. 118.

79/19–21   Quoted in Hal Burton, ed., *Great Acting* (1967), p. 29.

CHAPTER 3

88/21–28   Paraphrased from the writings of Piaget by Howard Gardner, in *The Quest for Mind* (1972), p. 63.

106/5–6   Constantin Stanislavski, *Building a Character* (1949), p. 118.

117/32–118/2   Quoted in Hal Burton, ed., *Great Acting* (1967), p. 133.
135/29–34   In *Screen Actor* (Spring 1974), pp. 21–22; emphasis added.

CHAPTER 4
155/4–6   Michel St. Denis, *Theatre: The Rediscovery of Style* (1960), p. 71.

CHAPTER 5
178/25–27   Stuart Little and Arthur Canot, *The Playmakers* (1970), p. 103.
186/14–18   Howard Gardner, *The Quest for Mind* (1972), p. 63.
187/5–188/1   For an elaborate demonstration of the suicide vs. society principle, see Karl A. Menninger, *Man Against Himself* (1938).
206/18–20   Quoted in Edwin Duerr, *The Length and Depth of Acting* (1962), p. 490.

CHAPTER 6
216/13–15   Quoted in William Fadiman, *Hollywood Now* (1972), pp. 88–89.
218/4–15   Roger Bannister, *The Four Minute Mile* (1962), p. 212.
220/4–12   John Lahr, *Astonish Me!* (1972), pp. 211–213.
221/1–7   Jean Louis Barrault, *Reflections on the Theatre* (1951), pp. 126–129.
221/14–16   In Jacques Petit and Jean-Pierre Kempf, eds., *Claudel on the Theatre* (1972), p. 14.
222/2–7   Helene Deutsch, *Confrontations with Myself* (1973), p. 15.
222/21–25   Peter Brook, *The Empty Space* (1968), p. 24.
223/8–14   Ronald Hayman, *Techniques of Acting* (1969), pp. 142–143.
225/21–24   Ernest Becker, *The Denial of Death* (1973). The quotation from Shaler's *The Individual: A Study of Life and Death* (1900) is in Becker, p. 11.
228/20–23   Quoted in *Time* Magazine, August 11, 1974; emphasis added.
230/8–19   Quoted, from several sources, by Frank Lentricchia, *Robert Frost* (1975), pp. 167–168.
230/36–231/5   W. B. Yeats, "Lapis Lazuli" (1938).
230/12–16   Peter Brook, *The Empty Space* (1968), p. 27.
230/28–29   Quoted in Howard Greenberger, *The Off Broadway Experience* (1971), p. 50.
234/22–24   Robert Cohen, *Acting Professionally*, 2d ed. (1975).
235/17–20   Howard Greenberger, *The Off Broadway Experience* (1971), p. 47.

SUGGESTED READINGS
FOR THE ACTOR

The following books provide a wide variety of information and perspectives on the art, craft, and profession of acting.

ACTORS ON ACTING

Naturally, the prime source for material on acting should be works by actors themselves; not all actors are writers, however, so this list is more limited than one would wish. Many books said to be written by actors are in fact ghost-written, and many are devoted mainly to theatrical gossip and reputation-mending. The following list is restricted to good books actually written by fine actors, and collections of comments by actors on their work.

Uta Hagen (with Haskel Frankel), *Respect for Acting* (New York: Macmillan, 1973). A fine book by one of the premiere actresses of the American theatre; separate chapters on thirty pertinent topics such as identity, thinking, improvisation, circumstance, the objective, the obstacle, and style. "The expression 'to lose yourself' in the part or in the performance . . . has always confused me. I find it much more stimulating to say that I want 'to find myself' in the part" (p. 34).

Richard Boleslavsky, *Acting: The First Six Lessons* (New York: Theatre Arts Books, 1933). One of the classics, and a wonderfully readable analysis, written in the form of a dialogue between the artist, Boleslavsky, and a "creature" who studies from him. Chapters (lessons) on concentration, emotional memory, dramatic action, characterization, observation, and rhythm. "I believe that inspiration is the result of hard work, but the only thing which can stimulate inspiration in an actor is constant and keen observation every day of his life" (p. 99).

William Redfield, *Letters From an Actor* (New York: Viking, 1967). A fascinating series of letters written by Redfield during rehearsals for the Richard Burton *Hamlet* (directed by John Gielgud) in which Redfield played Guildenstern. Redfield comments perceptively on British and American actors and acting. "I call it hard work and emotional nudity. Politeness in the theatre can be an enemy to excitement and creativity."

Lee Strasberg, *Strasberg at The Actor's Studio*, edited by Robert H. Hethmon (New York: Viking, 1965). The edited and transcribed tapes of acting classes at actor-teacher Strasberg's celebrated New York studio. Interesting for the problems raised by the students, many of whom are professional actors, as well as for Strasberg's answers. "The basic difficulty in all acting is that the actor must create on the stage, almost as much as in life, the sense of spontaneity. In all great acting that is done. In all great acting there is the element of spontaneity within a performance that yet keeps a shape and an outline. In great acting there are constant improvisational elements that come through" (p. 299).

Joseph Chaikin, *The Presence of the Actor* (New York: Atheneum, 1972). An intriguing book with fresh insights by the founder-director of The Open Theatre, who is an excellent actor in his own right. "During performance the actor experiences a dialectic between restraint and abandon; between the impulse and the form which expresses it; between the act and the way it is perceived by the audience. The actor is playing in present time, and comes to an unmistakable clarity that the act itself is being created and dissolved in the same instant" (p. 10).

Michael Redgrave, *The Actor's Ways and Means* (London: Heinemann, 1953). The distinguished mid-century British actor's frequently interesting if often awkward attempt to combine "method" with theatrical "instinct." "The essence of acting is the power to act. The basic will of the actor must be, quite simply, to act: not to think, not to feel, not to exhibitionise, not to make some personal statement—though he may do one or all of these—*but to act.* It is as compelling as the word to 'open fire.' The curtain is up. Go on and act" (p. 29).

Constantin Stanislavski, *An Actor's Handbook,* edited and translated by Elizabeth Reynolds Hapgood (New York: Theatre Arts Books, 1963). The best single-volume compendium of Stanislavski's teaching. The student interested in the Stanislavski method, of course, should read Miss Hapgood's more complete translations of Stanislavski's major works: *An Actor Prepares* (New York: Theatre Arts Books, 1936), and *Building a Character* (New York: Theatre Arts Books, 1949). These two works, written together at the end of Stanislavski's life and planned for simultaneous publication, constitute the two "sides" to the Stanislavski system. That they were published thirteen years apart has occasioned much of the confusion surrounding that system. The reader is also referred to Stanislavski's autobiography, *My Life in Art,* translated by J. J. Robbins (New York: Theatre Art Books, 1948); and to another compilation of writings from various sources; Constantin Stanislavski, *Creating A Role,* translated by Elizabeth Reynolds Hapgood (New York: Theatre Arts Books, 1961).

Liv Ullmann, *Changing* (New York: Knopf, 1977). A deeply penetrating book by an actress of great accomplishment in both film and stage, serious and comic roles. "Onstage what I am acting is reality for me. In the same way that my reality is acting. Each is a part of the whole" (p. 210).

Anthologies of actors on acting

Toby Cole and Helen Krich Chinoy, *Actors on Acting* (New York: Crown, 1970). The revised edition of a masterful collection of comments by actors throughout the ages.

Roy Newquist, *Showcase* (New York: Morrow, 1966). Interviews with

Edith Evans, George Grizzard, Julie Harris, Jack Lemmon, John Gielgud, Peter O'Toole, and Jessica Tandy, among others.

Leonard Probst, *Off Camera* (New York: Stein and Day, 1975). Interviews with Al Pacino, Paul Newman, George C. Scott, Dustin Hoffman, Lynn Redgrave, Marlo Thomas, Zero Mostel, Woody Allen, and others.

Lewis Funke and John E. Booth, *Actors Talk About Acting* (New York: Avon, 1961). Interviews with Anne Bancroft, Bert Lahr, Paul Muni, Shelley Winters, Sidney Poitier, Alfred Lunt, Morris Carnovsky, and others.

Hal Burton, *Great Acting* (New York: Hill and Wang, 1967). Interviews with Laurence Olivier, Ralph Richardson, Peggy Ashcroft, Edith Evans, and others.

Hal Burton, *Acting in the 60s* (London: British Broadcasting Company, 1970). Interviews with Richard Burton, Albert Finney, Eric Porter, Maggie Smith, and others.

The Drama Review No. 71 (September 1976). An issue devoted to "Actors On Acting," featuring interviews with leading members of avant-garde American and European theatre companies of the 1970s.

Lillian Ross and Helen Ross, *The Player* (New York: Simon and Schuster, 1962). Interviews with Anthony Perkins, Anthony Quinn, Kim Stanley, Jane Fonda, Walter Matthau, Eileen Heckart, Maureen Stapleton, Robert Shaw, and others.

DIRECTORS ON ACTING

Walter Felsenstein, *The Music Theatre of Walter Felsenstein*, translated and edited by Peter Paul Fuchs (New York: Norton, 1975). A brilliant book by the German opera director, generally considered the finest in his particular craft; a man who brought great truth into the staging of highly stylized operatic works. "The heart of music theatre is to turn music making and singing on the stage into a communication that is convincing, truthful, and utterly essential. Music theatre exists when a musical action with singing human beings becomes a theatrical reality that is unreservedly believable" (p. 15).

Peter Brook, *The Empty Space* (New York: Avon, 1968). A passionate book detailing the author's search for an "immediate" theatre. Exceptionally lucid analysis of the contemporary stage. "Acting begins with a tiny inner movement so slight that it is almost completely invisible. In early theatre rehearsals, the impulse may get no further than a flicker. For this flicker to pass into the whole organism, a total relaxation must be there, either god-given or brought about by work" (p. 99).

Michel St. Denis, *Theatre: A Rediscovery of Style* (London: Heinemann, 1960). A sensitive attempt to define "style" in the theatre, and to suggest its components and ramifications. "There is no meaning or psychological construction in a play which can be separated from its style. The one contains the other. Style has its own meaning. The text has its own power, it creates its own effect: it must not come into conflict in any way with psychological motivation. This is the most thrilling problem that modern actors and directors have got to solve" (p. 79).

Robert Lewis, *Method or Madness?* (London: Heinemann, 1960). A clear and entertaining discussion of the Stanislavski method, its interpretations and misinterpretations, by one of its practitioners. Lewis brings historical information, common sense, and his own experience as a director and acting teacher to this readable "codicil" to the Stanislavski system. "The fear of being phony has become one of the phoniest things in the theatre" (p. 165).

Tyrone Guthrie, *Tyrone Guthrie on Acting* (New York: Viking, 1971). A witty and always engaging treatise by the late English director, celebrated for creating highly theatrical and vivid revivals of the great classic plays. "Good acting, is, first, convincing; then, enlightening; finally, compelling. Likewise, bad acting is unconvincing, unenlightening, and boring. A really good actor will never be utterly terrible in anything; and a really bad one, though he may do well in certain parts, will never cause an experienced observer to mistake success for talent" (p. 13).

Jerzy Grotowski, *Towards a Poor Theatre* (New York: Clarion, 1968). An intense view of theatre, one which Peter Brook calls "holy," explained in a series of interviews by a unique Polish director-teacher. "Acting is a serious and solemn act of revelation. The actor must be prepared to be absolutely sincere. It is like a step towards the summit of the actor's organism in which consciousness and instinct are united" (p. 210).

VOICE

The scientific study of voice operation is still in its infancy, and there remains a great deal about the human voice that is simply unknown. The four authors below, however, have enjoyed distinguished careers as vocal teachers, and each has trained many performers; their works are valuable, and for the most part complementary. All books include vocal exercises.

Arthur Lessac, *The Use and Training of the Human Voice* (New York: DBS Publications, n.d.). A book about the entire "vocal life."

Kristin Linklatter, *Freeing the Natural Voice* (New York: DBS Publications, 1976). Emphasis on naturalness in speaking, and the uniqueness of each person's resonance, diction, and regional dialect.

Cecily Berry, *Voice and the Actor* (London: Harrap, 1973). The most widely used British text, written by the voice director of the Royal Shakespeare Company. Easy to read, easy to follow, and extremely useful.

Cornelius L. Reid, *Voice: Psyche and Soma* (New York: J. Patelson Music, 1975). Primarily for singers, Reid's book is rather iconoclastic, and presents evidence—some of which is scientific—that "pulls the rug out from under those who cherish what are mistakenly believed to be 'traditional' practices, proving that 'breath control,' 'voice placement,' and nasal resonance are without validity" (p. 3). A fascinating, provocative study. "Psychologically, singing is an aggressive act" (p. 12).

MOVEMENT

Four studies of movement that are useful to actors, and which include exercises in movement:

F. Mattias Alexander, *The Resurrection of the Body*, edited by Edward Maisel (New York: Dell, 1971). This is a reprint of the teachings that developed the "Alexander Technique," as used in many European and American theatres.

Nancy King, *Theatre Movement: The Actor and His Space* (New York: DBS Publications, n.d.).

Richmond Shepard, *Mime: The Technique of Silence* (New York: DBS Publications, 1971).

James Penrod, *Movement for the Performing Artist* (Palo Alto: Mayfield, 1974.)

GAMES AND IMPROVISATIONS

Viola Spolin, *Improvisation for the Theatre* (Evanston, Ill.: Northwestern University Press, 1963). The groundbreaking work on games and improvs—by a master teacher. "Growth will occur without difficulty in the student-actor because the very game he plays will aid him. The objective upon which the player must constantly focus and towards which every action must be directed provokes spontaneity. In this spontaneity, personal freedom is released, and the total person, physically, intellectually, and intuitively, is awakened" (p. 5–6).

Louis John Dezseran, *The Student Actor's Handbook* (Palo Alto: Mayfield, 1975). A book of games and exercises as used by many American actors, directors, and acting teachers. "Perhaps the most significant aspect of theatre games is that you will learn to teach yourself by creating a situation similar to the one in which your character finds himself" (xii).

ACTING TEXTBOOKS

These books provide step-by-step instructions in acting, often with viewpoints somewhat different from those expressed herein:

Robert L. Benedetti, *The Actor at Work* (Englewood Cliffs, N.J.: Prentice-Hall, 1976). Emphasizes the actor's development of expressiveness, skill in analysis, and instinct for role-playing.

Charles McGaw, *Acting Is Believing*, 3d ed. (San Francisco: Rinehart Press, 1975). First published in 1955 and regularly revised. Emphasis on the actor's will to action, on "doing, not being," and on "inter-influence."

Jerry L. Crawford and Joan Snyder, *Acting in Person and in Style* (Dubuque, Iowa: Wm. C. Brown Co., 1976). Emphasizes "personalization"—the actor's "truthful use of himself" in both scripted and improvisational material.

THEORETICAL APPROACHES

A relatively new development in the English-speaking theatre is the emergence of "performance theory," a body of investigation which brings anthropological, psychological, sociological, and political perspectives into a theory of theatre. Although these investigations do not always offer much in the way of practical suggestions or information to the actor (and some do), they do provide a deep background for the actor's ultimate creative potential, as well as for his understanding of the larger importance of acting and its extraordinary possibilities.

Antonin Artaud, *The Theatre and Its Double*, translated by Mary Caroline Richards (New York: Grove Press, 1958, original French edition, 1938). The seminal work of "Theatre of Cruelty," in which the theatre is compared, in a famous metaphor, to the plague. "One cannot imagine, save in an atmosphere of carnage, torture, and bloodshed, all the magnificent Fables which recount to the multitudes the first sexual division and the first carnage of essences that appeared in creation.

The theatre, like the plague, is in the image of this carnage and this essential separation. It releases conflicts, disengages powers, liberates possibilities, and if these possibilities and these powers are dark, it is the fault not of the plague nor of the theatre but of life" (p. 31).

Richard Schechner, *Environmental Theatre* (New York: Hawthorn, 1973). "Performance theory is a social science, not a branch of aesthetics. I reject aesthetics" (vii). Schechner is the founder-producer-director of the Performance Group (New York), and a director-theorist of the first order. This book is a rich study of both the pragmatics and principles which he has developed. Chapter heads: Space, Participation, Nakedness, Performer, Shaman, Therapy, Playwright, Groups, and Director. Many fascinating and useful exercises.

David Cole, *The Theatrical Event* (Middletown, Conn.: Wesleyan University Press, 1975). A highly theoretical study of acting and ritual, comparing the actor both to the shaman (a psychic voyager to the land of the gods) and to the hungan (a man psychically possessed by the gods). "In the figure of the actor—at once a role-possessed body and an embodied role—imagination and presence come up against each other in a way that allows us to test the strengths of each against the claims of the other" (p. 5).

Michael Goldman, *The Actor's Freedom: Towards a New Theory of Drama* (New York: Viking, 1975). A brilliant discussion of the centrality of acting and performance to dramatic literature itself. Goldman goes beyond the common idea that plays are "meant to be acted," and impressively demonstrates that plays are *about* acting. "The characters of drama are actors" (p. 93).

Bertolt Brecht, *Brecht on Theatre*, Translated by John Willett (New York: Hill and Wang, 1964). A compendium of Brecht's writings on epic theatre and the theory of "alienation" or "distancing." See also Willett's *The Theatre of Bertolt Brecht* (London: Methuen, 1960). "The essential point of the epic theatre is perhaps that it appeals less to the feelings than to the spectator's reason. Instead of sharing an experience the spectator must come to grips with things. At the same time it would be quite wrong to try and deny emotion to this kind of theatre." (One of Brecht's first essays, as quoted in *The Theatre of Bertolt Brecht*, p. 170).

ACTING AS A CAREER

Robert Cohen, *Acting Professionally* (Palo Alto: Mayfield, 1975). The second edition of a book detailing career opportunities—and what to do about them—in New York, in Los Angeles (Hollywood), and in the American regional theatre.

Clive Swift, *The Job of Acting* (London: Harrap, 1976). A British survey on the same topic. Mr. Swift is himself a well-established British stage and television actor. "Acting is energy. In the theatre people pay to see energy" (p. 5).

Donald Farber, *Actor's Guide* (New York: DBS Publications, 1971). A legal guide to contracts, unions, and so forth.

BOOKS ON HUMAN INTERACTION AND BEHAVIOR

The books below deal not with acting as a theatrical art or craft, but with human behavior in everyday life. The list is a short one, consisting of those few books which are both immediately useful to the actor and also starting points for a more intense investigation.

Paul Watzlawick and others, *Pragmatics of Human Communication* (New York: Norton, 1967). An outstanding introduction to communication theory, patterns of human interaction, content and relationship modes of communication (relacom), cybernetics, and feedback. Includes a "communicational approach" to the play *Who's Afraid of Virginia Woolf?* A clear, if complex study that serves as background to other books below.

Erving Goffman, *The Presentation of Self in Everyday Life* (New York: Anchor, 1959); *Interaction Ritual* (New York: Anchor, 1967); and *Strategic Interaction* (New York: Ballantine, 1972). Goffman's work explores the performance aspect of daily behavior, the strategies and tactics of face-to-face interactions, and the "face-work" of humans in interacted situations.

Eric Berne, *Transactional Analysis in Psychotherapy* (New York: Castle, 1961); and the more popular sequels, *Games People Play* (New York: Castle, 1964) and *What Do You Say After You Say Hello?* (New York: Grove Press, 1970). Berne is the originator of transactional analysis, as well as one of the first proponents of game theory, and his approach to human interaction emphasizes intentions and performances. In *Games People Play* Berne analyzes human interactions on a game model; in *What Do You Say After You Say Hello?* he does so on a "script" model. The findings of Berne have been skillfully related to acting in a series of articles by Professor Arthur Wagner in *The Drama Review* (Summer 1967, Spring 1969). Interviewed by Wagner, Berne has commented, "The problem for actors is difficult. The question always is, where are they? Who and where is the real guy? I think things would be clearer if one looked at the actor's work not as playing a character but as dealing a series of specific interpersonal transactions" (*TDR* 36, Summer 1967, pp. 89–90).

Albert E. Scheflen, *Body Language and Social Order* (Englewood Cliffs, N.J.: Prentice-Hall, 1972). An illustrated and documented study of the use of body position, gesture, and expression for tactical purposes in human interaction. An introduction to kinesics, turn-taking, and the use of verbal and nonverbal cues to create ongoing, orderly situations (such as conversations, parties, and meetings).

Charles Darwin, *The Expression of the Emotions in Man and Animals* (Chicago: University of Chicago Press, 1965). A reprint of Darwin's classic 1872 study.

INDEX